The Rivers of Life – and Death

by

William T. Harper
Revised Edition, © 2013

Dedication

Dedicated to all those with whom I have enjoyed my time on the water – my family and friends, the "stink-potters," the "rag-sailors," the towboaters, the paddlewheel skippers, and even the GIs and the U. S. Navy crews on the troop ships that took me across both the Atlantic and Pacific Oceans, courtesy of Uncle Sam.

Likewise, this effort would not be nearly as complete as this author hoped it would be without the help of the Non-Fiction Critique Group Members in the Brazos Writers organization in Texas – specifically Barbara Althaus and William Klemm, PhD. Their eagle-eyes and their cogent comments have highly enhanced this author's efforts.

w.t.h.

Table of Contents

List of Illustrations

Chapter I
Tragedies and Triumphs

January 9, 2005 was, without a doubt, one of the darkest days in the American towboating industry's 200-plus-year history on the nation's inland waterways. Four towboat crewmen drowned when their boat washed over a dam on the Ohio River. Other dark days have been:

June 16, 1964
April 6, 1969
August 1, 1974
May 28, 1993
September 22, 1993
July 15, 2001
September 15, 2001
May 26, 2002

Those nine days saw towboats and their barges slam into highway and railroad bridge pilings, collide with another vessel, run over a fishing boat, and wash over a dam. The resulting catastrophes ended the lives of 114 unsuspecting motor vehicle occupants, railroad train passengers and crew, fishermen, and mariners in those nine separate accidents.

The absolute blackest day – and not to diminish any of the other eight – was **September 22, 1993**. On that day, the towboat *Mauvilla*, pushing six barges in dense fog, nudged a railroad bridge, causing the derailment of Amtrak's *Sunset Limited* passenger train, thereby plunging forty-seven hapless souls to their deaths in an alligator- and snake-infested murky bayou near Mobile, Alabama. One-hundred-and-three others were injured in the carnage.

The other eight days, listed in magnitude of tragedy and briefly stated, include:

April 6, 1969 – The towboat *Warren J. Doucet*, pushing three barges loaded with 27,000 barrels of crude oil, and a Chinese freighter, *Union Faith*, collided with an ensuing fireball explosion claiming twenty-five seamen's lives.

May 26, 2002 – The towboat *Robert Y. Love*, traveling north-bound on the Arkansas River near Webbers Falls, Oklahoma, rammed an Interstate-40 bridge pier, collapsing a 503-foot section of the bridge. Eight passenger vehicles and three tractor-semitrailer combinations drove into that black hole, resulting in fourteen fatalities and five bone-crushing injuries.

September 15, 2001 – The towboat *Brown Water V* crashed into one of the concrete piers supporting the Queen Isabella Causeway connecting South Padre Island to the Texas Gulf Coast mainland. Ten automobiles carried eight stunned people to their watery grave. Others survived.

June 16, 1964 – The towboat *Rebel, Jr.* hit the Lake Pontchartrain Causeway in New Orleans, Louisiana. Six passengers in a Trailways bus that plunged into the Lake were killed.

July 15, 2001 – Six recreational fishermen died when their 17-foot boat was run over by the towboat *Elaine G* and its fourteen barges on the Ohio River, about 25 miles northeast of Louisville, Kentucky.

January 9, 2005 – The towboat *Elizabeth M.*, pushing six coal barges through the icy Ohio River near Pittsburgh, Pennsylvania, was swept into and over a river dam and falls. Four of the seven crew members aboard the boat perished.

August 1, 1974 – Another towboat, the *Miss Andy*, also plowed into the Lake Pontchartrain Causeway north of New Orleans, killing three motorists in two cars.

May 28, 1993 – The towboat *Chris* collided with a support pier of the Judge William Seeber Bridge in New Orleans. The impact caused about 145 feet of bridge deck to collapse. Two automobiles carrying three people fell with the four-lane bridge deck resulting in one death and serious injuries to the other two people.

*   *   *

Through these pages, the nine horrific tragedies stretching back over forty-nine years (1964-2013) are re-visited. This collection of reports was triggered by what so many of America's television viewers, this writer included, saw and were shocked by on August 1, 2007. That day, as many of us sat down to watch the evening news on our TV sets just before dinner time, we saw new and gripping pictures of devastation flashing across our television screens. These live shots weren't of another war in some far off place. They were the recordings of the collapse of the Interstate-35W bridge into the Mississippi River just south of the St. Anthony Falls Lock and Dam in Minneapolis, Minnesota. For this former Minnesotan who had spent the better part of thirty years living in the Twin Cities area, the televised carnage, indelibly magnified by the flaming tractor-trailer and the battered yellow school bus, was overwhelming.

This correspondent has traveled almost all 2,350 miles of that great river as it flows from its source in Itasca, Minnesota (1,475 feet above sea level) to its mouth at the Gulf of Mexico (0 feet above sea level). This book is meant for those who have also traveled on and/or marveled at any of this nation's inland waterways – the Mississippi, the Missouri, the Arkansas, the Illinois, the Ohio, the Gulf Intracoastal Canal, etc. For those who have navigated the locks or merely putt-putted up and down those waterways – whether commercially or as a pleasure boater – the stories herein – told below in reverse chronological order – are for you. It may also be that this book will find its way into the crews' quarters on many of the 3,000-plus towboats and tugs that ply those waterways. To some of them with whom we have traveled the Inland Waterways, we say "Hello" again. To all of them, we say "God Speed."

And last but surely not least, these words may ironically bring some small sparks of knowledge to everyone about how that breakfast cereal on your table this morning got there.

*   *   *

What is the life of a towboater who brought that Pennsylvania coal down the rivers to the electric power plant that lights your home? Patti Marciano in a PBS report describes it this way:

> As a towboater, your job is to safely and efficiently steer barges loaded with grain and other products from point A to point B, pick up a new load and go back again. Be careful not to let the barges break away from the boat or each other. Work six hours on, six hours off, for 28 days straight. Never leave the boat. Carry heavy equipment and endure the danger of being struck by a deadly tow line or falling overboard and being sucked under by the undertow. You're fairly well paid, your "room and board" is taken care of. You've got a bed, meals, and a shower. But you don't see your family for a month at a time. Sometimes you feel like you're in prison.
>
> There's no such thing as "stopping for the night." You keep the boat and barges

moving, through the early morning sunrise and moonless night darkness. When your co-worker wakes you up at 11 o'clock at night to start your shift, you rise, no matter how tired you are, because your colleague is even more tired, having been at it for six hours and it's his time to rest now.[1]

*   *   *

One of the oddities emerging from these stories is their similarities. A couple of the allisions[a] were carbon copies of each other. On at least three of these occasions, the man at the wheel fainted or "passed out" or "blacked out" prior to a crash. For better or for worse, holidays such as Easter, Memorial Day, and Labor Day entered the equations.

Another similarity is the almost universal lack of adverse weather conditions identified as causing these accidents. In only two cases was fog a factor; in six of the other seven tragedies, weather conditions were close to ideal. In two of the stories, it was only because of fortuitous fishing contests that the death tolls were not much higher. And, in a couple of these stories, the classic management-labor differences are apparent with the former assigning "human error" as the cause and the latter citing "terrible working conditions."

With all the economic benefit emanating from this nation's inland waterways, with all the joy and pleasure they give its recreational boating people, with all the physical and psychic scenic pleasure they give its citizens, those very same rivers, streams and canals are, indeed, The Rivers of Life. Unfortunately, in all too many cases, they are also The Rivers of Death.

---

[a] A noun "allision" means a vessel striking a fixed object vs. the more common verb "collision," a vessel striking another moving object.

*   *   *

But, why should anyone have to die to be a mariner? That is a question National Mariners Association (nee Gulf Coast Mariners Association) Captain David C. Whitehurst asked at the opening of his prepared remarks at a New Orleans workboat show in 2006.

> "Why would anyone seek employment in an industry that has one of the highest death rates per-capita of any industry in the United States? It is an industry where every year a hundred vessels sink, capsize, and burn. It is an industry where the entry-level deckhand has a chance of dying by drowning, getting crushed between barges, docks or lock walls or being injured by flying rigging and deck fittings. Many mariners suffer debilitating back injuries by carrying or pulling on heavy ratchets and wires. Some of these wires were previously retired from use as elevator cables.
>
> The American Waterways Operators (AWO) identified falls overboard as the leading cause of death by drowning. In the towing industry, injuries are three to eight times the national industrial average. And, finally, why would anyone want to seek employment where illegal drugs are so commonly used in such a potentially dangerous setting?"[2]

Some industry figures estimate the death rate of tow workers could be as high as 72 out of 100,000, or roughly equal to the commercial fishing industry – the second most dangerous profession after the timber industry, according to the U.S. Bureau of Labor Statistics. A breakdown of towing casualties indicates that sixty-two percent are caused by human error.[3] Working on a towboat is – as the old saying goes – "a dirty job but somebody has to do it." Not only is it a dirty job, but often it's a back-breaking, hard job. It's hard labor in Louisiana's sultry summertime heat and it's even harder in the early freezes of Minnesota's unrelenting wintertime. On many of those days there aren't enough of those "somebodies" around who are willing to do those dirty jobs. Moreover, if ever enough of those "somebodies" are not around, this nation's economy could be in far more trouble than it was during the Great Depression of the 1930s.

The rivers' system of locks and dams which make so much of that travel possible, forms a "stairway" that, in the case of the Mississippi River, starts at St. Anthony Falls, site of the I-35 Bridge collapse in Minneapolis. The "stairway" then drops the level of the Mississippi River 420 feet en route from Minneapolis to just north of St. Louis, Missouri. Without a lock and dam system, none of the thousands of towboats and their barges plying the river daily – such as we'll be discussing in these pages – would be able to deliver their cargo.

While the August 1, 2007 Interstate 35 tragedy had no towboat involvement, many of its aspects were frightfully similar to those nine events listed above. It also revealed economic considerations perhaps un-thought of looming ominously in the background – boating accidents, acts of terrorism, etc. What if some of those darkest days in towboating mentioned at the outset herein happened in another place, a more vulnerable place, what then?

Suppose, for instance, the I-35 incident had happened another 650 miles or so down the Mississippi River with circumstances say, similar to the May 26, 2002 allision that took out a huge chunk of the Interstate-40

15

Bridge at Webbers Falls, Oklahoma in a catastrophe which killed fourteen people (and is covered later in these pages). In the Minnesota bridge collapse, despite the tragic loss of thirteen lives, commercial traffic on the Mississippi River was virtually unaffected – because there was so little of it that far up that river.

What if the 4,260-foot, $118-million "Super Bridge," the Clark Bridge crossing the Mississippi River near Alton, Illinois just north of St. Louis, were to come crashing down?

The Clark Bridge over the Mississippi River north of St. Louis

Closing the Mighty Mississippi at that location would preclude hundreds of barges full of thousands of tons of grain from the nation's heartland from reaching the Gulf of Mexico and on to the world's markets. The commercial havoc such disruption would play on this country's and the world's economic system is inconceivable. Hundreds of millions of tons of commerce could be backed up on the inland waterways for months. It could make the Great Depression's stock market crash of 1929 look like a mere sell-off of a few penny-stocks.

16

As towboats can, have and do cause major calamities by alliding with overwater highway bridge supports, they also often do severe damage to the locks through which they pass with and without their cargo barges. In 2005 for instance, the Pittsburgh District navigation facilities experienced about one towboat accident each month. The frequency of damage to the District's river locks due to navigational accidents recently increased at an alarming rate with seven towboat accidents reported since December 1, 2005.[4] Imagine what a shut-down of a major lock on the inland waterways system would do? A University of Missouri study did just that and arrived at this conclusion: "Lock failure on either the Mississippi or Illinois rivers carries with it the potential economic damage that could exceed more than half a billion dollars for corn and soybean producers..." over just the October through December of 2005 period.[5]

According to Captain Milford Lawrence, "There is more corn produced in the upper Midwest than anywhere else in the world. More grain is moved on the Mississippi River than on any other river system in the world. The sight of ocean-going barges from around the world picking up Midwestern grain in New Orleans is sobering. Few farmers begin to realize the number of people around the world that are fed by Midwestern corn."[6]

For those inclined to think the possibility of shutting down the Mississippi River because of a boating accident is a "cry-wolf" scenario, consider this edited story about a towboat incident from *USAToday*:

> "The entrance to the Mississippi River was closed to ocean-going vessels for a second day Sunday.... There was no way to tell when the river may reopen, said Coast Guard Petty Officer Jonathan McCool.... The collision came just a day after the river

had been reopened following a collision
[three days earlier] between a tanker and a
freighter. At one point, about 40 ships were
backed up, including at least three large
cruise ships carrying some 7,900 passengers.
McCool said.... 'It is like a chain. Once you
take one link out of the chain, the whole
system is disrupted'."[7]

But even once is more than enough. It
happens!

Remember the words of famed author William
Faulkner who knowingly said, "A mule will work for you
for ten years for the privilege of kicking you once."
Likewise are the Fates flowing along with the Inland
Waterways. What follows on these pages are not just a
Nobel Prize-winning writer's ruminations and fictional bad
dreams. They're living nightmares.

*   *   *

Chapter II
The Rivers Giveth...

In his book *Rising Tide*, John M. Barry writes, "The valley of the Mississippi River stretches north into Canada and south to the Gulf of Mexico, east from New York and North Carolina and west to Idaho and New Mexico. It is a valley 20 percent larger than that of China's Yellow River, double that of Africa's Nile and India's Ganges, fifteen times that of Europe's Rhine. Within it lies 41 percent of the continental United States, including all or part of 31 states. No river in Europe, no river in the Orient, no river in the ancient civilized world compares with it. Only the Amazon and, barely, the Congo have a larger drainage basin. Measured from the head of its tributary the Missouri River, as logical a starting point as any, the Mississippi is the longest river in the world, and it pulses like the artery of the American heartland."[8]

The Inland Waterways are truly gigantic, as is their influence on this nation's and the world's commerce. John Skorburg, writing in the Heartland Institute's *Environment News,* July 1, 2004, said, "U.S. agriculture depends heavily on the inland waterways to transport farm commodities to overseas markets. One-third of U.S. agricultural production is exported, and more than 60 percent of those exports depend on barge transportation through the Mississippi and Illinois rivers." There are something like 27,000 barges hauling mostly petroleum products, chemicals, coal, wood products, metals, and grain on the Inland Waterways.

The Mississippi drainage basin, where many of the towboat accidents reported on in these pages occur, can best be described as a misplaced, gnarled, giant California redwood tree lying vertically across the country's midsection. Its Mississippi River roots are firmly planted in the Gulf of Mexico, just about 100 water miles south of New Orleans. The main trunk of that "tree" reaches north on a winding journey of 2,320 miles to its source where it trickles as a tiny walk-across stream coming out of Lake

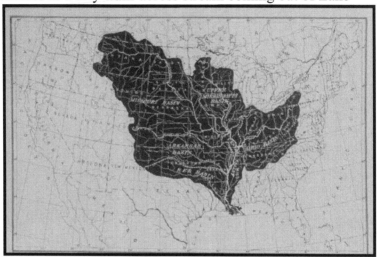

**The drainage basin of the Mississippi River
– 1,240,050 square miles. (NASA photo)**

Itasca in northern Minnesota. The Mississippi River System and the Inland Waterways that serve it, spreads its branches – the Mississippi, the Minnesota, Missouri, Arkansas, Ohio, Kentucky, Cumberland, Tennessee, Monongahela plus the Ouachita, Green, Illinois and the Kanawha – into twenty-two states and forty percent of the U. S. population. Not in your wildest nocturnal nightmares could you imagine the devastation to the economy of the United States if that commerce were interrupted in any significant way – either by forces of nature, accidents, or (think 9/11) evil-doers.

As we "climb" that tree into the pages of heartbreak and heroism herein, we'll branch off both east and west from New Orleans along the Gulf Intracoastal Waterway (GIWW). It meanders about 1,300 miles paralleling the coast of the Gulf of Mexico from near Tallahassee, Florida to Brownsville, Texas. It makes its way via a series of man-made canals, sheltered bays, nearly continuous barrier islands, and rivers. Close to the extreme ends of both those seemingly idyllic limbs, we'll visit sites where fifty-five people lost their lives in towboat accidents. Right there in the middle of the GIWW, we'll look at a pair of calamities in New Orleans' waterways, and two more north of "The Big Easy" on Lake Pontchartrain. Further up the tree, we'll stop along the Arkansas River in Oklahoma and also climb all the way up the Ohio River to Pennsylvania to review other calamities. We'll complete the trip to tragedy and triumph back to the Ohio River, this time near Louisville, Kentucky, to re-examine the *Elaine G* catastrophe.

Along the way, we meet more than a few of the people who work, live, and sometimes even die on those towboats. They are a breed apart. As a far more skilled writer than this one put it, "Among marine people the riverboat man seems to be an especially skilled breed, as much at home with his towboat in midstream as he is bow-on to a shallow bank. More of a rugged country boy than a seaman, he often thinks of the river with its numerous small river towns and 'honky-tonks' more in the nature of a marine highway than as a body of navigational water. Special tribute is his for making seem easy what to an offshore person usually is difficult work...."[9]

*   *   *

The progenitor for today's towboat and their barges, the flatboat, came into being as American settlers weaned themselves away from their Atlantic Seaboard roots and started their westward expansion into our "Manifest Destiny." The flatboat was the cheapest to build of the many types of boats used in Colonial days and it became the standard conveyance for families seeking more living space and a new life. All the boats in that period were hand-powered, with poles or oars for propulsion and

21

steering. They simply floated along with the current. They were not intended for round trips since the settlers used them only to get to their new homes and then broke them up and used them for their lumber to build those homes and shops in which to buy supplies. This situation changed dramatically in 1811 with the launching of the first steam-powered boat on the western waters, the *New Orleans*, built

The flatboat is how the towboat industry started.[10]

near Pittsburgh, Pennsylvania. Steamboats made it possible to increase the speed of the trip down-river and, more importantly, made the return trip possible. Commerce on the rivers increased and by the end of 1835 more than 650 steamboats had been built in what was then the American west.

The jargon of the towboat industry is almost a language unto itself. It is suggested the reader turn to the Glossary of Terms at the end of this book for the definition of some of those terms. One of the first things one needs to know on this subject is the definition of a towboat versus a tugboat – both of which are often used as synonyms for each other. There are differences. According to *Webster's Ninth New Collegiate Dictionary,* a towboat is "a compact, shallow-draft boat with a squared bow designed and fitted for *pushing* tows of barges on island waterways."

This is a "towboat" – on the Mississippi River at St. Louis.[11]

WordNet, a lexical database for the English language at the esteemed Princeton University, commits the "sin" of misidentification when it offers the following definition for a towboat: "Noun – tugboat, tug, towboat, tow-er (a powerful small boat designed to pull or push larger ships)."

That so-called "powerful small boat designed to pull or *push* larger ships" is the definition of a tugboat – as shown below – not a towboat.

Therefore....score: one for Webster; zero for the WordNet. Putting it even more succinctly, one writer warns, "Do not call a river man's towboat a tugboat. It neither tows nor tugs, but rather, it pushes. And although it pushes, it still is a towboat...you figure that one!"[12]

You can also "score one" for some of the more "enlightened" towboat-owning companies who put creature comforts for their crews high on the list of boat designs. Many towboats get pretty elaborate. Some of the older "river-rats" talk about towboats that have gold door handles, carpets, built-in vacuum systems, maids and everything else. On some of those boats, they say, you didn't dare go aboard until you take off your work shoes and put on house slippers. One of those "maids" is liable to work on the back of your head with a broomstick if you come on board with your work shoes on – so they say.

The two little boats here are "tug boats" doing their job.[13]

Similarly, when today's old-timers talk about "maids" on towboats, they usually do it almost with a condescending sneer even as females on the rivers are becoming less and less of an oddity and more and more found in responsible positions. In the towboat fleets of the 21st Century, you may find as many males working as galley cooks as you find females piloting the boats the guys are cooking in. Some "brown water jockeys" will be quick to tell you, "I have nothing against women working and making a living and stuff like that."

Others will tell you something else. As did one longtime towboat captain while pushing chemicals along the Lower Mississippi and relating a story about one of his predecessors: "He didn't care who you put on the boat – as long as it wasn't a woman." The subject is, indeed, touchy (but not, as far as we could tell, "feely").

*   *   *

Long-gone Joe Waller was first hired on towboats during World War II after he ran away from his Houston, Texas home in 1943 at age 13. "When my momma found out where I was at," Waller said with a grin, "she sent a truant officer down there and the company made me quit." Undeterred, Joe ran off again looking for another job. He met up with "one old Cajun boy operating a 'shifting' boat [a boat that moves other boats and barges in and out of piers and dockages as they're loaded and unloaded] and he was so desperate for help because of the wartime shortage that he don't care how old I was."

Nate Thibideau was that "old Cajun boy" and Waller signed on his "little old wooden boat – about forty-feet long and nine- to ten-feet wide – with something like a 110-horsepower Atlas engine in it." To say the accommodations were sparse was to put it mildly. The boat had "no bunks. It was just a piece of junk. What they called the galley was just a part of the engine room with a floor in it and a two-burner butane gas stove. It wasn't much of a boat. I worked from six in the evening until six in the morning. But, I always had some change in my pocket."

Sixty years later, Joe Waller was still clearly remembering his days as a towboater and his feelings about women on boats could not have been less clear. Joe was not the above-mentioned Captain Thibideau who didn't care who worked on his boats "as long as it wasn't a woman." But he sure supported that thesis.

"The industry tried getting more women signed on aboard towboats," Waller recalled, "but these boats are not equipped with private bathrooms and private rooms and everything private. Sometimes we have three men in a room, sometimes two, sometimes four up in the focsule." Even worse, he said, "The bathrooms would consist of two commodes, two wash basins, and two showers and they're not stalled off or anything like that."

He cited as an example a woman who applied for a job as cook and he, then a towboat captain, had to turn her down because of her false expectations. "She later went to a labor board on me," Waller said, and "when I was asked why I turned her down, I told the board that I didn't think she understood what the job was. Somebody had filled her head full of baloney because I said that these are sea-going tugs; they're not luxury liners. They're work boats. I mean they're <u>work</u> boats. When we pick up a barge, I mean, we <u>all</u> come out and work. All of us. Once we get under way, we stand watches (pre-assigned shifts). The cooks get up at 3:00 in the morning to prepare breakfast for the watch-changes between 5:30 and 6:30 in the morning. And then she has lunch ready to serve between 11:30 and 12:30 and the same thing for the evening meal. At night, they're on their own."

On those boats, Waller told her, "We don't have private quarters. You might be in a room with two men, you might in there with one man, you might be in there with three men. And we don't have private bathrooms and we sure don't have room to build one! So I want that understood. If we go somewhere and the crew goes out and gets drunk or you go out and get drunk, and one of them crawls in bed with you, don't you call the home office. Now that's the bottom line. That's the way it is, lady. There is not going to be any doors put on the bathroom stalls or anyplace else."

Backing off somewhat, Waller confided that he had "nothing against women working and making a living and stuff like that. But, you see, they get to hollering that they want 'equal rights.' No they don't. They want special privileges. 'Equal rights' means you want the same thing everybody else gets. But I've seen them out there waiting to tow one of those big off-shore drilling rigs out there and some of those women have welding jobs. But, they want somebody else to carry those automatic welding machines and drag their cables for them and all that kind of stuff. So tell me where that 'equal rights' stuff is. Again, I've got nothing against a gal making a living. But, if she can't cut it, 'go to the house.' That's what they'd tell one of them men. And that means you're gone. You're fired."

There is no escaping the feeling that in Joe Waller's mind – and those of many of his contemporaries – towboating was and is a man's world. Period.

*   *   *

As of June 2008, on our nation's inland waterways and coasts, America's tugboat, towboat and barge industry transported twenty percent of America's coal – enough to produce ten percent of all the electricity used each year in the U.S. It also moved more than sixty percent of U.S. grain exports, helping American farmers compete with foreign producers. Our current fleet of nearly 5,200 modern tugboats and towboats and more than 27,000 barges moves almost 800 million tons of raw materials and finished goods each year. Across the nation's 25,000-mile waterway system, the towboat industry adds five-billion dollars a year to the U. S. economy.

Water transportation is the most economical mode of commercial freight movement. This is due to the enormous capacity of a barge. For example, one typical inland barge has a capacity five times greater than one railroad car and sixty times greater than one semi-trailer truck. String together one forty-barge tow such as the one shown below, and it equals ten freight trains of 100 cars each. It also replaces of 2,400 semi-tractor-trailers burning diesel fuel along the nation's highways thereby moving goods off the already-congested roads and rails and away from crowded population centers. Barges provide a lower cost mode of transportation for a wide range of commodities. Shipping the same 2005 commodity volumes to the same destinations would cost an additional $580 million by rail and $1.6 billion by truck, according to figures in the study.[14]

The practice of towboats pushing as many as forty barges has been condemned by National Mariners Association (nee Gulf Coast Mariners Association) Captain David C. Whitehurst (mentioned on page 14 above).

This modern towboat is pushing forty barges down the Mississippi River.[15]

"These unsafe tows," Whitehurst contended in 2006, "frequently strike bridges and damage shore facilities. This is unsafe for the crews on the vessel as well as the innocent motorist that cross these bridges. When these tows break up, rigging goes flying everywhere, barges sink, other river traffic is delayed, and embattled crews must work day and night to reassemble the tows in all types of weather."[16]

In a related matter, towboat operator Larry Gwin filed a suit against his employer – American River Transportation Company ("Artco") which was operating towboats on the Mississippi River between St. Paul, Minnesota and New Orleans. He charged the company fired him because he refused to perform duties he considered unsafe. In 1999, Artco initiated a "six long" program meaning that its lower river vessels would push forty-eight barges, six long and eight wide.

For five-and-a-half-years, Gwin captained the *Daniel MacMillan*, the largest size towboat on the river at 10,500 horsepower and routinely pushed forty-barge tows between St. Louis and New Orleans. After being told the "six long" program was voluntary, Gwin decided not to participate in the program because he thought the program was unsafe.

A February 1, 2002 company evaluation then rated his performance as "fair" in the category titled "does he/she operate the vessel to its full potential." Gwin wrote to his Artco supervisor saying, "You have asked me if I was willing to take 46 barges southbound. I advised you that the safe number of barges to navigate southbound on the Mississippi River is determined by the river conditions, but never more than 40.... Some of the reasons I gave you for not wanting to take more than 40 barges southbound include my concern for the life and safety of my crew and my livelihood, i.e., my license...."

In January of 2003, Gwin received another evaluation that rated his performance as "good" in eleven of thirteen categories but only "fair" rating for "learns new skills" and again, "does he/she operate the vessel to its full potential." Thirty days later, Artco discharged Gwin through a letter indicating that he had been terminated because of "a reduction in Artco's business." Gwin sued Artco claiming it is illegal to discharge a seaman for refusing to perform duties ordered by his employer if the duties would result in serious injury. A jury found for him and awarded him monetary compensation after a 12-day trial that began on February 27, 2006. After Artco appealed the verdict, the United States Court of Appeals for the Seventh Circuit upheld the verdict on April 10, 2007.[17]

Gwin was not alone in his position. Towing companies often push pilots to their limits, said retired pilot Arthur Harman Sr., of East Liverpool, Ohio, who navigated Pittsburgh's rivers for thirty years. He said he'd been denied work because he wouldn't steer in fog or take on more cargo than he thought was safe.[18]

*   *   *

Captain Waller cites an even greater extreme than the forty barges shown in the preceding picture. He claims the record for the largest number of barges in one tow is eighty-seven! Waller said it was set by Alvin Murphy when he was working on a trip from New Orleans to St Louis. Just imagine. Eighty-seven barges! That's a long look from the wheelhouse to the front of the tow – almost 1800 feet (three city blocks) and about 500 feet more than quarter-of-a-mile! Under normal operating conditions (which include all kinds of weather), a watchman – with radio communication with the helmsman – is required to be on a barge at the head of a long tow. The next time you're driving down an Interstate highway and you see a sign about an exit ramp quarter-of-a-mile away, look ahead at that distance and imagine the head of a tow up there at the approaching overpass.

Look again at the picture on page 28 and imagine, if you can, a string of barges twice as long as the one in that picture. Captain Waller, scratching his head and chuckling a bit, described it. "The record for the largest number of barges in one tow was set by Alvin Murphy – eighty-seven barges! They were standard, 195x35-foot grain barges and he had them stacked up eight or nine deep and ten wide."[19]

Musing on, Waller remembered that "Ol' Alvin was one heck of a guy. He usually had his wife riding with him because he didn't like readin' the river chart books. He was an ol' Cajun boy who couldn't read or write. His wife would read the chart books for 'im and when she couldn't be with 'im, she'd tape-record the notes – listin' the light numbers and the mile-markers[b] – and ol' Murphy would listen to the tapes while navigatin' the rivers."[20] They obviously didn't have as many regulations nor regulators back in the days when Alvin Murphy was plying the inland waterways. One can only hope that Ol' Alvin had 20-20 eyesight.

*   *   *

In 2002 as noted above, 799 million tons of materials were transported via barge at an average of 1,500 tons per barge and fifteen barges per fleet. That's 35,500 barge trips per year or nearly 100 trips each day.[21] Consequently, waterways are very busy with all kinds of traffic. So it is hardly surprising that accidents involving barges/tows sometimes occur. America's 25,000 miles of navigable inland waterways connect ports along the Gulf Intracoastal Waterway with such cities as Mobile, Alabama; New Orleans and Baton Rouge, Louisiana; and Houston, Corpus Christi and Brownsville, Texas.

Those ports, in turn, connect with major inland ports such as Memphis, St. Louis, Chicago, St. Paul, Cincinnati, and Pittsburgh. All of them, in turn, connect with the Lower Mississippi River and the Tennessee-

---

[b] Mile-markers along the banks of major waterways are used much the same as those on the nation's Interstate Highway System.

Tombigbee Waterway, allowing ocean shipping to connect with the barge traffic going up and down these water highways and thereby making them vital to both the domestic and foreign trade of the United States.

Additionally and based on several working trips on commercial boats on the Mississippi, we'll also report on towboat people, their life-styles and working conditions. And, in a 1,700-mile trip down the "tree" trip from Chicago, Illinois to Freeport, Texas taken by this writer in a forty-seven-foot sail-less sailboat, we'll pass along some pleasant and even frightening observations about the Tom Sawyer-Huck Finn life on this nation's Inland waterways. Life isn't always easy and it's hardly ever glamorous.

Daily salaries for deckhands on average are $150; they range from $250 to $500 a day for pilots and captains. Some workers are on the river for 14 days, and off seven. Some are scheduled to be on the river 21 days, and off 14. Some have seven days on, seven days off. Turnover is high, not only because of the safety issues, but because of the isolation, loneliness and long times away from home. As was said so often in "Hill Street Blues," an Emmy Award-winning, long-running American television police drama, so, too, it applies to life on the nation's water-bound system: you have to "be careful out there."

*   *   *

32

Chapter III
And the Rivers Taketh Away....

Everybody and his brother it seemed knew the frigid, raging Ohio River was going to be trouble in the early hours of January 9, 2005 – especially those who were unfortunate enough to be working on that river on that morning at that place. All the towboat crews knew it. The towboat-owning company knew it. The U.S. Coast Guard, the U.S. Corps of Engineers, and the lockmasters at the Montgomery Lock and Dam on the Ohio River knew it. This was not the kind of black night to be out working on a river. Everybody there knew it. IT – was a disaster waiting to happen. And, IT did.

The towboat *Elizabeth M,* up-bound on the Ohio River that night with a crew of seven, picked up six 195x35-foot barges – each fully-loaded with 1,000 tons of coal destined for Braddock, Pennsylvania. There were apprehensions among some crew members, especially after other towboat crews down-stream warned them about the turbulent conditions ahead. Some towboats wouldn't even dare to venture out of port that night because of the rough river and the icy weather conditions. When ice forms on the broad, flat surfaces of river barges, it weighs them down considerably and added weight can lead to maneuverability problems – to say nothing of slippery deck conditions for the towboat crew.

"Work on a towboat can be dangerous in the best of weather," wrote Virginia Linn in the *Pittsburgh Post-Gazette.* "Throw in a mix of frigid winds and ice, high water and fast currents, and it becomes downright deadly. Most of the time," she continued in quoting local boat owner Phillip Johnson, "you get good serenity. Time to yourself and good thinking....Summertime it's beautiful, fall and spring it's beautiful. Wintertime can be pretty rough."[22] Most riverboat personnel would consider that a mild understatement, especially when "lines from the towboats to the barges can freeze or become slippery in snow; high waters can cause a towboat to lose control of its barges."[23]

Although the Coast Guard can shut down a river, usually it's the company's or the captain's call whether or not to challenge the elements. Decisions are based on Coast Guard rules, distance to be traveled, size, ability and availability of crew, weight of load, and the towboat's capacity to handle the barges under those conditions. Mostly, it's a "gut" call or just plain old "intuition."

The *Elizabeth M* (photo by Campbell Transportation Company[c]

Nonetheless and according to reports, the 108-foot towboat *Elizabeth M* corralled its six barges at George-town, Pennsylvania, around ten o'clock on the freezing, moonless night of January 8, 2005. The staging area for putting the tow together was about eight miles west of the Montgomery Lock and Dam on the Pennsylvania side of

---

c Towboat fleets often have a common name or category for their boats, such as family/longtime

employee names, company big-wigs – *Warren J. Doucet, Miss Andy, Chris, Elaine G.* and *Robert Y. Love*;

the "moon" boats - *Angola Moon*; the thoroughbred boats - *Count Fleet, Swaps, Whirlaway*, etc.; race

tracks - *Belmont, Hialeah, Pimlico*, and so forth.

its state border with West Virginia and about thirty-two miles northwest of Pittsburgh. Weather conditions meant a tough slog fighting against an estimated twelve-to-fifteen-knot current – three to four times the river's normal down-stream speed. The hills of western Pennsylvania and eastern West Virginia force the river into narrower and thereby swifter channels. Traffic through the lock was down to four vessels a day versus its normal seventeen for that time of the year. A river "advisory" was in effect. Recent heavy rains and flooding had turned what veteran tow-boaters mockingly called "the retirement river" into a raging torrent.

An indication of just how powerful the Ohio River was barreling down-stream was that it took the tow almost three hours to travel those eight miles. Normally, it would do it in half that time. Still, despite the falling 38-degree F. temperature, all appeared to go well as the *Elizabeth M* and its barges made their way toward the Montgomery Lock at mile-marker 31.7 on the Ohio River. The Montgomery is a busy lock, normally handling approximately 550 commer-cial lock-throughs a month plus another 275 pleasure craft during the summer months.[24] Those 275 pleasure craft a month (3,300 a year), as busy as it seems for the Montgomery Lock, pales considerably when compared to the Windy City's Chicago Lock which moved 37,366 vessels through one chamber in 2002.[25]

The Montgomery Lock and Dam is one of the U. S. Army Corps of Engineers' 257 owned or operated lock chambers at 212 sites along the inland waterways, 145 of which also serve as multi-purpose dams. For example, forty-six lock-associated dams currently produce hydro-power. The builders of these locks and dams are to be commended for their workmanship as some of them, built in the 1800's, are still operational. Even more amazing are Locks One and Two on the Kentucky River – just west of the town of Carrollton – which were built in 1839![26]

Meanwhile, on the *Elizabeth M*, things were going so well, the towboat's captain, George (Toby) Zappone – with twenty-four years of experience on the inland water-ways, twelve of them as a licensed captain – felt secure

The Montgomery Lock and Dam - in quieter times

leaving the boat's wheelhouse around midnight and turning the "con" (command) over to his relief pilot, thirty-six-year-old Scott Stewart. In addition to briefing Stewart on weather conditions, Zappone left orders that his brother-in-law, Rick Conklin – who was aboard as a pilot-in-training – "should not pilot the boat in high water." [27] Actually, Zappone was merely reiterating the policy of Campbell Transportation Company (owner of the *Elizabeth M*) which stated a "striker-pilot must serve watch under the direct supervision of the (ship's) Master."[28]

Things had progressed markedly "since the 1970s when pilots were 'a dime a dozen' and the Coast Guard handed out Operator of Uninspected Towing Vessel (OUTV) to just about anyone that wanted one."[29] Campbell Transportation, operating on the Upper Ohio River, had been in business for over sixty years that January morning with a fleet of thirty towboats and 420 open-hopper barges.

* * *

Kennon Bradley "Spiderman" Ashley, born in Natchez, Mississippi in 1976, wasn't anywhere near the Montgomery Lock and Dam that January morning in 2005 as he told the story of how he got his nickname almost exactly three years earlier down south on the Mississippi. "I got bit by a brown recluse spider right on my shoulder blade," said Ashley with a grimace. "I had a big hole in my shoulder blade and it swole up and hurt like the dickens so I had to go to a hospital. And wouldn't you know it," he continued, "about four months later I got bit on the opposite shoulder blade and the same thing happened."

When a landlubber with a tape recorder slung around his neck asked, "How come," the "Spiderman" looked at his questioner like he came from outer space. "Are you kidding," he answered incredulously, "It's 'cause there's bugs on boats and where there's bugs, there's spiders. Spiders eat bugs. Hell," he snapped, "on the Mississippi River, there's bugs ever' where!"

Another thing the "Spiderman" knows a thing or two about is locking through the Ohio River's standard 110x600-foot locks because there have been times when, because of another deckhand's illness, he's had to do the deck hands' job all by himself, often with jumbo barges (those larger than the standard 195x35-foot barges) to make it even tougher. Oddly enough, it is not unusual to run a boat short-handed. Deckhands come and go – sometimes the latter in mid-trip. Instead of the typical "grass being greener on the other side of the fence," the river boatman's saying is "the water seems deeper on the other side of the shore."

Ashley described short-handing. "It's as if you're out there by yourself and you gotta break the couplin's on the barges and get the lockmaster to pull them through, get back on the boat and put the other two barges in the lock, break the boat out, and get the lockmaster to pull them through too, then put the boat in the lock and take it through, then build tow again," said Ashley as breathlessly as if he had just completed the job.

To make things worse, he continued, "on that Ohio River, you come out of one lock and you're lookin' at another one and they're both 600-foot locks. So, if you're out there by yourself, you got four good, hard hours of work." He didn't feel he needed to explain to the note-taker that all the locks on the upper Ohio, the upper Mississippi and the Illinois rivers are also 600-footers. What the note-taker should have known was the crew doesn't have to break-up the tows as much in the larger locks as they do in the smaller ones (see Glossary). But even the 600-footers are now deemed too small. Most tows today are 1,200-feet. The Upper Mississippi River's smaller locks create significant delays because to pass through a 600-foot lock on a larger tow "you gotta break the couplin's on the barges" and can take about two-hours. With the new 1,200-foot locks, the process would take half that time or less.

*   *   *

As they approached the Montgomery Lock and Dam, the seven-man crew aboard the *Elizabeth M* wasn't facing "Spiderman's" troubles. They weren't short-handed. They didn't have to worry about bugs and spiders in that frigid weather. At about 1:00 a.m., the towboat and its barges made it safely to the Montgomery Lock's 110x600-foot chamber and started "locking through." John Thomas was the lead deckhand. His job, like that of most deckhands, meant constantly going across the decks tightening the ratchets on the wires connecting the barges to each other and to the towboat. There's always a certain amount of slippage in the cables due to metal contraction and expansion and river forces greater than a deckhand's working on the connected vessels.

Also, it is amazing to stand on the deck of a towboat and listen as one of the deck hands asks the towboat pilot to "please bring it (the load) up about four inches." Moments later, he calls again, "Ok. Take it up another inch." In addition, deckhands generally have to do just about all the unwanted jobs on a tow – chip paint, mop up, sweep up, clean out the toilets, etc. Some of them have to make the beds. And they have to learn how to lash the barges.

There's a natural – almost time-honored – progression up thorough the chain of command in towboating. It starts with being an apprentice deckhand, the greenest of the green. It usually takes at least one, maybe two 30-day hitches on the water to shed the apprentice label and assume the glories of a deckhand as outlined above, assuming you pass the critical eye of the boat's captain. Common sense also helps in passing the working tests.

The next step up the ladder is tankerman-trainee on those barges carrying various liquid cargoes of volatile chemicals. There is a formal school for tankerman training where candidates are taught techniques for loading and discharging barges. Another one or two hitches on the water are necessary before final licensing.

If a deckhand/tankerman has made it this far, the next job is a relief mate taking over when the regular mate is off duty. On some boats, the mate runs the deck crew independently and doesn't need to deal with the captain. On other boats, the mate is merely a middle man between the captain and the deckhands. Until the confidence of an established working situation is reached, the captain simply tells the mate what needs to be done and generally lets the mate do the job. Otherwise, the mate makes the decisions independently.

Generally under the supervision of the mate, the deckhands do the previously mentioned general maintenance when they are not engaged in "tow work" – building and breaking apart the tow by lashing barges together with wire cables and keeping the rigging tight during the river run. This is done by brute strength and with the aid of ratcheted winches. If a string of barges is longer than a lock, the deckhands break the strings into lock-size components, just as "Spiderman" described it above.

The mate graduates to relief pilot and then to pilot and to captain. However, on some towboats, after being licensed to command, a few skippers think the words "Captain" and "God" are synonymous. So much of any crew person's training in any step up the ladder on a towboat is on-the-job. Whether it's working in the engine room – as the plumber, the electrician, the pipefitter, the janitor – or in the wheelhouse, you learn a lot by simply doing. Working as a one- or a two-man "black-gang" member in the bowels of the a boat or in the airy "penthouse" topside behind "the sticks," most of the learning comes from watching "old hands" do their job.

Thus the crew of an Inland Waterways towboat will normally consist of a captain and a pilot (who relieves the captain – only of his navigational duties), a chief engineer and a cook with no relief crew for them but who work as needed, two shifts of two deckhands each (one of whom could be a tankerman certified for "red flag" cargo if needed), and two alternating-shift mates. Other than the cook and the engineer, a normal "on deck" complement for a 30-barge rig is four – captain or pilot, one mate, two deckhands.

There is a sizeable personnel turnover in these lower ranks, so much so there's a saying among the captains on some boats: "Have you hugged a deckhand today?" This kind of towboat work goes on year-round in the complete spectrum of weather conditions, some of the worst of which was being experienced in the early hours of January 9, 2005 on the Ohio River at the Montgomery Lock and Dam.

*   *   *

John Thomas aboard the *Elizabeth M* learned all that stuff years before and observing the Montgomery Lock entry procedure, he reported, it "went smooth as could be.... It was a beautiful approach."[30] The six barges were inside the lock, snugly tied to the lock's shore side on the right wall. The towboat nestled alongside them on their left side as river water flooded into the chamber to raise them all to the next "step" (level) of the Ohio River's "stairway" in the locking-through procedure.

At that early-morning hour, Captain Zappone, Tom Fisher and Jacob Wilds were the three members of the so-called "Captain's Watch," the 0600-Noon and the 1800-Midnight shifts.[d] They were "officially" off-duty. They had retired to their quarters to catch whatever sleep they could before reporting back on duty at six in the morning. The "After Watch" crew (Noon-6:00PM/Midnight-6:00AM) consisted of Stewart, Conklin, Thomas and Ed Crevda. People working shifts like that in such prolonged and close proximity often develop a "family" attitude among towboat crews.

"If I had to go out on a boat," one old salt told this writer, "and one of my kids was sick or something like that

---

[d] Sometimes called a "back watch" and a "front watch," the pilot usually has the back watch. His primary responsibility is to drive the boat. The "captain" has the front watch and he's ultimately responsible for everything.

and those other wives heard about it (and everybody knew everybody and their families), they'd come over and help my wife with the laundry or pick up the wash and take it home or take care of the kids or whatever was needed. People cared. Boating people are strange people," he continued. "But, they're good people. They're beautiful people. What makes us a family," he said, "is the close-living together; everybody sharing, and the fact that we're dependent upon each other." The "family" crew "dependent upon each other" aboard the *Elizabeth M* started bringing the tow out of the lock and heading it for Bradford, Pennsylvania.

Bringing the tow out of the lock. That's when all Hell broke loose.

*   *   *

It should be noted here that a common procedure for putting barges into a lock is to have the towboat push the barges in and, if there isn't enough room left in the lock for the towboat to stay behind the barges, it will disconnect and slide into the lock alongside the barges. That's what happened at the Montgomery Lock and Dam. In often conflicting reports at the time, the 600-foot-long string of six barges (three rows of two-abreast) was pushed out of the lock by the *Elizabeth M* and into the Ohio River's furious flow. Something called an "outdraft" current caught the shore-side, right-front barge and started pushing the string left toward the middle of the river.

An outdraft, said 30-year river pilot Fred J. Hunter at a subsequent U.S. Coast Guard inquiry, "just wants to suck you right out there"[31] into the middle of the river's flow. It intensifies during high water conditions. According to Hunter, the way to escape an outdraft is to build up a head of steam, steer directly into the current, and then head off toward the nearest shoreline. Montgomery Lockmaster

John Anderson said of such rogue currents, "You need to stay against the wall of the lock because the river has a lot of outdraft that will push you out, especially with the dam wide open."[32] That wide-open dam would later become a controversial factor.

According to the Coast Guard "inquiry,"[e] deckhand Thomas said pilot-in-training Conklin – instead of regular pilot Stewart – was at the controls of the *Elizabeth M* as it started to exit the lock, despite Captain Zappone's warning.[33] "Rick was at the sticks," said Thomas, who also said he heard Conklin on the radio. "I have no doubt in my mind." [34] (The Coast Guard's final report, issued on November 8, 2007, agreed Conklin "was at the wheel of the *Elizabeth M* when it first left the lock."[35])

As soon as the lock personnel cleared the tow to leave the chamber, *whoever* was at the helm – Stewart or Conklin – started shoving the barges forward while simultaneously sliding the *Elizabeth M* back to the rear of the tow where it would take up its normal pushing position. The intent there was to face-up (re-cable) the barges to the towboat "on the fly," as they say. It was a common maneuver. The trouble was, the forward, free-moving barges – no longer under the towboat's control – were caught by that outdraft as they left the lock and were forced dramatically left. "I noticed that the head of the tow looked weird. It was riding out (toward the center of the river)," Thomas testified.[36] The entire rig swung left and headed directly into the boiling river flow roaring down-stream toward the dam extending perpendicular to the lock across the entire width of the waterway.

As the tow started to get away, the towboat hit one of the lock's walls, setting off the general alarm on the

---

[e] a preliminary hearing held shortly after the accident which leads to a final report that in this case would not be issued until almost three years later.

boat. Although contradicting their testimony later, two Army Corps of Engineers lock workers testified they did not see or hear any of the barges hit the sides of the locks while exiting. On the other hand, the boat's survivors said the barges did hit the lock walls, snapping the barges' attaching cables to each other.[37] The official Coast Guard report said there were actually three allisions between the tow, the towboat, and the lock works.[38]

Now, it was "all hands on deck!" time. Captain Zappone testified he was below decks sleeping when the incident started. He dashed to the pilothouse dressed only in his shorts and T-shirt following the urgent clanging of general alarm bells. There he said he saw Stewart – not Conklin – at the wheel. Zappone took over momentarily but he had to scramble back to his cabin to get his eyeglasses.[39]

When the Captain returned to the pilot house, he said Stewart was still at the wheel. At that point, the *Elizabeth M* was just emerging from the lock as Thomas finally managed to get the runaway barges cabled back to the towboat. But now, it was too little, too late. The barges were being dragged inexorably by the outdraft current away from the relative calm of the east bank on the right side of the river. They were sliding into the center of the river where the down-bound current was strongest. The thick steel wire cables used to lash the barges to each other and to the towboat[f] started snapping like uncooked spaghetti straws. "We kept breaking lines left and right, from the current and the weight of the tow," said Thomas.[40] Weighted down with 6,000 tons of coal, some of the barges started coming loose from each other and headed straight for the dam's thundering spillway, now less than a quarter-mile away.

---

[f] Steel cables are called "wire," regardless of size and they usually come in thirty-five and sixty-five-foot lengths.

Zappone frantically fought back at the wheel. The captain tried to steer the still-attached barges to the mooring cells, the huge concrete piers in the water above and below the ends of the lock walls to which tows sometimes tie up while waiting to lock through. He hoped to get them tied off there. But when one of the barges still lashed to the towboat started to take on water and began to sink, with no other choice, Zappone ordered all barges cut loose. He then tried desperately to bring the towboat up against the side of one of the loose barges – now perpendicular to the river's flow – and push it away from its down-stream path to destruction.

However, that became a secondary objective. Ed Helenic, who started working at the lock the previous November, said he was baffled when he saw the captain turn his boat down-stream, toward the dam and the barges, in a river running twelve-mph, four times faster than normal. "I say to myself, 'What the hell is he doing'" Helenic wondered.[41] The answer to that question became Zappone's primary mission: get his deckhands off the barges and back on the towboat.

Montgomery lockmaster Anderson agreed with that opinion. "I think [Zappone] went around the barges for another push to save the men on the barges [who were still trying to lash them back together]," he said in one report. "You wouldn't normally risk your life to save coal barges."[42] Anderson, who had then worked at Montgomery Dam for fifteen years, said he'd never seen anything like the accident. "How far he went out there before he went into the river (current), I don't know," Anderson said. "What truly happened, what's going through that pilot's mind, I don't know. Only he can answer that."[43] Another viewpoint, a popular one among those in the towboat fraternity, was expressed by Greg Periman of Siloam Springs, Arkansas who has been working rivers since 1976, including those in the Pittsburgh area. "He probably thought he'd lose his job if he lost those barges," Periman said.[44]

In a white-knuckle effort, Zappone was "burnin' the beans" as diesel smoke poured from the towboat's stack. Using the boat's declared 2,200-horse-power engine, Zappone try to muscle the barges away from the outdraft and perhaps beach them on the near shore. According to one official, the *Elizabeth M*, with her updated engines, had enough power – on paper, at least – to push the coal-laden barges through the fierce twelve-to-fifteen mph current and away from the locks. "That's what it's designed to do," said Coast Guard Commander Wyman Briggs. "The river, though rough, was navigable."[45]

However, the Coast Guard's final report on the incident concluded that "engine governors had been installed [on the *Elizabeth M*], limiting speed to 1,200 rpm, insufficient to overcome the currents in the restricted area above the dam."[46] The *Elizabeth M* was built in 1951 by Dravo Corp. on the Ohio River's nearby Neville Island and, like most towboats, had engine governors installed to keep the engines from over-speeding and blowing up, the same as your small lawnmower motor.

Horsepower, real or imagined, was in contention here – as it would also be in some other incidents reported on these pages. There has long been an argument within the industry (between the towboat-owning companies and the crews that sail them) and without (between the regulators and the crewmen). On the one hand, there's the claimed (or "paper") horsepower that some boats are certificated with to enable them to be approved for larger and heavier loads. On the other hand, there is what one towboat captain calls the "honest" horsepower the boats actually have and it is invariably far less that the "paper" claim. As Captain Larry Gwin (pages 29-30) put it in his testimony in front of a U. S. Coast Guard advisory committee, "I have watched one industry publication 'increase' the paper horsepower on some 8,400 horsepower boats to 9,000 horsepower without a commensurate mechanical upgrade of any sort."[47]

Ironically, the *Elizabeth M* had another power failure the previous September 24. Coast Guard spokesman Lieutenant Junior Grade Justin Covert said that loss of power, "probably means loss of propulsion." *Elizabeth M* owner Campbell Transportation Co. inspected the vessel's hull and machinery in October, according to a company statement released five days after the crash. The boat was put back into service "in excellent working condition," the company said. The *Elizabeth M* spilled 1,000 gallons of diesel fuel into the Ohio River in 1998, when it grounded on rocks...(about which the company apologized) "for overlooking"[48] (i.e., failing to report to investigators).

At one point, crew members even had a brief moment to breathe an unjustified sigh of relief as they thought the situation had stabilized. "I didn't feel no need for panic," deckhand Thomas said later because "barges break loose all the time." As a matter of fact, two runaway coal barges threatened the Sewickley Bridge over the Ohio River east of the Montgomery L&D just six days later. There were nine or more other incidents, mostly on the Ohio, of barge breakaways, of boats or barges striking bridge piers, or similar safety problems involving tows, according to U.S. Coast Guard Lieutenant Kevin Lynn, of the marine safety division in New Orleans. [49] Still, deckhand Thomas said he "didn't feel in any type of danger. All [seven of the crew was] working together."[50] They were making some headway. Deckhand Jacob (Jake) Wilds had similar feelings of relief. There was a time, he said, when "crewmembers believed they had won the fight and were taking pictures with cameras and camera cell phones."[51]

Some headway was being made. But not enough.

*   *   *

With all the deckhands back on the towboat, Zappone continued to try to save the barges by pushing them upstream against the unstoppable flow instead of, perhaps, abandoning them and saving the *Elizabeth M.* He reportedly was afraid the runaway barges might slam into a highway or railway bridge abutment down-river. Exactly that happened on September 22, 1993 when the towboat *Mauvilla* had an "encounter" with the Big Bayou Canot railroad bridge ten miles northeast of Mobile, Alabama. That sent forty-seven people aboard Amtrak's "Sunset Limited" railroad train to a cruelly contrasting fiery-watery death. Another 103 passengers were injured, many seriously, as is recounted in Chapter VIII.

But Captain Zappone's decision to attempt to save the barges was crucial and risky, testified river pilot Hunter – with perfect 20/20 hindsight. "I could tell you right there, that wasn't going to work. Not with the horsepower [of the] vessel he had," the river man said. "In that state of river up there, it's treacherous, there's no doubt about it." [52] Conversely, one who was there – deckhand Wilds – said about efforts to still save the barges, "We cut [the barges] loose but we stayed with them. The Captain never let go. He kept trying to get them." Wilds' favorable comments about Captain Zappone would change later on.

The embattled skipper then brought the bow of the *Elizabeth M* to a position midway between the barges, now parallel to the dam, and again tried to shove them back to the nearest shore. In so doing, the *Elizabeth M* proceeded inside an Army Corps of Engineers restricted area guarding the dam. As Zappone tried to push the barges back upstream, the *Elizabeth M* was unable to make any headway. In reality, the towboat actually started losing ground.

Suddenly, the looming disaster at the Montgomery Lock and Dam was compounded. The onrushing river current started pushing some of the barges – each loaded with 1,000 tons of coal – down against the *Elizabeth M.* It too was being forced down-stream into the gaping maw of the 1,378-foot-long dam's thundering spillway. At the same time, Thomas did everything he could do to try to salvage the situation. He again jumped back and forth from the towboat to the barges in a vain attempt to secure lines to the rapidly accelerating family of doomed vessels. When it became apparent his efforts were fruitless, he made one last leap across the churning river back to the towboat. By now, just about everything was lost. In moments, those losses would rise exponentially.

*   *   *

Now the free-floating barges, with the towboat trapped between them and the dam's magnet-like pull, started – one by one – to either sink or wash over the dam. The crew's cries of "We need to cut loose! We need to cut loose!" filled the air. But it was already too late. Almost before the crew knew it, the towboat, too, was in the process of going over the dam. Three of the barges, now free of any restraint from the *Elizabeth M*, slipped around it and went over the dam. At this point, there was no getting free for the towboat either. There was no way out for the entrapped *Elizabeth M*. The towboat did manage to slip off to the left of the onrushing barges. As the river's vortex magnified at the face of the spillway, it quickly and totally overwhelmed the *Elizabeth M*'s engine capacity and the towboat, too, went over the dam, stern first.

With the dam highly illuminated as usual, the U. S. Army Corps of Engineers workers on the lock knew moments earlier trouble was brewing when they heard the engine on the *Elizabeth M* screaming at its maximum rpms in a futile effort to overcome the forces of both the river and the barges pushing the uncontrollable towboat down-stream. Unlike the "Little Engine That Could" of fairy-tale fame as it successfully overcame a mountain's vertical

49

gravity, the marine engine on the towboat couldn't; it failed in its horizontal effort.

As the catastrophe started to unfold, the crews on two other nearby towboats – the *Lillian G* and the *Sandy Drake* – initiated rescue efforts. They started throwing life preservers and everything else that would float into the river, hoping something, anything would reach the *Elizabeth M's* beleaguered crew and give them something to grab and stay afloat. Having heard the radio distress calls coming from the dam, the *Rocket*, another Campbell Transportation boat not too far down-river (but not close enough either) quickly got up a head of steam and drove up-river towards the face of the dam. The *Rocket's* pilot, Charles Montgomery, gave his three crewmen – Robert Corman, Donald Brown and Thomas Zeigler – a choice before departure. They could get off their sixty-six-foot towboat or they could head up-river against the raging current to try to rescue the *Elizabeth M's* crew. Without hesitation, the crew volunteered to head up-stream.[53]

All but one of the seven *Elizabeth M* crew members managed to get topside before the vessel slid over the spillway. During the jolting ride over the dam, deckhand Jacob Wilds said they were thrown around "like crash dummies." The boat inexplicitly (at the time) sank almost immediately as it plunged into the raging whirlpool churning more than five feet above the river's normal fifteen-foot height. Only the very top of the wheelhouse remained visible while the towboat sat on the river's bed facing up-stream. According to the Coast Guard's final report issued on November 8, 2007, "modifications made to the *Elizabeth M* in 1997 allowed the vessel to flood faster than it should have, and quickened its sinking."[54]

Word of the disaster, triggered initially by the lock workers, spread throughout the nearby marine area. As one

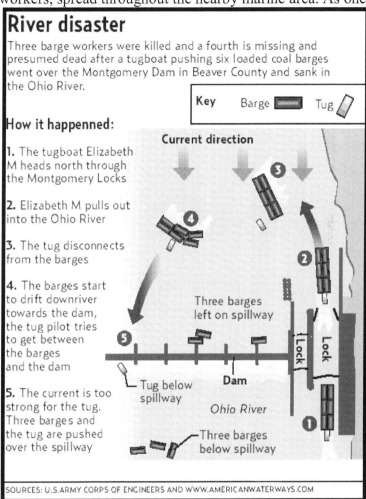

River disaster

Three barge workers were killed and a fourth is missing and presumed dead after a tugboat pushing six loaded coal barges went over the Montgomery Dam in Beaver County and sank in the Ohio River.

Key   Barge ▬   Tug

How it happenned:

1. The tugboat Elizabeth M heads north through the Montgomery Locks

2. Elizabeth M pulls out into the Ohio River

3. The tug disconnects from the barges

4. The barges start to drift downriver towards the dam, the tug pilot tries to get between the barges and the dam

5. The current is too strong for the tug. Three barges and the tug are pushed over the spillway

Current direction

Three barges left on spillway

Tug below spillway

Dam

Three barges below spillway

Ohio River

Lock

Lock

SOURCES: U.S. ARMY CORPS OF ENGINEERS AND WWW.AMERICANWATERWAYS.COM

**(It should again be noted: many times towboats
are mislabeled as "tugs")**

newspaper article reported, "Corps [of Engineers] employees rushed out onto the top of the dam and tossed out some life preservers." Heroes and heroics were abundant although the latter was tragically not universal – after the

The *Elizabeth M* shortly after going over the dam.
Photo: Bob Donaldson, *Post-Gazette*

Elizabeth M went over the dam. Don Hopey of the *Pittsburgh Post-Gazette* described the scene this way:

> Screams for help echoed from the towboat *Elizabeth M* as it sank into the swirling, frigid Ohio River after tumbling backward through the Montgomery Dam.... The crew's cries could be heard over the rushing wall of noise from the river as it sluiced through the wide open dam gates, and over traffic noise on [nearby] state Route-68.... "I could hear them screaming all the way across the road at my house," said Stanley Bostwick, a member of [a local] Volunteer Fire Department, who lives at least 200 yards from the dam. "When I got here the boat was still above water, but it was sinking fast."[55]

Chuck Ward, a local assistant fire chief, echoed that frustration. "What was so bad was that we could hear the guys on the boat screaming for help but we couldn't do anything," he said. Three of the six *Elizabeth M* crewmen quickly lost their grip on the boat's icy hand-holds and were immediately swept down-stream under the thrashing current. Ed Crevda was eventually pulled from the water but he died later that day in a nearby hospital. The bodies of drowning victims Tom Fisher and Scott Stewart were identified later that Sunday.

The body of the fourth fatality, Rick Conklin, wasn't recovered from the towboat's hull until the craft was raised from the water on March 4, 2005 – Conklin's father's sixty-sixth birthday. Immediately following the wreck, Conklin's 39-year-old sister, Lori Hoover of Fredericktown, Pa., was bereft. She wanted to know "why they were on the river. Barges can be replaced but not a life. It's too dangerous. It's not worth a life." As the days dragged on, she wished her brother "would reach his hand up out of the water and I would just grab it." Continuing the family's futile vigil, Ms. Hoover said, "I hope he's not dead, but if he is, I hope he's in the boat, then at least we can come to some kind of closure."[56] The Conklin family got that closure after almost two months of hopeless prayers.

But Captain Zappone and crewmembers Thomas and Wilds were spared. Zappone and Thomas were able to hold on to the towboat for what Thomas thought were "hours." For however long those "hours" were, the gallant deckhand held on to a pilothouse ladder with left arm and to his captain with his right. "We're gonna make it. We're gonna make it," Thomas kept shouting to Zappone. But, even as he screamed encouragement to the wounded skipper, who later had to have a finger amputated, Thomas was not sure he would be able to hang on much longer and he "made his peace with God."

"If I wasn't going to die that day, [the captain] wasn't either," Thomas said, as the U.S. Coast Guard later commended the humble deckhand for his heroism. Recalling that he gave his captain "my coat, my gloves, anything I could do to try to stop the bleeding," Thomas said Zappone "didn't even want to be saved. He was hurt so bad because he lost his crew members that he kept saying, 'Just let me go'."[57]

John Thomas, "Tony" to those who knew him, was a big, strong, strapping man – one who looked like he was born for the sometimes grueling river work; someone who looked like a character out of a Mark Twain novel. While he was holding on to Zappone, the captain was calling for help on a hand-held radio and fighting off the numbing effects of the icy-cold, chest-high water. "He was going into shock. He kept slipping into the water ... He wasn't concerned about himself. He kept talking about the guys, the guys," Thomas said of Zappone.[58]

Both of them were yelling to the lock and dam personnel – many of whom had come out across the top of the dam trying to lend assistance – hoping against hope to have a helicopter flown over to airlift the towboat men from their perilous perch. Soon, however, the *Rocket* hove (came) into view and drove precariously close to the cascade streaming down the face of the dam. "I could hear them saying they couldn't hold on much longer," remembered the rescue boat's skipper, Charles Montgomery. "They were hurt. They needed help."

As the *Rocket* approached, her crew prepared flotation devices and gathered blankets, Montgomery said. One crewman put a pot of chicken broth on the stove.[59] In a delicate maneuver in the churning river, the sister-ship got close enough to throw out life preservers and ring buoys. *Rocket* crewmen called for Thomas and Zappone to abandon their ship, dive into the river and catch one of those life preservers so they could be pulled to safety aboard the rescue vessel.

Even with ever-weakening grips brought on by the numbing cold, jumping into the icy river wasn't a pleasant prospect – but it was their only alternative because the *Rocket* couldn't get any closer to the *Elizabeth M*. Faced with their dangerous "fish-or-cut-bait" decision, Zappone and Thomas got into an argument about who would jump first. The captain felt the age-old seaman's adage that the skipper must be the last one to leave a sinking ship. Thomas wasn't having any of that. He was certain the wounded captain wouldn't have the physical strength to leap far enough to catch a life ring.

So, Thomas literally picked up the smaller skipper and threw him bodily at one of the many preservers the nearby towboat sent flying into the river. Assured that Zappone had caught on to a life ring still attached to the *Rocket*, Thomas then dove into the raging river and grabbed another one for himself and the two of them were dragged aboard the *Rocket* – all at considerable risk to that vessel and its crew.

At some early point in the struggle for survival, deckhand Wilds went back to his quarters to get his camera/cell phone and began taking pictures. However, he lost the cell phone as the tow went over the dam. Then, he said, Fisher, Crevda and he tried to get the *Elizabeth M*'s lifeboat released and into the river but couldn't get it deployed, in part, because it was submerged in water. "It's like a winch system," Wilds said later. "There's gotta be a quicker, better way to get that boat in the water."[60]

As the *Elizabeth M* early on settled to the bottom of the Ohio River, Wilds was washed overboard and blacked out as he was carried down-river, tumbling like a tree branch in the turbulent waters. "I remember drowning," he recalled. "I remember thinking I gave up. I gave my regards to God." He also thought about his nineteen-month-old daughter, Storm, and other people he loved. And then, suddenly he "didn't want to drown anymore." He called it a "miracle" when "my head popped above the water" and he yelled for help. Wearing his life-preserver, he stayed afloat

Days later, the *Elizabeth M* sits in about 15-feet of water.
Photo: Robin Rombach, *Post Gazette*

"for another hour," he said. Then crewmen from still another boat down-stream spotted him and pulled him out of the water.[61] Earlier, he saw something floating nearby in the water that he thought was a body but when he grabbed it he found it was a garbage bag.[62] His best friend and fellow-crewman, Tom Fisher, wasn't so lucky. His last words to Wilds as the towboat went over the dam were, "Don't worry, Jake."

For their acts of personal courage in extremely adverse and dangerous conditions, Captain Charles Montgomery, Bob Cornman, Don Brown, and Tom Siegler were presented with the Carnegie Medal for heroism on May 23, 2007. The Coast Guard also honored John Thomas with a Silver Lifesaving Medal.

Those Who Beat the River
John (Tony) Thomas, 39, Powhatan Point, Ohio
Jacob (Jake) Wilds, 26, Latrobe, Pennsylvania
George (Toby) Zappone, Crucible, Pennsylvania

Those Who Didn't

Rick Conklin, 40, Crucible, Pennsylvania
Ed Crevda, 22, West Brownsville, Pennsylvania
Tom Fisher, 25, of New Cumberland, West Virginia
Scott Stewart, 36, Elm Grove, West Virginia

*   *   *

As has been said, there is that general feeling that working on a towboat is like being a part of a family. What makes it like a family is the living close together; everybody sharing, everybody dependent upon each other – especially during the bad times. Living together for thirty-day stretches of hard work and short sleep can be difficult. Being out on the non-stop rivers where you can't just jump in the old jalopy and head for the nearest Walmart to find a tool to fix a problem, fosters an aura of independence in crew personnel, and interdependence between them.

Many try for this work, don't make it, and drop out – and as some crew personnel like to brag – leaving only the better ones shipboard. The mates are teachers, bosses, sometimes enforcers, referees, and usually good listeners. Man-to-man conflicts are rare among crew members. If they have problems – such hot versus cold working environments, conflicts in musical tastes, etc. – conflicts that can't be worked out, one of them will ask for a transfer to another boat.

Talk about conflicts in musical tastes, Mark Chandler, raised in Opelika, Alabama "by a workaholic minister," plays the French horn in his church orchestra. When many of the crews are in the Willie Nelson school of music appreciation, a French horn can be a problem. But Chandler, who "came to the rivers" in the late 1990s, does his practicing at home. He agrees with the closeness that crew life – the good and the bad – engenders. "One of the most awesome guys I've ever met on the river [was who] would teach me anything I asked him, he'd teach me. Every question I could come up with he would teach me to the best of his ability. A lot of things I got better than him at but he always had somethin' to teach me. He was really laid back, a really good-natured fellow. He always laughed. Always made things funny. He's taught me the bulk of what I know to this day."[63]

That sounds like a decent definition of "home" life.

*   *   *

Aftermath

Getting back to the tragedy and to give the reader another idea of the force of a raging river, consider the following:

On April 19, 1979 the *M/V Cahaba*, an 80-foot, 1,800-hp towboat approached the old Rooster Bridge, four-teen miles south of Demopolis, Alabama. With Captain Jimmy Wilkerson "at the sticks" (the helm), the *Cahaba* was bringing four standard 195'x35' barges filled with coal down the Tombigbee River to Mobile Bay when it approached the river's 202 mile-marker. Weather reports of the time indicated the river was abnormally high – a reported record high gage of 73 feet vs. the normal 13 feet – due to recent rainstorms. The Tombigbee River was running at an accelerated pace that had some towboats making an astounding 15-knots downstream that day.

The usual practice under such conditions at this place is for the towboat to head for the east bank of the river, out of the fierce current. The idea is to cut the barges loose and let them drift under the bridge span while the towboat captain then backs off, steers for the lift bridge opening on the river's west side, goes through, and doubles back to nimbly catch the barges drifting on the down-river side of the bridge.

On that bright April day in 1979, things definitely didn't go exactly as planned.

The *Cahaba's* two deckhands and its pilot were on the barges attempting to release the wires (cables) attaching the barges to the towboat. All but one wire was freed, leaving one barge still hooked up to the towboat. When

The *M/V Cahaba, right center,* approaches the Rooster Bridge pushing four barges, each loaded with 2,000 tons of coal.
(Photo from the Collection of John R. Miller)

Captain Wilkerson tried to back away from the bridge according to plan, the onrushing current and the still-attached barge with its 2,000 tons of coal, overwhelmed the *Cahaba's* 1,800-hp engine.

This series of photographs taken by a cameraman, who just happened to be waiting on the bridge because of the open lift, dramatically shows what happened next:

**The rear end of the still-attached barge is dragging the bow of
the under-powered *Cahaba* directly into the Rooster Bridge.**
(Photo from the Collection of John R. Miller)

**The *Cahaba* slams into the bridge but the towboat is now
perpendicular to the raging current and is helpless.**
(Photo from the Collection of John R. Miller)

The current drags the *Cahaba* under the Rooster Bridge and...

... the towboat pops up again on the bridge's down-stream side.
(Photos from the Collection of John R. Miller)

With the crew members still on one of the drifting barges (left center) and with Captain Wilkerson still "at the sticks," the *Cahaba* rights itself with its engine still running.
(Photo from the Collection of John R. Miller)

It should be noted that there were no injuries sustained, that the barges were rounded up by another towboat and delivered to their destination, that the *Cahaba* was deliberately run ashore, ultimately was refurbished, re-named, and sold to another company.

All's well that ends well – most of the time.

*   *   *

Unlike the *Cahaba* incident, throughout the thirty-four months leading to the Coast Guard's final report on the *Elizabeth M* catastrophe (released on November 8, 2007), charges and countercharges flew back and forth – as might be expected. Lawyers for the victims, the survivors, the towboat company, and various maritime organizations racked up hundreds of "billable" hours recounting conflicting claims and counter-claims. It was not surprising to some that the ultimate verdict in the Coast Guard report was that Captain Zappone be prosecuted. However, he ultimately faced no criminal charges for his actions during the disaster because the U.S. Department of Justice found insufficient evidence to prosecute.

Unclear communication was one of the factors that caused the *Elizabeth M* and its doomed crew to be in such a perilous position in the first place. Campbell Transportation Company had issued handwritten orders by FAX that another one of its vessels, the *Richard C*, should meet the *Elizabeth M* at Georgetown and help it build the tow. The *Richard C* was then supposed to accompany its sister ship up-river to the Montgomery Lock and continue to stand by along the way to Bradford, Pennsylvania for further assistance should the river or the near-freezing weather conditions warrant same.

The problem was, however, the FAX did not clearly state the intent of the orders and the type of help the *Richard C* was to offer. Furthermore, the *Richard C* did not have ample time to even get to Georgetown. Meanwhile, the towboat *Rocket* was at Georgetown where its crew assisted the *Elizabeth M* in making up its tow.

It can be incredibly hard work making up a tow. The cables (wires) are heavy, the winches are geared 'way down and take innumerable turns to let off or take up slack. It's a lot of lifting and tugging for the deck crew. Most times the deckhands pull as hard as they can on the winch wheel handles and still have to stand on top of the cross bars and "put their back into it" to snug up the wires as tight as humanly possible. Trying to cinch up two massive steel barges each filled with 1,000 tons of coal is not an easy job – and it is not made any easier by freezing weather and slippery footing.

By the time the *Richard C* got to Georgetown, the *Elizabeth M* had already cinched up its tow and was underway up-bound with its six barges. Ironically, the down-bound *Richard C* passed the up-bound *Elizabeth M* about midway between Georgetown and the Montgomery L&D. The controversy over interpretation of the confusing FAX highlighted the week-long Coast Guard inquiry shortly after the disaster. Robert Hudson of Racine, Ohio, captain of the towboat *Richard C*, said he thought he "was supposed to meet the *Elizabeth M* at Georgetown to get in tow with them to shove six loads (of coal) up-river." Captain Zappone read the message to "mean that the two vessels were to meet sometime further up-river to push another tow." But Hudson contradicted that testimony, saying the two towboat captains spoke after receiving the order and Zappone talked about how the barges would be assembled for the *Elizabeth M*. The varying readings of the FAX were, said Zappone's attorney, Fred Thiemann, "reasonable interpretations of the same order." [64] But Campbell Transportation Company officials claimed Zappone defied orders to rendezvous with the *Richard C*.[65]

Hudson, who went off duty around 11 p.m. January 8, said he did not know why the two crews failed to meet as intended by the FAX. When asked whether he thought a helper boat was needed to handle a current that was four times faster than normal, Hudson answered, "Necessary? No. Prudent? Yes."[66]

Ultimately, both captains were rebuked in the November 8, 2007 Coast Guard report. It said that Captain Zappone "engaged in misconduct and negligence, acts that played a role in the sinking, and recommended a suspension or revocation of his pilot's license, as well as a criminal investigation." Steering his boat into the restricted area above the dam was the primary reason for this rebuke. The same recommendations were issued for Captain Hudson, his for failure to assist the *Elizabeth M* in the up-stream operations.[67]

The Coast Guard said there was plenty of blame to go around although all of it could never be assigned because of the unfortunate deaths of some of those intimately involved in the accident. The reference here points to the deceased Rick Conklin and Scott Stewart and which one of them was at the helm when the tow left the Montgomery Lock. "There were," the report concluded, "many opportunities to make decisions and take actions which could have prevented all or part of this." Zappone's license was suspended for eighteen months commencing on January 9, 2005 (the day of the accident) and he served another eighteen months on probation with his boating activities being monitored. Two months after the release of the final report, Zappone was permitted to again command a vessel.[68] Hudson was given a "letter of warning" for failing to have the *Richard C* take appropriate actions when he knew the *Elizabeth M* had departed alone.

The Coast Guard's investigation into the incident concluded in October 2007. A number of deficiencies aboard the towboat, including "modifications [to the towboat]...that were not completed in accordance with the manufacturer's specifications or good marine practice [that] reduced the vessel's survivability and degraded the vessel's propulsion system capabilities." Specifically, one marine survey [inspection] following the accident noted..."two cutouts approximately 25 by 25 inches on the main deck in the vicinity of the steering and an open grating replacing approximately 30 inches of the stern section of the deck. These and other modifications compromised the vessel's watertight integrity. The vessel was also found to be over-ballasted and hatch dogs [locking devises] to be unserviceable, making it susceptible to flooding. Mechanically, engine governors had been installed, limiting speed to 1,200 rpm, insufficient to overcome the currents in the restricted area above the dam."[69]

Over the past decade-plus, annual fatalities among towing crew members have been as low as nine in 2003 and as high as 29 in 1997. Officials say the most common deaths are falls from barges by deckhands.[70]

*   *   *

As might be expected, there was a lot of bitterness and rancor on the part of some of the families and friends of the lost mariners. Bill Downer was a friend of Scott Stewart, the "After Watch" pilot who had, ironically, survived another towboat-over-the-dam incident at Reedsville, Ohio in 1996. Downer was angry when he said, "Whoever ordered [the *Elizabeth M* and] those barges up that river is the person who needs to be held responsible." Stewart's brother-in-law, James Hall, wanted to know "what was the urgency for that coal to get up the river? Give me a break," he complained caustically.[71]

Deckhand Jacob Wilds – despite his earlier praise for Zappone's efforts – later charged the captain put cargo ahead of the crew, making several desperate maneuvers to snare runaway barges, several times putting *Elizabeth M* between the loose barges and the dam.[72] Wilds lost his best friend, Tom Fisher, whom he called a hero in the tragedy when the *Elizabeth M* went over Montgomery Dam. "The captain was crazy. He went on the backside of the tow. He made a big mistake. He risked our lives about ten times that night, and he killed my friend," said Wilds.[73]

There were those who challenged the impact the raising of the dam's gates from eighty-three feet to eighty-nine had on the calamity. In so doing, some contended, the lockmasters at Montgomery might have contributed to the accident. However, in the Coast Guard's final report, Army Corps of Engineers Colonel Michael Crall said "the effect of raising the gates, letting more water run through them, would have had a negligible effect on the current."[74]

But another Coast Guard investigation report dated May 1, 2006 yet never publicly released – except to the *Pittsburgh Post-Gazette* via a Freedom of Information request – claimed, "While the *Elizabeth M* was in the lock chamber, the dam gates were raised from 83 feet to 89 feet. An increase in the flow rate over the dam would have increased the outdraft current at the upper approach to the lock."[75]

That's exactly where the *Elizabeth M* lost control of its barges. According to Stephen Moschetta, an attorney for a Washington, Pennsylvania firm specializing in marine cases, "It's surprising. It created a greater chance that what's in the lock chamber would be pushed out toward the middle of the river.... Whether it's negligence I don't know, but it didn't help. It could have been an aggravating factor."[76]

Also commenting on the opening of the dam gates was Karen Auer, a spokeswoman for the Corps of Engineers. She noted, "It's possible it could have increased the outdraft currents..." and it may had "some slight effect but not as much as at lower water levels."[77] This cited newspaper account continued with Ms. Auer's statement that an internal Corps review found that standard procedures were followed on the night of the accident and all lock and dam personnel acted properly. Ms. Auer said it is not standard procedure to notify boats in the lock chamber that the dam gates have been raised or lowered, even when the river is flowing swiftly at high levels, and the *Elizabeth M* was not notified.[78]

The simmering debate on the effects the opened gates on the Montgomery Dam had or didn't have on sweeping the *Elizabeth M* to its doom would go on to no satisfactory conclusion. Another question seemingly unresolved was why didn't the Montgomery Lock and Dam employees on duty that night immediately shut down the gates to shut off the flow when they saw the trouble Captain Zappone and his crew were in?

In what was seen by some as an effort to shift the blame to Captain Zappone, Campbell Transportation Company President Don Grimm said during the Coast

Guard's inquiry into the accident, "...there was some errors in judgment, obviously."[79] Adding to the confusion, about ten days after the accident the Associated Press reported, "The *Elizabeth M* had been in an accident seven years ago that damaged the hull of the vessel. The owner of the company has said in the past that the 54-year-old boat was never involved in an accident."[80] Grimm was further reported as saying, "...if the *Elizabeth M* had been in an accident, he was not aware of it and that it would be difficult to know everything about the company's fleet of 30 boats."[81] Evidently, it wasn't difficult for the Coast Guard to know the company's fleet in general and the *Elizabeth M* in particular because it reported "the boat was involved in reportable marine casualties in 1992, 1998, 1999, 2000, 2001, and 2004."[82]

In a later story with which psychoanalysts – amateur and otherwise – could have a field day, surviving deckhand Jacob Wilds was arrested on assault charges almost exactly two months to the day after he was pulled from the raging Ohio River. On March 7, 2005, State police allege Wilds assaulted his one-year-old daughter; the mother of the child, Cindy Piett, and Cindy Piett's mother, Lani Piett.[83]

One has to wonder: was Wilds inherently angry, as witness his charges against George Zappone, the boat's skipper? Was he overcome with remorse over the loss of his best friend, Tom Fisher, in the accident? Or was he wracked with guilt about things he thought he could have or should have done to help save his fellow crewmen? In any case, it's ironic that he assaulted his "daughter, Storm, and other people he loved" who gave him the will to fight back against the Ohio River. It was for them on January 9, 2005, that he "didn't want to drown anymore."

In the immediate aftermath of the *Elizabeth M* tragedy, Dave Sneberger, assistant operations manager for the twenty-three locks and dams in the Army Corps of

Engineers' Pittsburgh District said, "I've been around since 1971 and with the loss of life, I've never seen anything like this. We've had deckhands fall in, but this has to be one of the worst."[84] For the survivors as well as the victims of the *Elizabeth M* catastrophe, it was "the *absolute* worst." For four of the towboat's seven crew members, the river – as usual – won.

*   *   *

Chapter IV
"A Rendezvous with Destiny"

Jeanine and Richard Cawley and their dog "Willow," were riding home in their 2001 Dodge pickup and fifth-wheel trailer after visiting their daughter in Nebraska, friends in Pennsylvania and his brother in Virginia. They were headed west on Interstate Highway 40, away from the cloudy day that was breaking behind them on the morning of May 26, 2002. They crossed into Oklahoma just north of Ft. Smith, Arkansas. Their ultimate destination was getting back to their 13,000 neighbors in Lebanon, Oregon, still some 2,000-plus Interstate miles northwest on those concrete ribbons. The couple, he fifty-nine and she a year younger, moved to Oregon after getting fed up with their winters in Nebraska. They were in no particular hurry; just a couple of sight-seers in their late fifties eyeballing the rolling countryside. At about 7:15 that morning, they decided to take a break and pulled into a highway rest stop just east of Sallisaw, Oklahoma. They left some fifteen minutes later.

They waited five minutes too long.

*   *   *

With his newly-minted official orders in his briefcase announcing his promotion to the rank of major in the U.S. Army, former Captain Andrew Franklin Clements was practically "low-level flying" eastward along Interstate-40, zooming toward Ft. Smith over the Memorial Day weekend, 2002. He was approaching the I-40 Bridge at Webbers Falls, Oklahoma – which opened in 1967 – the

71

same year little Andy Clements was born. He was heading back to his wife and their four kids – daughters Alexandra and Christina, nine and two; and sons Michael and Andrew David; four, and two months – in Woodbridge, Virginia. There they, his new house, his new rank, and his new military job were all awaiting him.

Alongside the 1991 West Point graduate on the front seat in the 2002 van was the family German Sheppard dog "Ostar." How many "conversations" had those two had as they reached the sixty-percent mark of their 2,929-mile transcontinental journey in the aptly branded vehicle, a Honda Odyssey? An Army "brat" himself due to his father's military career, Clements, according to friends and neighbors, was "the type of person who would help you even if he didn't know you [and he was] a good family man."[85]

*   *   *

The towboat *Robert Y. Love*, with Captain William Joe Dedmon at the wheel, was chugging northwesterly up the Arkansas River heading for Catoosa, Oklahoma. The 104x30-foot craft pushing two empty side-by-side asphalt tank barges, was a conventional twin-screw, diesel-driven inland boat owned by Magnolia Marine Transport Co. (MMT), headquartered in Vicksburg, Mississippi, and its parent company Ergon, Inc. MMT's primary business was transporting asphalt or black oil through the Mississippi River system and the Intracoastal waterways of the Gulf of Mexico.

Dedmon came aboard the *Robert Y. Love* at 6:40 the night before, May 25, 2002, while it was transiting the river's James A. Trimble Lock 13, near Van Buren, Arkansas. He was relieving his predecessor who shipped out on vacation. Ahead lay 152 miles of waterway en route to Catoosa, where he would load up his two 297x54-foot barges (MM-60 and MM-62) and head back down-stream. Dedmon, from Florence, Mississippi, picked up the remainder of the "Captain's Watch" at 1910 hours (7:10 p.m., all times CDT). Three-and-one-half-hours later, he

**Towboat *Robert Y. Love*, a 104x30-footer
with twin GM diesel engines[86]**

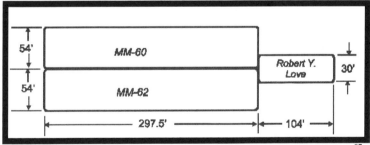

Schematic of *Robert Y. Love* and the two barges it was pushing[87]

was relieved by his "After Watch" pilot, James Wilkinson. A little more than six hours after that, at 0530 hours on May 26, Dedmon returned the favor.

*   *   *

What better way for a mom and dad to spend a holiday weekend than to go visit their son and daughter-in-law? That's what Jerry and Patricia Gillion were doing when they left their home in Spiro, Oklahoma and headed west-northwest to son Troy and Shelley Gillion's home in Broken Arrow, Oklahoma, just a hundred miles or so "down the road a-piece," as they say in that part of the country. The Gillions were a close-knit family and hundred-mile-plus trips on the highways in the southwest were like a short hop to the neighborhood Walmart store for them. Their route would take them across Interstate 40 and the Muskogee Turnpike, and those two super-highways would make their 100-mile trip fly by for the two "very special people who loved life and laughed a lot"[88]

*   *   *

Gail Shanahan was returning to Stockdale, Texas from the Old Fort Futurity and Super Derby in Ft. Smith with her best friend and another horse trainer, forty-five-year-old Maggie Green. Gail, a forty-nine-year-old widow, was looking forward to her coming re-marriage. As they approached the Webbers Falls Bridge over the Arkansas River, they still had another 500-plus miles to go. They were full of anticipation about how they were going to spend the $7,000 that two of their horses had won in the Derby competition the night before.

Even with the horse trailer and the four horses in it they were pulling with the 2001 Dodge 3500 truck, they had gotten an early start and at 7:30 that Sunday morning westbound on I-40 they expected to be home north of San Antonio during daylight hours. Their friend Kay Blandford of Southerland Springs, Texas, was also heading home from the rodeo but she was twenty miles back. Gail Shanahan had flown up to Ft. Smith and was about to fly back when she changed her mind and decided to ride with Margaret Green and keep her company on the long haul.

74

Besides, May 26th was Margaret Green's birthday.

*   *   *

The *Robert Y. Love* cleared the Robert S. Kerr Lock 15 on the Arkansas River at Sallisaw, Oklahoma around five o'clock on the morning of May 26, twenty-four miles down-stream of the I-40 Bridge. It was the hustle and bustle of locking through brought Captain Dedmon out of a dead sleep. He was wearied by the extensive traveling he had to do to pickup his boat the previous evening near Fort Smith. It is not uncommon for such long jaunts to match up crews with their boats. Emergencies notwithstanding, when crew members' 30 days are up, some towboat companies get them off or on the boat no matter where the crew member happens to be. It's usually by crew van or SUV but if it's too far for highway transport, the company provides air transportation. That can run to $5,000 or so to take crew from, for instance, Vicksburg, Mississippi to Pittsburgh, Pennsylvania, and bring another back.

Dedmon, after his wearying trip, dressed and stumbled somewhat groggily to the ship's galley, shaking off the effects of a couple of Benadryl pills he had taken for a sinus headache prior to going to bed the night before. He grabbed a soft drink from the refrigerator. The jolt of caffeine was all the sixty-one-year-old skipper needed to wake himself fully. Fifteen minutes later, he went to the wheelhouse to relieve relief pilot Wilkinson. With thirty miles of waterway ahead of him until the next lock at Webber Falls, Oklahoma, the captain settled in for the expected five-hour leg up the river. Other than the gray weather, he had no waterway concerns at that time. Dedmon and the *Robert Y. Love* were making good time. Traffic on the river was its usual minimal – averaging only three tows a day through the locks.

*   *   *

One of the Mississippi River's largest tributaries, the Arkansas River, flows 1,450 miles from the Rocky Mountains in Colorado, through Kansas, Oklahoma, and

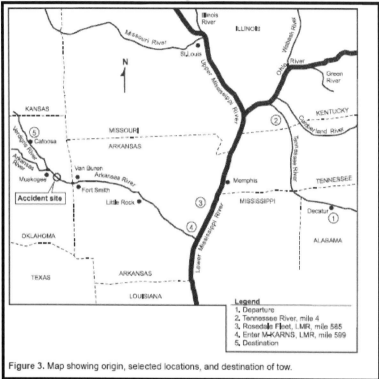

Figure 3. Map showing origin, selected locations, and destination of tow.

Arkansas to its confluence with the Mississippi River. The McClellan-Kerr Arkansas River Navigation System (the M-KARNS) is a 445-mile-long inland waterway with 18 locks and dams that enable vessels to overcome a 420-foot difference in elevation from the Mississippi River to the head of navigation at Catoosa, in east-central Oklahoma. The McClellan-Kerr Arkansas River Navigation System is named in honor of former U. S. Senators Robert S. Kerr from the Sooner State, and John McClellan from Arkansas.

The Army Corps of Engineers operates the locks and dams twenty-four hours a day; the U.S. Coast Guard maintains the channel markers and other navigation aids.

The M-KARNS begins in Arkansas at mile 599 on the Mississippi River, about half way between New Orleans and St. Louis. Via the White River and a man-made canal, the waterway reaches west-northwest toward the Arkansas River. There the M-KARNS and the Arkansas River become one and the same for the next 377 miles running through Arkansas and into Oklahoma.

In Oklahoma the waterway leaves the Arkansas River once again, at Muskogee, and follows the Verdigris River north for the last 50 miles to the head of navigation at Tulsa's Port of Catoosa, 445 miles from the Mississippi River. The channel depth is maintained at nine feet or more and its width is mostly 250-300 feet. All along the route, its thirty-eight bridge channel clearances are generally 300 or more feet wide horizontally and fifty-two feet or more vertically.

*   *   *

James Johnson and his wife Misty were taking their three-year-old daughter Shea Nicole on a holiday ride from their Lavaca, Arkansas home up to Tulsa, Oklahoma. The reason for the 150-mile trip was to take the little girl to the Tulsa Zoo and see some of the 1,500 animals housed there. The multi-million-dollar penguin exhibit that opened in 2002 was a special attraction. The shortest distance between those points would be to take the Muskogee Turnpike northwest after getting off eastbound Interstate-40 at the Webbers Falls exit, moments after crossing the bridge there over the Arkansas River.

At around 7:40 that morning, tiny Shea may well have been asleep strapped safely in her car seat and dreaming about "lions, and tigers, and bears, oh my!"

*   *   *

Interstate-40 near Webbers Falls, Oklahoma, an east-west, two-way, four-lane, divided highway with posted speed limits of seventy miles-per-hour, was a vital link in the Interstate Highway System started during the administration of President Dwight Eisenhower. Even-numbered routes – such as I-40 – run basically east and west; odd numbers run north and south. Standard three-foot high barriers divided the east- and west-bounders on the twelve-foot wide traffic lanes.

Wayne Martin and his wife Susan, both forty-nine, happened to be among the east-bounders on the morning of May 26, 2002. They were driving their new 2002 Chevy 1500 pickup from their home in Norman, Oklahoma – where he served as a police detective and a member of the department's emergency dive team – to a family re-union in Clarksville, Arkansas. It was a 250-mile straight-arrow shot across I-40. They left home around 5:30 that morning. Two hours and 140 miles later, they were just minutes away from the I-40 exit at Webbers Falls, Oklahoma.

There was a rest stop just a few miles further on down the road. But at the time, Mother Nature didn't call.

*   *   *

Once Captain Dedmon cleared the Ft. Smith area on the Arkansas River and crossed into Oklahoma, there were only a couple of bridges he'd have to pass under before arriving at Lock 16 at Webbers Falls. And with the river running south-southeast at approximately two-miles-per-hour (other reports had it considerably higher), Dedmon would have no trouble shoving the *Robert Y. Love* against that current and up the river. Because of the M-KARNS lock and dams, the river he was traversing was mostly a series of placid reservoirs. Dedmon was easily making at least six- to seven-miles-per-hour. Sunrise was still an hour away and although the skies were overcast, there was ten-mile-visibility and the winds were light and variable at three- to five-miles-per-hour. The outside temperature was a pleasant sixty-four degrees Fahrenheit.

For a river boat captain, you could hardly ask for a better day on the water.

*   *   *

David John Mueggenborg and wife, Jean Elizabeth Mueggenborg, buckled up their seat belts and, unlike east-bounders Wayne and Susan Martin, they *left* a family reunion in Arkansas and headed west-bound for their tiny hometown of Okarche, Oklahoma (population: 1,110). In their five-year-old Ford Crown Victoria, they were driving on Interstate 40 towards Oklahoma City, 200 miles west and then it was another thirty-five miles northwest to home near Broken Arrow. Like so many of his rural neighbors (fifty-percent of them of German decent), David Mueggenborg worked as a farmer "from can-see to can't."

With he having served six years in the Air National Guard and she, born the daughter of an army lieutenant colonel at Fort Ord, California, much of their travel hours were whiled away talking about things military in nature. But on this morning of May 26, 2002, the fifty-two-year-olds, farmer and wife, no doubt were more concerned about staying ahead of the storm clouds they saw forming out behind them to the east as they crossed the Arkansas-Oklahoma state line in the west-bound lanes.

Like most farmers, Mr. Mueggenborg did not want to be away from his crops too long.

*   *   *

79

Paul Tailele was driving his 2001 Volvo big rig westbound on I-40 on the morning of May 26, 2002. He had left West Virginia the day before and was headed for his home in Magna, Utah, stopping off in Las Vegas, Nevada. He wasn't interested in the blackjack games there. The 39-year-old truck driver was in a bit of hurry to get back to "Sin City" to see his kids. Although divorced from his former wife, Ronette, they were, as she said, "not very good mates but we were good parents."

Tailele, known as "Junior" to his friends, often scheduled his trips so he could be home for son Jeremy's football games and daughter Shakira's basketball games. Even though it was a Memorial Day weekend, the Hawaiian-born trucker of Samoan decent was still putting the pedal to the metal to get home to the kids – games or not. Somewhere around 7:40 on that morning, he put through a cellfone call to his daughter. Maybe he forgot it would be 5:40 in the morning in Las Vegas!

Shakira wasn't disturbed by the early wake-up call. She'd talk to her Dad no matter the time, no matter where he was.

*   *   *

Cary Cochran, who started piloting towboats in the mid-1970s and with whom this writer did some towboating on the Mississippi in 2001, remembers well his first trip as captain. It all began at MM 175 near Donaldsonville, Louisiana on the Lower Mississippi River. He ran a "light boat" (no cargo) from there to Baton Rouge where he picked up five empty oil barges and carried them to right below New Orleans. It was about a 24-30-hour trip. "Too scared" to remember much about his feelings during that first trip, he does recall his first encounter with a bridge – the one going over the river at Greenville, Mississippi. When he steered his boat under it the first time, he was

again "awed and amazed." He has since become a bit
cynical about river-crossing bridges. Before a bridge across
the river is built, buoys are placed in the river at the spot
where piers are contemplated. Then commercial boating
interests are asked to comment on those placements.
Cochran's comment:

"It seems they put bridges in the ungodliest
places."[89]   ·

*   *   *

Such did not seem to be the case when Captain Joe
Dedmon approached the 1,989-foot long I-40 bridge over
the Arkansas River. Had he been asked that day, he no
doubt would not have placed that bridge in the "ungodly"
category. As a matter of fact, he didn't have a care on his
mind about navigating these (or any other) waters. The
sixty-one-year-old skipper had been working on inland
waterways vessels for forty years. Just five days earlier, on
May 21, 2002, he celebrated thirty-one years as a Coast
Guard-licensed Operator of Uninspected Towing vessels,[7]
after starting as a deckhand on the Mississippi River in
1957.

He now had fifteen months in as captain of the
Robert Y. Love. He knew his ship well. He had been under
the I-40 Bridge "hundreds of times and it was an easy
bridge to navigate."[90] Once he was lined up, all it took was
"a little right rudder to steady the tow before placing the
rudder amidships (zero rudder angle) and passing under the
navigation span." [91] Nothing to it. The only potential
problem that morning was the presence of dozens and

---

[7] "Uninspected" vessels are subject to a number of Coast Guard
safety-related regulations including required safety equipment such as
fire extinguishers, lifesaving equipment, emergency radio beacons,
and ventilation for tanks and engine spaces.

dozens of small bass boats engaged in a fishing tournament north of the bridge. But, it was an organized event – the Jimmy Houston Outdoors Team Tournament – which meant somebody in charge would see to it that the little boats wouldn't be in the big boat's channel. The *Robert Y. Love* was lined up perfectly in the middle of the channel. Dedmon took note of the green, unlighted buoy on the left side of the river.

Dedmon and the towboat *Robert Y. Love* were one-third-of-a-mile south of the bridge. Four minutes away.[92]

*   *   *

Richard and Jeanine Cawley travelled westbound on Interstate 40 as they approached the bridge over the Arkansas River near Webbers Falls, Oklahoma, en-route to their Lebanon, Oregon home. Going in the same direction on the same highway were **Jerry and Pat Gillion**, off to see their son and his wife. **Gail Shanahan and Margaret Green** and their four horses in the trailer headed for Texas were approaching the bridge, too. The **Johnson family**, bound for the Tulsa zoo with their three-year-old baby girl strapped in her car seat, were only fifty short miles underway from the home they left that morning east of Ft. Smith. **Paul Tailele**, pushing the pedal to the metal in his big rig west-bound on the concrete ribbon, pulled his cellfone out of his pocket and called his daughter Shakira. **David and Jean Mueggenborg** were watching the threatening weather clouds form in the eastern skies behind them, wondering how the weather might affect their crops at home.

Captain (Major) **Andrew Clements** was eastbound on the Interstate, coming up on the bridge over the Arkansas River, heading home for a new life in Virginia. **Wayne and Susan Martin** were right there along with him, looking forward to a family reunion in Arkansas.

It was a long holiday weekend and these people were taking advantage of it on Interstate 40 as they approached the Arkansas River Bridge near Webbers Falls, Oklahoma at 7:45 on the morning of May 26, 2002. They were in just eleven of the daily average of 19,000 vehicles that crossed that bridge. They were coming from the east. They were coming from the west. They were converging. Like the disparate, compacting winds of a hurricane. As President Franklin Delano Roosevelt said sixty-six years earlier – long before any of them were born – they all had "a rendezvous with destiny."

*   *   *

Captain Dedmon sat behind the controls of the *Robert Y. Love* in the cramped though comfortable surroundings in the wheelhouse, which was equipped with two VHF-FM radio-telephones, a single-sideband radio, radar, a global positioning system (GPS) unit, swing meter, depth sounder, steering controls, and engine controls. It was all right there in front of him. And notice in the page 84 picture, there is no huge wooden steering wheel – as seen in all those old movies about "life on the Mississippi." There's hardly a helmsman on the waters today who has ever used a steering *wheel*. It's all hydraulics and electronics. A towboat's wheelhouse today (again, see page 84) is getting to look like a computer techie's giant arcade.

Dedmon's course was set to steer the tow smack-dab through the middle of the 322-foot channel opening between columns four and five of the twelve holding up the Interstate-40 roadway, fifty-plus feet above the river. It's rare for a pilot or a captain on the Inland Waterways to have any apprehension approaching the I-40 bridge, especially under such ideal conditions. It was a long way away – both physically and psychologically – from the trickiness of the Eads Bridge over the Mississippi River at

St. Louis, Missouri. Some call that the trickiest area on the Upper River because its superstructure below the road deck is an elongated arch that slopes quickly downward to the

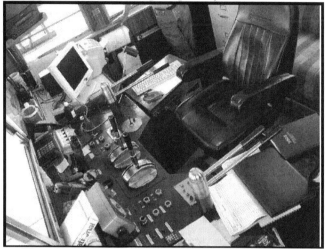

The wheelhouse aboard the *Robert Y. Love* shows its cramped quarters but efficiently laid-out controls. The view forward from the Captain's chair is to the left.[93]

bridge's supporting piers. When a boat is running, pushed by a swift current in very high water, if you don't nail it

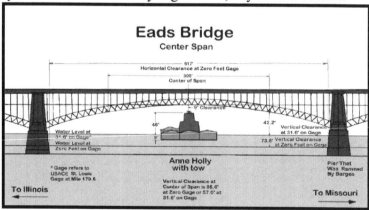

right in the middle with a normal towboat, there's little margin for error.

The photo of the *Robert Y. Love* wheelhouse (above) is fairly indicative of the way computers and other electronic equipment is sprinkled around a towboat captain's work area. In many boats today, they no longer rely on radio-telephone communications with their home offices; it's all done by computers. Crew changes, schedules, time-clock entries are managed by computers. For instance, nowadays the cook fills out a paper form indicating what is needed in the way of galley supplies. He passes it on to the captain who transmits it to company headquarters on shore via electronics such as Boatrac or FAX. There the order is filled and the supplies are brought to the boat when it arrives at home port or are even delivered to the boat by the supplier in mid-stream, on-the-fly. For those somewhat less than technically literate with electronic equipment and who may not have yet read "Computers for Dummies," the fallback position for them is backing oneself up with paper and pencil log notations.

More and more, the pilot-house is also like a pent-house. Some towboat cockpits now resemble a high-rise office – surrounded with picture-windows, stereo systems, book cases, family pictures, etc. Some wheelhouses are huge, giving the helmsman lots of room to flick back and forth on the boat's steering "joystick" to make minor course changes. Those who remember old movies with "Cap'n Andy" (a.k.a. movie actor Joe E. Brown) steering Jerome Kern's magical "Showboat" down the Mighty Mississip while spinning that huge mahogany steering wheel would be greatly disappointed with today's boats. One captain this writer met on the Mississippi who's been around for years and years, told me he's never, ever used a steering wheel. It's all done with levers.

The crew's quarters of today are also a long-way removed from the galley-slave visions of days past. Some are sizeable and come equipped with large-screen televisions pulling in cable channels via satellite dishes.

They have VCR, CD, and DVD players with a library full of films. In one we saw, there was a whole series of pocketbooks in the crew's lounge with titles such as *Atlas Shrugged* and *The Fountainhead* by Ayn Rand, *The Immigrants* by Howard Fast, James Mitchner's *Alaska*; *Rainbow Six* by Tom Clancy, *The Chamber* by John Grisham, Milton and Rose Freidman's book, *The Freedom to Choose*, Ken Follett's *Lie Down with Lions*, and *The Bankruptcy of America: How the Federal Budget is Impoverishing the Nation*.

(For more practical viewing – though maybe less enjoyable for the crew – there are also training videos available including "How to Select and Safely Use Portable Fire Extinguishers," and some of the "Inland Waterways Video Safety Series." There are also films like "Welcome Aboard" and one from the Texas A&M University's Oil Spill School. On some boats, you will even find this book – *The Rivers of Life – and Death*.) Today's towboat lounge presents a very comfortable setting with over-stuffed couches, reading lamps, and a ship-to-shore telephone so crewmen without a cell phone can keep in touch with their families.

The mess hall on a towboat is, as might be expect-ed, the social center of life on the waterways. And just like it is at many homes across the nation, there are three days on most boats that are "designated" – fish on Friday, steak on Saturday and chicken on Sunday. A lot of the menu selections "depend on the captain" who may want chicken twice a week. That means the cook then only has to plan menus three days a week. Southern people on these boats "are mostly into 'soul' food and the younger ones are into MacDonald's and Wendy's."

The big meal is served at 1100 hours rather than 1700 because either the captain or the relief pilot is going to bed on the later break. Crew members also use the galley as some sort of a doctor's office, their local barber's chair, a psychiatrist's couch. They think the cooks "know everything" and so they bring their questions of life to them. And the crew members also come in to the galley and "vent" to the cooks about the boating life gripes. Some cooks – especially females – become the "Ann Landers of the waterways."

*   *   *

Somewhere around 0700 hours on May 26, 2002 aboard the *Robert Y. Love*, Captain Dedmon and deckhand Eli Hogsett started an extended conversation, mostly about kids. It went on for half-an-hour or so as they motored up-river. On some boats, hanging out in the wheelhouse is like gathering around the office water-cooler. Crew members, just like their business counter-parts, talk about families, homes, cooking, gardening, etc. But sometimes, some captains will have no part of such socializing. One had a sign on the cockpit door reading, "If you have no business up here, you have no business up here."

After their chat, the captain instructed Hogsett to go below and wake up the relief mate because they were approaching Lock 16, mile 366.6, about one hour away. (Corps of Engineer regulation 33CFR207.275(g)(5) then required at least two hands be on deck to handle lines while locking through.) The mate was awakened at about 0725. Hogsett then completed some minor chores and went to the galley where he and the mate talked and drank coffee for a few minutes.

That Captain Dedmon was alone in the wheelhouse, as captains and pilots of towboats often are, wasn't unusual.

What was unusual was that captains and pilots aren't often in the wheelhouses of their towboats, unconscious and slumped over the boat's controls.

Captain Dedmon was. Just minutes after Dedmon sent the deckhand below, the captain inexplicably "blacked out" and fell, but not completely to the deck of the wheelhouse, because of the limited space between the vessel control console and the deck. With no one at the helm to steer it, the tow continued to gradually veer left and struck pier three, 201 feet west and outside the navigation channel, at an approximately fifty-six-degree angle. At the estimated speed of six-seven miles-per-hour, Steve Tipton, a University of Tulsa engineering professor, said the impact of the collision would have been roughly equivalent to sixty-two 2,000-pound cars slamming into the structure simultaneously at 60 mph. "It [6-7 mph] would look deceivingly slow, like you might be able to reach out and stop it yourself," he said. "But it actually would have had a tremendous amount of power to it."[94]

None of the crew had any idea that a catastrophe was coming. There was no sharp swerve of the boat. There was no abrupt revving of the engines nor any sound of acceleration to get back on course; no deceleration into reverse to back away either. There were no emergency bells clanging; no alarm bells indicating Dedmon was trying to avoid a crash. None of the crew had any idea what was happening in the wheelhouse. But suddenly, they felt a jolting impact as huge galley refrigerators and other equipment fell to the deck. They heard a "big bang." They bolted outside the galley where they saw a 503-foot section of the I-40 Bridge plunging into the Arkansas River and on to the bow of their barges.[95] They also saw a tractor-semitrailer and a pickup truck drive off the Interstate.

Nine more vehicles followed. Fourteen people died.

*   *   *

In a cold, clinical, almost matter-of-factual manner, this is what happened as the *Robert Y. Love* approached the

Interstate-40 Bridge over the Arkansas River near Webbers Falls, Oklahoma on Sunday, May 26, 2002, commencing at about 0730 hours according to the National Transportation Safety Board (NTSB):[96]

> The captain stated that after he told the deckhand to awaken the mate, he precautiously watched to make sure the deckhand [climbed safely down the steep and narrow] stairs from the wheelhouse, then returned his attention to maneuvering the tow. The captain reported that the last thing he remembered before the accident was aligning the tow to pass under the I-40 bridge main navigation span (between piers 4 and 5) and passing a green navigation buoy (channel marker) to port (left), approximately 0.35 miles from the bridge.
>
> After the accident, the captain stated that his unconsciousness occurred "all at once" and further stated, "I remember looking out to the side of the buoy and then looking back at the bridge, and after that I don't remember nothing." His first recollection after the allision was being in a crouched position between the operator's chair and the vessel control console and realizing that his head and arm were wet from the soft drink he had placed on the console.
>
> He stated he could not visually focus on anything at first nor "get oriented right." He managed to get to a fully standing position to be able to see over the console and out of the wheelhouse window. After he saw the highway bridge deck collapse onto the deck of the barges, he sounded five blasts on the vessel's whistle (a mariner's danger signal). While still experiencing problems focusing upon what was happening, he

recalled seeing an 18-wheeler, and possibly a pickup truck, go off the bridge.

He said that he then "started blowing the [towboat's] whistle again, just to try to get somebody's attention to stop...[the traffic] on the bridge." He further explained that though he was familiar with the boat, he had to "fumble around for the general alarm to get it set off." The captain could not recall the allision. He said that he had applied a few degrees of left rudder to align the tow for passage through the bridge navigation span and that when he regained consciousness, the rudder was still in the left position.

The mate who was on duty indicated that he ran from the galley to the wheelhouse and when he got to the door, the captain was screaming, "make them stop! Why won't they stop coming [referring to the vehicles on the bridge]?" The captain asked the mate, the first person to arrive in the wheelhouse, to send a distress message to the Coast Guard. The mate made the call on the VHF-FM radio (channel 16) and then telephoned the company office on the company cellular telephone to report the allision. The radio distress call was heard and logged at 0745, simultaneously, by the watch-stander at Coast Guard Group Lower Mississippi River (Group LMR), Memphis, Tennessee, and by the lock operator at Lock 15, mile 336.2 [thirty miles to the southeast].

The remainder of the crew heard the towboat's whistle sound, followed by the sounding of the general alarm bell. While making routine engine room rounds, the chief engineer [James Lowery] heard the bell. He reported hearing the accident about 0750 and that the impact caused him to fall to one knee. He immediately returned to the engine room to check void spaces for flooding and was in the engine room for 10 to 15 minutes. The engineer stated that he did not notice any engine speed changes before the accident and that had the engine speeds changed before the accident, he would have easily noticed the change.

The pilot and the other mate were off-duty and asleep in their quarters during the allision. The pilot, who was in his bed when he felt a bump, heard the towboat's whistle sounding and then heard the general alarm sound. He looked out his window (his room was on the port side of the main deck, aft) and saw the bridge deck lying on the barges. He said he immediately ran out of the deckhouse and went to the head of the tow to check the condition of the barges. About 45 seconds to a minute and a half later, after checking the tow, the pilot arrived in the wheelhouse and found: "The captain was visibly shaken...He was standing, and he was in tears, shaken." The pilot then relieved the captain from watch and the mate from handling communications.

Later medical tests showed Dedmon's "black-out" as being "consistent with an episode of syncope, in which blood flow to the brain is interrupted for any of a variety of reasons. This interruption results in loss of consciousness and falling. Normally, after such a fall, an individual is in the horizontal position, allowing blood to flow to the brain and recovery to occur quite rapidly. However, the captain was supported in a crouched position as a result of the limited space in the wheelhouse in which to fall, and this position did not permit an immediate return of blood flow to his brain."[97]

(It should also be noted that the NTSB Board later concluded "the captain experienced a sudden loss of consciousness, possibly as the result of an abnormal heart rhythm. The Safety Board also concluded that the captain had no apparent symptoms of clinical significance prior to the accident, and a reasonable clinical evaluation of the captain before the accident was unlikely to have detected the medical conditions that were discovered through post-accident testing. However, it was later reported the 61-year-old Captain Dedmon had heart blockage [according to] an investigator for the National Transportation Safety Board and reported in the *Muskogee Daily Phoenix*. NTSB [also] said it was not known if Dedmon's condition had anything to do with the blackout or the crash.)[98] There was no requirement for towboat captains then to submit to annual physicals, ala airline pilots, according to Captain Richard Block, Secretary of the National Mariners Association.[99]

As relief pilot Wilkinson explained it, "The captain was visibly shaken. He did not know what had happened. He apparently had blacked out or passed out. He couldn't hardly talk," Wilkinson said. "He was visibly shaken, in tears." Chief engineer Lowery went below decks to check for leaks after the collision and when he next saw Dedmon, the engineer said, "He didn't have very much to tell me because he just was in a daze or something or other. I told him everything looked good downstairs, wasn't no leaks. And he never did answer me." After the crash, Hogsett went forward and checked on the barges. When he returned to the wheelhouse, he saw Dedmon still in shock. "The captain, he told me... 'I don't know what happened.' Hogsett said, 'All I know (is), I hit the bridge'."[100]

*　　*　　*

The aforementioned Joe Waller, a long-time towboat captain, wouldn't have been surprised to hear about a towboat captain doing strange things while at the helm. He remembered that he once had to relieve a captain who went "plumb crazy in the wheelhouse from some medicine he was takin'." According to Waller, the captain was "a good ol' boy and everybody liked him real well. But he'd been takin' stuff (prescription medicines) and he'd go to sleep at the table and fall face-first in his food. He was drowning in his own food on his plate." Waller recalled that he was asleep in his bunk when one of the deckhands burst into his cabin and said, "Man, get up here. The captain's goin' crazy."

When Waller got up to the wheelhouse, they told him the captain had taken the boat up and down through a Natchez, Mississippi bridge four times. Waller, the relief pilot, went to the helm and said, "Captain, I gotcha now. I'm relieving you." He called the port captain who supported his action and told him, "Don't let him at the wheel no more." The captain had gotten hooked on some pain medicine, Waller said, "and he never did come back to the boats."[101]

*   *   *

Kirk Washburn and Alton Wilhoit started out in their bass boat – one of 170 by one count – that morning, just five minutes after sunrise. They were contestants in the national Jimmy Houston Outdoors Team Tournament on the Arkansas River just north of Webbers Falls, Oklahoma. They must have liked that storm building to the east of the river because, some say, bass bite more when a storm is near. With a little bit of "fisherman's luck," Wilhoit and Washburn caught a two-and-one-half-pound bass as they drifted stern-first down-river toward the I-40 Bridge. Washburn looked behind him and saw the *Robert Y. Love* south of the bridge plowing north in their direction. With the tow in the center of the channel and the bass boat in the weed beds along the east shore, neither craft was a threat to the other – just as the tournament organizers planned.

What the tournament organizers hadn't planned was the morning's tranquility being shattered with a sound like a sonic boom when Captain Dedmon and the *Robert Y. Love* hit that I-40 bridge piers and sent the roadway crashing into the river. Washburn and Wilhoit stowed their fishing gear and quickly motored toward the accident site. They watched in horror as a truck heading west flew off the bridge. Then, another semi sailed into the murky water and vanished.

Six weeks after the collapse of the I-40 Bridge cancelled their fishing tourney, Kirk Washburn (l) and Alton Wilhoit (r) were reunited with Rodney Tidwell, whose life they saved on that Memorial Day weekend in 2002.[102]

Washburn dialed 9/11 on his cell phone and alerted a nearby "unbelieving" sheriff to what had happened. Washburn and Wilhoit then stood waving their arms in an effort to ward off more tragedy. But when their boat drifted directly under the bridge and a truck plunged off narrowly missing their boat, they knew they were in the wrong place at the wrong time.

They motored back up the river and Wilhoit took the tournament-required flare gun they had on their boat and fired it at an approaching semi. His aim was dead-on. The flare actually struck the truck's windshield. The trucker slammed on his brakes, stopping just before his wheels went over the edge of the fallen bridge deck.

Moments later, according to Mike Lambeth writing in a fishing enthusiast's magazine, "...the anglers idled toward the barge, looking for survivors in the water.

> Then they heard a resounding yell, "Hey!" Mississippi truck driver Rodney Tidwell, west-bound for Reno, Nevada in his big rig, had miraculously surfaced and, though badly injured, beckoned for help. Washburn and Wilhoit quickly tied a flotation cushion to a rope and tossed it out as the injured trucker struggled to remain afloat. Tidwell was pulled to safety by his two 'heroes' and later admitted he couldn't have treaded water much longer.
>
> "Thirty feet away," Lambeth continued, "the bleeding and badly injured body of Arkansas truck driver James Bilyeu surfaced. His desperate pleas for help weakened as the current pulled him under the front of one of the barges. Washburn and Wilhoit saw Bilyeu, but were penned in by the strong current to the bridge's mangled concrete pylon and its protruding rebar. [They] encouraged the trucker to hang on to some floating boxes nearby. It was then that

[other tournament fishermen] Norman Barton Jr. of Sallisaw and Randy Graham of Wagoner, Oklahoma, arrived....

"[Now] the badly injured Bilyeu was nowhere in sight. Graham maneuvered their boat [to] the front of the barge, and noticed a strange object. The object turned out to be the blood-covered [but thankfully live] head of Bilyeu. Norman and Randy tossed the victim a cushion on a rope and pulled him to safety. With injured survivors onboard, the boats headed to the ramp a little over two miles away. They cared for the victims the best they could. Emergency help was on the scene when they arrived.... Washburn and Wilhoit humbly insist that they are not heroes. In fact, they were doing what anyone else on the scene would have done. They regret they couldn't have done more."[103]

As for his role in the heroics, Norman Barton said, "I've learned a lot from my little brother. He's an emergency medical technician and a firefighter by trade. One of the things I've always heard is, 'Keep 'em talking, don't let 'em pass out.' And I knew [James Bilyeu] had been in that cold water and had been in shock and scared to death and was hurting real bad.... I was afraid," Barton continued, "he might slip away from us or slip unconscious there for a little bit. But fortunately, he didn't. He stayed awake."[104]

*   *   *

At a memorial service for the bridge victims a year later with James Bilyeu attending, he said, "If it hadn't been for

Norman and Randy, I was going down for the last count. I owe them my life."[105] At what was left of the Interstate 40 Bridge on that Sunday morning of May 26, 2002, "heroes" and "fishermen" seemed to be synonymous.

*   *   *

In many ways, James Bilyeu, Rodney Tidwell and, as is later recorded herein, Richard Cawley were lucky in their rescues. There were fishermen in the area who had the know-how, the equipment, and the will to save them. For those who went under the water and were submerged in their vehicles but may have had enough air trapped in their cars to sustain for some period of time, they were doomed by several unpredictable factors. For instance, immediately after the bridge was hit, the crew of the *Robert Y. Love* tried to launch its skiff to get to those vehicles in the water. But their little boat got tangled up in some of the bridge debris and it couldn't be released.

The inability of trained underwater divers to get to the victims, despite the quick appearance of some of them on the scene (eight minutes in at least one case), was caused by the crash site waters being filled with rebar, concrete, vehicles and the fuel that had spewed from them. Heavy thunderstorms with lightning were another problem, as was the swift current due to a large amount of recent rainfall that made the river water very murky. Still further was the precariousness of the accident site itself.

With a huge slab of Interstate-40 remnants sitting precariously atop the *Robert Y. Love* barges (as shown in the page 99 photograph), engineers had to order underwater divers and other rescue team members to temporarily restrain their recovery efforts. The concern was that even a fraction of an inch of movement by the massive concrete bridge deck would break it free from it tenuous attachment to the rest of the roadway and bring those tons of shattered highway and re-bar crashing down. The Oklahoma Department of Transportation (ODOT) quickly mobilized a team of seventeen surveyors who set up and manned equipment to monitor the bridge on a twenty-four-hour basis for structural integrity, the potential for more damage, and to ensure the safety of rescue teams.

Within one hour of arrival, the surveyors were able to provide bridge engineers with position data hourly.[106] Divers were standing by but couldn't enter some parts of the river until that shaky part of the bridge was stabilized.

"They can't go under it because it's moving and shaking," Rebecca Smith, spokeswoman for Muskogee County Emergency Management Services, said. "At this point, I believe we are moving more into a recovery mode than a victim mode.... The vehicles that have been underwater have been there about five hours now."[107] All lingering hope of crash victims still in their cars surviving on wished-for air bubbles therein vanished when the effects of hypothermia were considered. Immersion in water at 65 F – a relatively mild air temperature – can lead to deadly hypothermia very quickly – thirty to sixty minutes most times. It became painfully obvious that a "recovery mode" couldn't do much to rescue those poor souls trapped under the chilling waters of the Arkansas River for so long a time.

It was also decided, among other things, to lower the depth of the river via management of the dams above and below the crash site, thereby reducing the current pressure pushing against the barges and the *Robert Y. Love*. U. S. Army Corps of Engineers navigation manager Gregory Barnes began calling dam operators up-stream to shut down water flow to the accident site. Water flow in the Arkansas River at the time of the accident was 54,000 cubic feet per second (cfs). By 1500 hours, the Corps had reduced the flow to 40,000 cfs; by 1700 hours, it was down to 38,000 cfs, and by midnight the flow was 21,000 cfs.[108]

By early that evening, engineers had also secured the barges in place using cables stretched taut to the still-standing bridge piers to anchor them. It was only then that the dive teams could safely enter the river. Rescue efforts were hampered by grid-locked highways and a lack of shoreline near the bridge, according to Michelann Ooten, an Oklahoma Emergency Management spokeswoman. [109] There would be no more survivors.

Part of the Interstate-40 Bridge sits on top of the barges that hit it. (Courtesy: Linda Copeland, *Sequoyah County Times*.)

The murmur of boat engines and human voices seemed to add to an eerie quiet. There was no smoke, no fire, no sirens. A green sheen of spilled motor fuel coated the river. Firefighters, rescuers, and divers waded in the water while crowds gathered on the riverbank and abutments. A mangled vehicle stuck out of the water. Maggie Green's horse trailer was lodged between the broken piers. The cargo of Paul Tailele's tractor-trailer floated downstream in the water. [110]

*   *   *

Eleven vehicles either fell with the collapsed sections of the bridge or drove off the bridge and into the void. In one of those cars were Richard Cawley and his wife of more than thirty years, Jeanine. He never had a chance to even get his foot on the brake pedal before they were airborne and she screamed, "'Oh my God, the road's gone!" He later said it seemed like they were in the air "forever." With the Cawley's experience being typical, it was evident that drivers could not see the bridge void in time to react and avoid driving into it – as was also the case at the Queen Isabella Causeway calamity in Texas, covered in Chapter VI herein. The slight incline of the roadway over the navigation channel again decreased the forward-sighting ability. Obviously, the drivers involved in this accident did not have sufficient time to stop their vehicles even if they did detect the collapsed sections of the bridge.

After hitting the water, Cawley unbuckled his seat belt but couldn't unbuckle his wife's. He managed to get out of the pickup but it rolled onto his arm, pinning him. By the time he got his arm unstuck he had to go up for air. He dove back down to their truck and its fifth-wheel motor home but the wreck had rolled over even more and Jeanine was now inaccessible.[111]

As Cawley struggled in vain to save his wife, John Swain and his son, Gabe, were fishing in the tournament on the Arkansas River when they heard a sound neither will ever forget. "I just turned to Gabe and said, 'What was that?'" Swain said. "It was a sound like something I've never heard before. I've heard collisions and explosions, even a train wreck. In Vietnam, I heard artillery shells, rockets and mortars explode. But I'd never heard anything like that. It was sort of a collision and explosion in one. It just reverberated through the trees."

As the I-40 bridge collapsed, "Gabe said, 'Oh my God, dad, they're going off the bridge.' He saw four cars go off," said the father echoing the son. Swain headed for a cluster of boats already at the wreckage site. He maneuvered his boat through the debris. One of the boaters told Gabe and John to look for a man who was in the water.

The man in the water they found was Richard Cawley, clinging to a coiled hose floating among the debris. Cawley said he couldn't hold on much longer; his arm had sustained serious injury. Gabe and John, maneuvering their boat through a swift current, took care not to further injure Cawley while they hoisted him into the boat. John held the man during the ride back to the tournament launching area, placing his head in the crook of his arm. From his first aid training, he fashioned a tourniquet and kept Cawley conscious. "He kept talking about his wife, how he couldn't get her out (of the submerged truck)," Swain said. "I just told him they were trying to help her." (John and Gabe Swain were later honored by the Tulsa Squadron, part of the national group U.S. Power Squadrons that promote boating safety.)[112]

*   *   *

In the world of possibilities, it is also altogether feasible that sixty-eight-year-old Max Alley and his wife of fifty years, Goldie, could very well have eventually passed Jerry and Pat Gillion – as all four were routed along the Muskogee Turnpike, though in opposite directions. Max and Goldie actually did see Major Andrew Clements car just in front of them as they approached the I-40 Bridge over the Arkansas River. Max, an evangelist, and Goldie, his gospel-singing accompanist, were motoring from their home near Broken Arrow, Oklahoma.

They were heading clear across the Sooner State to the Arkoma Assembly of God Church just west of Ft. Smith, Arkansas on that May 26. They left home early that morning because they wanted to get to Arkoma in time for

Sunday School and preach about the "tricks of the devil." As for Goldie's singing, she often said, "God doesn't care about your talent. He cares about a willing heart."[113]

Before the day got much older, the Alleys learned more about some of Old Lucifer's tricks and God's willing heart. In the picture below, that's the Alleys' Chevrolet pickup truck on the section of the bridge that dropped twelve feet straight down under them, giving him time to slam on his brakes and stop before going over the brink.

Max Alley's back, being broken in two places, and Goldie's two cracked ribs didn't keep them from getting released from the Muskogee Regional Medical Center on the night of the crash. None of those injuries kept the lucky preacher and his wife from later spreading the word of their miraculous escape on that Sunday morning. And, as Goldie Alley says, "It's still so good to be here. The things I used to gripe about I can't even gripe about anymore."[114]

A section of I-40 dropped straight down (left-center) and gave the occupants of the pickup truck thereon – Max and Goldie Alley – a chance to stop before diving into the river.
(Courtesy, Tom Gilbert, *Tulsa World*)

Eleven vehicles crashed into the Arkansas River when the Interstate-40 Bridge collapsed near Webbers Falls, Oklahoma, on May 26, 2002.

Those Who Didn't Make It
Jeanine Cawley, 58, Lebanon, Oregon
Major Andrew Clements, 35, Woodbridge, Virginia
Jerry Gillion, 58, Spiro, Oklahoma
Patricia Gillion, 57, Spiro, Oklahoma
Margaret Green, 45, San Antonio, Texas
James Johnson, 30, Lavaca, Arkansas
Misty Johnson, 28, Lavaca, Arkansas
Shea Nicole Johnson, 3, Lavaca, Arkansas
Susan Martin, 49, Norman, Oklahoma
Wayne Martin, 49, Norman, Oklahoma
David Mueggenborg, 52, Okarche, Oklahoma
Jean Mueggenborg, 51, Okarche, Oklahoma
Gail Shanahan, 49, Stockdale, Texas
Paul Tailele, Jr., 39, Magna, Utah

The medical examiner ruled the manner of death as accidental drowning on thirteen victims, with one (Andrew Clements) succumbing to blunt trauma to the head.

Four more vehicles were involved containing:
Those Who Made It
Goldie Alley, 65, Broken Arrow, Oklahoma
Max Alley, 67, Broken Arrow, Oklahoma
(in the pickup truck he was able to stop)
Truck driver James Bilyeu, 62, Conway, Arkansas
Richard Cawley, 59, Lebanon, Oregon
(husband of Jeanine Cawley listed above)
Truck driver Rodney Tidwell, 37, Ripley, Mississippi

In the aftermath of his son's death caused by the collapse of the Interstate-40 Bridge, Major Andrew

Clements' father, Ronald, mournfully asked, "What were the odds of something like this happening?" What indeed?

Over the span of the 1,700 miles his son had driven since leaving California, suppose he had, just once, spent sixty seconds longer at one of the many gasoline stations at which he had stopped along the way? Suppose the Cawleys had decided to wait for the next rest stop after the one at Webbers Falls on their westbound trip? Suppose Gail Shanahan had flown back to Texas as she originally planned? Suppose little Shea Nicole Johnson would have had a usual three-year-old's tummy ache before she left home with her Mom and Dad and their departure was delayed a tad? Suppose Paul Tailele had pulled his truck over to the shoulder to make that early-morning phone call to his daughter. And suppose May 26, 2002 hadn't fallen on a holiday weekend? Just suppose....

"What," asked Ronald Clements, "were the odds of something like this happening?"

*   *   *

In the wake of the *Robert Y. Love*/Interstate-40 disaster, a device know as a "Deadman's" alarm has been proposed for installation in many types of towboats on the nation's Inland Waterways. According to Captain Whitehurst of the National Mariners Association (NMA), these proposed "alarms go off first in the wheelhouse to wake the pilot on watch. Then if the pilot does not push a button to disarm the alarm," said Whitehurst, "a really loud-as-hell-alarm goes off alerting the boat crew that the pilot is asleep or there's another emergency in the wheelhouse."

Some of these alarms are activated by motion detectors. "Others work with the steering," reported Whitehurst. "If the sticks (steering gear) are not moved in a specified time frame, the alarm goes off!" The system is much the same as that in the engineer's cab on railroad trains. It's even so simple it's found on newer automobiles; when you don't quickly turn off your turn signal, it beeps back at you to remind you it's still blinking away. It is ironic that this new "Dead Man's" alarm system brings to mind the name of the skipper of the ill-fated towboat *Robert Y. Love*, Captain William Joe Dedmon.

As of the spring of 2013, the "Dead Man's" alarm was mandated via IMO resolution MCS.128(75) – Performance standards for a Bridge Navigational Watch Alarm System (BNWAS). Holding back its institution in the "regs" for years was because at first it was only directed at towing vessels pushing "red flag" – hazardous cargo – barges.

Why the ruling wasn't initially universal is a question asked by Captain Whitehurst when he correctly noted, "dry cargo tows have KILLED also!" Some, such as NMA's Secretary Captain Richard Block, "suspect the [delay] may [have been] financial – that a one-time mechanical 'fix' is cheaper than hiring a third licensed operator to share some helmsmen's punishing twelve-hour daily workload.

Block also charged the companies were urging "a 'mechanical solution' to a 'human' problem." Continuing Block said, "It wasn't until the early 1990s that the Coast Guard recognized that at least eighty percent of the accidents involved human failure rather than mechanical failure." That revelation led to the very successful "Prevention Through People" program instigated by then-USCG Admiral James Card. Nonetheless, said Captain Block in referring to the then absence of "a third licensed operator" on board and the physical/mental burden it puts on only two helmsmen, it still meant their "twelve-hour day [each] means an eighty-four-hour work week no matter how you slice it."[115]

(And that's why the "Dead Man's" alarm was needed.)

*   *   *

Chapter V
The Imposter

In researching the "Rendezvous with Destiny" segment of this work, one out-of-place name kept popping up. It was that of William J. Clark, the so-called "mystery man" all conspiracy theorists have come to love. Clark's one of the strangest stories to emerge from the Interstate Highway-40 disaster. Later labeled "The Imposter," William James Clark was for several years one that many people knew *of* but few people knew *about*. Conspiracy theorists embraced him. One such, radio talk-show host Jerry Pippin, even did an on-air ninety-minute interview with Clark in April of 2008.

(Other far-out stories, by the way, featured on Jerry Pippin's radio broadcasts included "The definitive work on the JFK assassination," and "The Twin Towers – An Inside Job?" Pippin has convinced those who have seen UFOs at Roswell, New Mexico they don't need new prescriptions for their eyeglasses, and yes, that Elvis Presley is alive and well and grinding his hips nightly in a swinging singles bar in the middle of Pennsylvania's Amish country.)

Here's a thumbnail version of "The Imposter" by the Associated Press, a somewhat more reliable source, on June 5, 2002:

> "The FBI is investigating a man who called himself an Army captain and looked through a briefcase and laptop computer belonging to a victim of last month's deadly interstate bridge collapse. The man, wearing fatigues and a beret, showed up within two hours of the Interstate-40 collapse and told the [Webber Falls] mayor he was

in charge. He identified himself as Captain William Clark." Mayor Jewell Horne said she was so busy answering phones and directing rescuers that she "didn't have time to think a lot" or check the man's credentials. Two volunteers from the Tulsa medical examiner's office eventually called authorities to check on him, she said.[116]

The victim noted in the above story was U. S. Army Captain Andrew Clements, cited elsewhere in these pages. Here's the way the Pippin program framed it on April 2, 2008 (one day after April Fool's Day, we might add):

> "William J. Clark came on the air to tell his side of the I-40 Bridge Collapse back in 2002.... The tale involves his side of the story on how he pretended to be an Army captain and took over the rescue efforts when a tug boat [sic] knocked down the bridge over the Arkansas River near Webbers Falls on I-40 in Oklahoma.
>
> The bridge is not far from a nuclear waste dump that was left unguarded with huge numbers of radioactive waste in barrels in the open with only an empty guard shack....The whole story is more than it seems. Not just a tragic accident, but some weird goings on that sounds like an X-Files episode.
>
> What was really going on in the Heartland at 7AM that fateful and disastrous morning? Were 14 more American lives sacrificed in the War on Terrorism, or was something even more sinister going on?" Clark answered that "sinister" supposition by charging that "a tugboat captain evidently

108

lost his mind, literally, and drove a barge…"
into the I-40 Bridge piling.[117]

In what might be called "a fairness disclaimer,"
Pippin's website did claim early in the interview that
"Clark is probed about his hearing voices, [and] memory
loss." Pippin then goes on to tie that into the memory loss
claimed by *Robert Y. Love* Captain Joe Dedmon, leading
him to ask, "Could this be some sort of mind control
activity using dubious characters to do undercover black
ops?" In his ninety-minute interview, Pippin claims to
"probe all the possible scenarios with Clark who gives
candid answers."[118] In this case, we'll leave the decision up
to the readers of *The Rivers of Life – and Death*.

Paraphrasing poet Elizabeth Barrett Browning in
this story, one can ask: How can I deceive thee? Let me
count the ways.

In the interview with Pippin, Clark says he drove on
the accident scene "about 7:20 a.m.," after an "uneasy
feeling" caused him to pull off the road twenty minutes
earlier. If he got to the Webber Falls accident scene as he
says he did at about 7:20 a.m., he got there twenty-five
minutes before Captain Dedmon and his towboat arrived.

Clark next makes the preposterous claim that he
dove into the "30-40 degree" water and he got two people –
a woman and her daughter – out of a submerged vehicle by
breaking a car window. (Pippin didn't remind him that had
the water been at less than thirty-two degrees, he might
have needed an ice auger to get into the wet stuff.) As
noted in the story above, all four of the survivors who went
into the Arkansas River in their vehicles were rescued by
nearby fishermen and none of those saved was female.

When Pippin asked Clark if he ever met towboat
Captain Dedmon, the imposter answered, "You mean the
one who had alcohol on his breath? I know he had alcohol
on his breath…."[119] First of all, after later admitting he had

in fact *never* met the captain, how did he *know* he "had alcohol on his breath"? And secondly, in conformance with all maritime rules of road in accidents on the inland waterways, Captain Dedmon readily submitted to the required alcohol and drug tests administered and they came out negative.

In keeping with his radio host's conspiracy theories theme, Clark got the pot boiling by claiming, "The federal government knew, a year before [the accident] even happened, the date it was going to happen. There was even a big Senate Oversight Committee on it where the CIA even admitted that they had information that was given to them a year prior; even six months prior, they had more information." [120] A good reporter/interviewer would have asked where such charges could be substantiated. Pippin didn't ask.

Clark was arrested in the Ontario, Canada, town of Tobermory, north of Toronto, on June 9, 2002 on fraud and theft charges as he waited to board a ferry. Canadian authorities charged him with possession of property obtained by crime, and also weapons offenses. He similarly faced charges under the Canada Immigration Act and was wanted by the FBI. Relatives and investigators said Clark had a history of assuming false identities to gain free meals, free rooms or merchandise. He was accused of renting eight hotel rooms in Van Buren, Ark., after the bridge accident, then skipping town without paying the $900 bill. [121]

On August 26, 2003, a U. S. federal judge sentenced thirty-seven-year-old William James Clark to three years in federal prison for falsely impersonating a U.S. Army officer and seventy months for possession of a firearm after a felony conviction. U.S. Attorney Sheldon J. Sperling said "Clark had identified himself as an Army officer working on the bridge disaster in order to obtain a pickup [truck] from a Searcy (Ark.) car dealer, clothing, supplies and food from a Fort Smith (Ark.) surplus store, and motel rooms from a Van Buren (Ark.) motel. Clark repeatedly called a victim's widow and falsely represented that he knew her husband, a deceased Army captain who perished in the tragedy. The court rendered a more severe sentence due to (the) defendant's continuing possession of a firearm during the criminal episode (and) to include the defendant's flight to Canada," Sperling said.[122]

Thus, William James Clark, "The Great Imposter," was returned to prison for relatively minor crimes; nothing at all like the magnitude one would expect from a conspiracy theorist's claim of a "second shooter" on the grassy knoll firing at President John F. Kennedy in Dallas in November of 1963. But even those stints behind bars for Clark became fuel for the conspiracy theorists who try to justify some of their fantasies by declaring his arrest, conviction, and incarceration are also parts of a great government cover-up policy.

And so it goes.

*   *   *

Chapter VI
Death in *Laguna Madre*

Captain Rocky Lee Wilson had no qualms when he handed over command of the towboat *Brown Water V* to his relief

The Queen Isabella Causeway[123]

captain, David D. Fowler, a few minutes before midnight on September 14, 2001.   The towboat with its five-man crew – the two captains and three deckhands – was starting on the first leg of a transit through the Gulf Intracoastal Waterway (GIWW) from Brownsville, Texas to the barges' ultimate destination in Tennessee. Both captains – with Wilson being the Master (senior officer aboard) – were experienced riverboat pilots. Fowler for instance, as the junior officer on board, had his Operator of Uninspected Towing Vessels License for twelve years.[124]

High above the handoff of the helm on the *Brown Water V* and almost exactly two hours after Fowler took over, revelers, workers, and other homeward-bounders in their automobiles were headed west over the 2.37-mile long Queen Isabella Causeway. The bridge connects South Padre Island to the mainland at the southernmost tip of

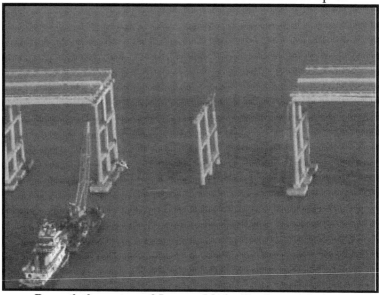

Beneath the waters of *Laguna Madre* lies the wreckage of eight vehicles and 350 tons of roadway[125]

Texas. Before anyone knew what was happening, ten of those vehicles took eight unsuspecting motorists to their death in the waters of the *Laguna Madre* eighty-five feet below the Causeway. The "Mother Lagoon" is known, ironically, as a 130-mile long sport fisherman's *paradise*.

Some of the bodies were trapped under 350 tons of concrete wreckage for more than a week before being recovered. Three other people were injured, and to this day, the details of that tragedy are still, again, fuzzy. Exactly what happened remains a mystery to some due to conflicting testimony, differing interpretations, and even non-existent explanations. Some people at the time were sure the tragedy was another terrorist attack, following the September 11 horrifics at the Twin Towers in New York City, the Pentagon in Arlington, Virginia, and that barren field in Shanksville, Pennsylvania, just four days before. Those suspicions were well-founded as the Causeway overrides with the Gulf Intracoastal Waterway – a major American fuel transportation route.

*   *   *

Long before, in 1770, the first Spanish colonial settlers had begun to fish and visit the *Laguna Madre*. In June 1845, a post office was established and the name of the community officially became Point Isabel. By 1850, Point Isabel was exporting $10 million worth of cotton annually. On March 23, 1928, Point Isabel was officially incorporated as its current name, Port Isabel.

The Queen Isabella Causeway, from its entry on the Port Isabel side, rises gently upward and easterly out over the *Laguna Madre*. At about its midway point, the road curves off to the southeast and connects with South Padre Island. It's about a two-and-one-half-mile trip. The GIWW channel passes beneath the overpass at about a half-mile from the Port Isabel shore side. South Padre Island's commercial and social lifeblood is the tourism industry, served mostly by the island's 2,500 permanent residents. It is also a vacation Mecca, notoriously (some claim) known for its beach parties by college and high school students celebrating the now-infamous Spring Break.

*   *   *

The weekend of September 14-16 marked the unofficial end of the 2001 tourist season and its final event was the celebration of *Diez y Seis de Septiembre* (the 16th of September), commemorating the 1810 start of Mexico's War of Independence against Spain. Tourists headed south to the Island from all over Texas, and north from the Mexican states bordering the Lone Star's, such as Coahuila and Nuevo Leon. Rooms at the Island's hotels were about seventy percent booked, a bonanza after the Labor Day celebration two weeks earlier.

Following the frantic check-in of hundreds of weekend guests on Friday at the oceanfront Holiday Inn SunSpree Resort, 22-year-old night manager Julio Mireles could hardly wait for his shift to end in the early Saturday morning hours so he could head home to Los Fresnos and get some sleep. His friend, Michael Lorber in his car, followed Mireles' out of the hotel parking lot, past the adjacent Schlitterbahn Waterpark with its tube chutes and surfing waves. Turning right onto Padre Boulevard went the two cars, motoring north on Texas Highway 100, where they and the road both turned left, heading for the Causeway. It usually was a fast, 30-minute drive from the Island almost straight due west along Highway 100 to Los Fresnos. With the Island's bars closing at their usual two-o'clock "witching hour," Mireles and Lorber were not alone on the bridge.

The Queen Isabella Causeway becomes part of Highway 100 as it crosses over the *Laguna Madre*, the 130-mile-long sea-water-salty bay that averages a mere two feet or so in depth. The Lagoon parallels the Texas coast running north-south along the Gulf of Mexico, barely

116

dipping into Mexico itself. Splitting the entire length of the *Laguna Madre* is the Gulf Intracoastal Waterway with its twelve-foot minimum depth. The trouble was, Julio Mireles and Michael Lorber were on Highway 100 and the *Brown Water V* with its string of four heavily laden barges was beneath it, some 375 feet off course. Then, at about two o'clock, the tow struck one of the Causeway's unprotected piers some 175 feet west of the navigation channel on the now-Saturday morning, September 15, 2001.

With Mireles' car in the lead as they roared up the incline and over the longest bridge in Texas, Lorber suddenly saw the taillights of his friend's car drop out of sight and down into the inky darkness. It plunged headlong eight stories into the abyss caused by a 160-foot section of missing roadway. Those motorists driving from the mainland side – what few there were at that hour – could see the missing spans just before the peak of the bridge and were able to stop in time. However, those driving from the Island could not see the missing spans until after they had crested the peak of the bridge and were about 200 feet from the edge of the gap.

For those headed for the Mainland, it was a situation eerily similar to what happened on Interstate Highway 40 eight months later, as reported Chapter IV in this book. The stopping distance for an average passenger car traveling at a speed of fifty-seven miles-per-hour (lower than the posted speed of sixty mph on the Causeway) is approximately 514 feet, according to an NTSB report.[126]

In the fifteen minutes before emergency personnel were notified and closed the approaches to the bridge, ten west-bound cars drove off the bridge into the water resulting in eight fatalities. Lorber's car was not one of them. He was able to slam on his brakes and stop at the brink of doom. As the search and rescue operations (soon to become "recovery" ops only) continued late Saturday afternoon, Michael Lorber was still sobbing over what he knew was the loss of his friend, Julio Mireles.

Looking out at the Coast Guard boats and some civilian craft searching fruitlessly for survivors in *Laguna Madre*, Lorber cried, "He's still in there." A little later, while viewing the same scene, Matt Pechacek, another friend of Lorber's and Mireles' demanded to know "why isn't there a million boats out there" looking for the lost hotel night manager and the other victims.[127] A third slab of highway crashed down earlier that Saturday morning, ending any hopes of a speedy recovery effort. It would be ten days before the last body, that of 22-year-old Julio Mireles, was pulled out of the murky waters.[128]

*   *   *

Efforts to recover the bodies of those trapped in their cars under those hundreds of tons of concrete and rebar were led by the Texas Department of Public Safety Dive-Recovery Team (DPS/DRT). Its members were certified deep-water divers with special training in cave- and swift-water-diving. The DRT was hampered in its recovery efforts by tidal currents that moved the sunken vehicles and poor visibility in what was an excavated fifty-foot deep waterway there.

"It took about twice as long as we thought," said DPS Lieutenant Lynn Dixon, who headed the fourteen-diver rescue team. The bottom of the bay beneath the bridge was littered with chunks of concrete and lengths of metal beam and rebar. "There was so much debris, it was difficult to orientate yourself," said Dixon.[129] The team was recognized as one of the best such units in the nation. In addition to its search and rescue efforts during the Queen Isabella Causeway collapse, the DRT played an integral role in the Space Shuttle *Columbia* disaster during February 2003.[130] Also assisting the Department of Public Safety experts and several Texas A&M University oceanographers in the underwater search was an eleven-member U. S. Navy dive team equipped with hand-held sonar and metal-detecting magnetometers under the command of Chief Warrant Office Patrick Culver.

*   *   *

The night of September 14-15, 2001 was crystal clear. The waning moon wouldn't rise until after five in the morning. There were no severe weather anomalies. The wind was out of the east-northeast blowing between eight and eleven miles per hour. It was a "gentle breeze" according to the Beaufort Wind Scale, the mariners' Bible for measuring and labeling wind velocity. There was no precipitation. There was no fog. The current in the Waterway was, however, "was running pretty hard," according to Captain Fowler. It brought the incoming tide from the Gulf of Mexico almost two-and-one-quarter feet above Mean Lower Low Tide.

Somehow, the *Brown Water V* got frightfully off the channel's course as it ran under the Causeway. Somehow, its lead barge *NM 315* allided with one of the piers holding up the Causeway. Somehow, 160 feet of four-lane highway concrete, rebar and railings would eventually go crashing down. And somehow, another eighty-foot section would splash into the murky water later in the morning.

The *Brown Water V* towboat was owned then by Rockport, Texas-based Brown Water Marine Services Inc. ("Brown Water" is a name given to inland rivers and waterways to distinguish them from "Blue Water" oceans.) The towboat was classified as a U.S. Coast Guard documented, uninspected towing vessel. According to the National Mariners Association, in 1972 Congress required vessel officers to be licensed, but it did not require their towing vessels to be inspected. This "uninspected" status continued until 2004 with a minor exception of a few large coastal and ocean towing vessels exceeding 300 gross registered tons. [131] Furthermore, charges NMA, "Few regulations assure crewmembers that their tug or towboat is safely constructed or adequately maintained. In fact, many are old and poorly maintained."[132] (Later in this Chapter and elsewhere in this book, variations of these claims are cited.)

The four barges being pushed single file by the towboat (there's that anomaly again) were owned by American Commercial Barge Line LLC, Jeffersonville, Indiana. Overall, "the string" (the towboat and its four barges) was 851 feet long and the barges were carrying slightly more than 6,000 tons of steel coil and phosphate. An incoming tide and a following current pushed the towboat and its barges to the left and out of the channel. The impact with which lead barge *NM 315* hit one of the Causeway's pilings was something even the gold vaults at Fort Knox, Kentucky may not have been able to withstand.

The forces of impact are noted above on page 88 where in a somewhat similar situation it "would have been roughly equivalent to sixty-two 2,000-pound cars slamming into the structure simultaneously at 60 mph."

*   *   *

Barry Welch began his career in the Art of Dermagraphics when he was just nineteen-years-old. Never heard of the "Art of Dermagraphics"? Then you've probably never been in a tattoo parlor. Thirty-four years later, and known as "Harpoon" Barry, Welch was still making body art in his shop on South Padre Island. "I was drawing before I was able to walk," Barry once claimed.[133] The 53-year-old, one-legged needle-master was a local legend among the Gulf of Mexico surfers as he swooped down the wave faces "hanging [in his case] five" instead of ten. It was that wooden leg that gave him his incongruously graphic nickname. "Harpoon" Barry and his 23-year-old wife and co-worker Chealsa [sic], celebrating the end of another summer holiday season of increasingly popular dermagraphics on the Island, decided to get out and go out for a night on the town on Friday, September 14, 2001.

They made the rounds of their usual haunts and sometime shortly before two o'clock on Saturday morning, decided they had better head back to their two-year-old son, Billy, who was in the care of his by now anxious baby-sitting grandmother, Jackie McClendon. Grandma McClendon, Chealsa's mom was, ironically, a receptionist at the same Schlitterbahn water park Julio Mireles passed when he left the Holiday Inn for the last time – just about when the Welches were heading south on Padre Boulevard on Texas Highway 100, for the Causeway, and their home in Port Isabel mere minutes away across the lagoon.

Barry and Chealsa climbed up the gentle incline toward the apex of the bridge over the Gulf Intracoastal Waterway in their SUV with its headlights stabbing into the ebony blackness of the still moonless night. With startling suddenness, the familiar roadway was no longer beneath them. There was only their watery grave below, leaving Billy Welch an orphan. In the immediate aftermath of the tragedy, Billy's grandmother, exasperated by the recovery process said, "A 900,000-pound slab of concrete is sitting on my baby [girl]," as she watched the operations from shore side.[134] "This will not be my daughter's final resting point. Do whatever, but get my daughter out of there. It's taking too long."[135]

A week later, grieving over the loss of her daughter and overwrought with sarcasm, Jackie McClendon lashed out as she paced the deck of owner Gary Wages' Beefeater's Smoke House restaurant where she could look out at the recovery cranes. There would be no closure until they got her daughter out. "You're in shock, then you get mad, then you learn to deal with it," she said.[136] With all the high technology available, she asked, why couldn't there have been some sort of warning system? "I feel like somehow...instead of having that big sign that says, 'Watch out for Pelicans,' [it] could have said, 'Danger, Bridge Down'."[137]

*   *   *

The *Brown Water V* – with Captain Rocky Wilson at the helm supervising the lashing of the four American Commercial barges to each other and also to the towboat – let go all lines from its Brownsville departure point shortly after nine o'clock on the evening of September 14, 2001. The float plan was to move the 6,000 tons of steel and phosphate up the Gulf Intracoastal Waterway and on to Tennessee. The GIWW is a shallow, inland canal running from Brownsville, Texas, to St. Marks, Florida. It gives mariners thereon a much smoother waterway than they might face with some storms out in the Gulf of Mexico, usually less than a few miles away. The Texas portion of the canal system extends 426 miles, from the Sabine River at the Louisiana-Texas border to the mouth of the Brownsville Ship Channel at Port Isabel.[138]

The string headed easterly for about thirteen miles – a fairly straight shot – where at just about midnight, it encountered the southern-most end of the GIWW. With the hands of the ship's clock pointing straight up and "eight bells" ringing, Wilson turned the wheel over to his relief pilot, David Fowler. Wilson and deckhands J. W. Blocker and Ross L. Valigura went below to catch some sleep. Fowler and deckhand Levie Old took over the wheelhouse. With nothing to do while Fowler steered the string, Old – with the relief captain's permission – slipped back into slumber nearby in the pilothouse where he was available "in case he [was] needed." [139] It was not an abnormal situation. Fowler soon turned the string north into the GIWW. As usual, the "S" curve taking him between Long

122

Island to the right and Port Isabel to his left, awaited. Not exactly the kind of thing that will "make my day" for any towboat skipper pushing 800 feet of barges, especially with conflicting currents (as shown in the chart below).

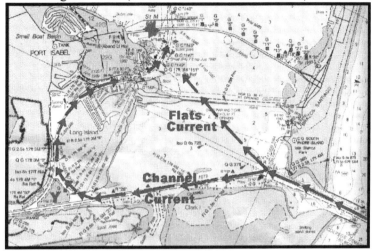

To the left of the "Y" on this chart (lower left corner) is where *Brown Water V* came out of the Brownsville Channel and headed into the "S" curve and the Queen Isabella Causeway (top center)[140]

Even before, and certainly after the tragedy, there were many who questioned why the difficult "S" curve has not been dredged in a straighter path. Another indication of the dangers in the "S" curve showed up on May 2, 2002, just eight months later when a fuel barge hit the nearby Long Island Swing Bridge the *Brown Water V* cleared the previous September. No one was injured in that allision but the connection from the island to the mainland, just about a mile south of the Queen Isabella Causeway, was shut down temporarily. Peter Benavides, a Cameron County commissioner with the Causeway tragedy still fresh in his mind, said "the incident was another warning that something needed to be done about the narrow passageway."[141]

Some towboat captains complain bitterly about swing bridges on the upper rivers. "They're real old and they haven't gotten around to replacing them with the new standard 300-foot channel span," one skipper grumbled. "Some of them," he continued, "only have 120-foot, 140-foot spans and with a bad current up there, they're tricky to get in and out of." Tricky is hardly the word. Running up and down rivers such as the Illinois and the Arkansas with a standard tow three-wide, that's over 105 feet in width. Guiding that load through an opening with less than eight feet of clearance on either side and with a river running is a lot more than "tricky." It's one of the reasons why long-time skippers have short-time hair.

An Army Corps of Engineers official testified that straightening the "S" curve "would destroy a portion of the sensitive *Laguna Madre* wetlands. There is strong environmental support backing this decision." This is not an unheard-of problem. As at least one respected waterways publication editorialized, "At some point, the environmentalists – who apparently have a terrible grip on government – and legislators decided it was not a good idea to spend money on our waterway system...."[142]

Nonetheless, the *Brown Water V* successfully cleared that Long Island Swing Bridge at one-forty-five a.m. on September 15, 2001. Fifteen minutes later, the South Padre Island-Mainland road came tumbling down!

*   *   *

To hitch-hike on the title of Sebastian Junger's 1997 classic book about men against the sea, it was *The Perfect Storm* awaiting Fowler as he headed for the Queen Isabella Causeway. More importantly, so it was also for so many of those driving overhead on the roadway eighty-five-feet above the Gulf Intracoastal Waterway.

According to some reports, some of the navigation lights on the bottom of the Causeway – those showing the center of the channel's width beneath the bridge – were out. The tide in the GIWW was more than two feet higher than normal at the time. "We do know the tides were extremely high and there were some strong currents. ... If there were any mitigating factors, those would be the ones," Bob Cornelison, director of the Port Isabel Navigation District, said later.[143]

The National Oceanic and Atmospheric Administration (NOAA) concluded the high tide was probably due to tropical storm *Gabrielle* in the Gulf of Mexico.[144] What are lemons for some is lemonade for others. A Currituck County (North Carolina) spokesperson, commenting on *Gabrielle* after it hit the Atlantic Ocean coastline, was most pleased because the tropical storm "has given us a little practice run for hurricanes. You don't wish to have a storm," she said, "but if you have to have one (*Gabrielle*) is a good one to have."[145]

Be careful what you wish for.

The higher the tide, the stronger the currents affecting the tow. Captain Alton Chadwick, an "expert" witness called at a hearing into the incident, guesstimated "the current at the time of the [allision] was between four and five miles per hour."[146] As noted above, Fowler reported the current "was running pretty hard." Deckhand Levie Old said it "was flowing really good...real strong." Captain Rocky Wilson called the current "the strongest I've seen it." And Senior Chief Paul Inskeep, Officer in Charge of the Coast Guard Cutter *Mallet* out of Corpus Christi, Texas, and on the scene within two-and-one-half hours of the allision, said the current "was [still] running very hard."[147]

Not only was the current running "really good," "real strong," "very hard," and "the strongest I've seen it," but there were two currents affecting the *Brown Water V* and its barges. As they emerged from the protection of

Long Island and into the open waters of *Laguna Madre*, those currents went crosswise – with one flowing "really good" northeasterly from behind the tow and the other hitting it "very hard" on its starboard (right) beam in a northwesterly direction (again, see chart on page 123).

Combined and if not compensated for by the helmsman, the currents were pushing *Brown Water V* and its four barges up-stream and to the left, away from the GIWW channel under the Causeway. Aiding the currents in the broadside push against the towboat was the ENE-wind blowing at about eight-to-eleven miles-per-hour. Throw in claims by some investigators who said the *Brown Water V* was underpowered. According to a plaintiff's attorney in a later legal hearing (and as in the *Elizabeth M* story reported in Chapter III herein), the accident wouldn't have happened if the tow was adequately powered. "With the currents that night, they weren't prepared with enough horsepower to steer away or back off," the attorney said.[148]

In subsequent hearings seeking the cause of the disaster, it was shown that the channel *Brown Water V* was supposed to be in was dredged to its required twelve-foot depth, was free of shoals, and a series of channel markers ("red nuns" and "green cans" that are supposed to mark the meanderings of waterway's safe passage) were properly placed. At least most of them were. The suddenly infamous buoy No. 147 was shown by Coast Guard officials to have been almost a football field's length away from where it should have been to allow a mariner space for the very wide turn vessels must make to navigate the channel's "S" curve. No one at the hearing could say why that particular channel marker was where it was.

The water next to No. 147 was shallowed by a seven-foot shoal and hitting it could knock a vessel or a tow off course. Brown Water Towing attorneys argued this was "an accident waiting to happen," asserting the buoys lure vessels outside the channel into dangerously shallow waters. The fact the buoys were located outside the channel was, however, noted on current-issue charts.[149]

Captain Fowler told the Coast Guard he ran aground briefly after hitting a sandbar or shoals on the right side of the channel. Company lawyers insisted the tow then lost its steering, and strong tidal currents swung the four barges Fowler was pushing into the unprotected concrete causeway pilings. That shallow area became the focus of much testimony. The Cameron County District Attorney's office announced it would review the criminal investigation of the collapse.

Even without the thunder and lightning, without hurricane-force winds, without Sebastian Junger's raging North Atlantic seas, at two o'clock on the morning of September 15, 2001 at the intersection of the Gulf Intracoastal Waterway and the Queen Isabella Causeway at Port Isabel, Texas, it was indeed – just as it was for Junger's fishermen – a catastrophic "Perfect Storm."

* * *

Another of the many mainlanders who made a living working on South Padre Island, Hector Martinez was the head-waiter at the Sea Ranch Restaurant, a favorite dining place for Winter Texans, Mexican nationals, and even the spring-breakers. Unknowingly, he too joined death's caravan of cars leaving the Island for home. His body wasn't recovered until the following Tuesday.

Gasper Hinojosa also was a victim, about whom there are those who argued that missing street lights on the bridge might have affected his vision of the roadway. As were some of the channel-marking lights under the bridge out, so too were some of the roadway-illuminating lights out over it. Usually, the lights were glowing "like a Christmas tree" waiting for Santa's arrival. Although some "thought the darkness had something to do with the September 11 terrorist attacks," actually "aging lamps and corrosive salt air make it difficult to keep the lights functioning," state and local officials later explained. [150] Likewise, Hector Martinez' survivors charged the sudden difference – from a well-lighted to a darkened highway – impeded his forward vision, which became a factor in his death plunge.

Hinojosa, a 52-year-old avid fisherman, was survived by his wife Raquel Teran Hinojosa. He worked nights as an assistant manager at the South Padre Island's Whataburger stand and may have been the first to drive into the chasm. His car was found smashed and lodged into a bridge support – the only vehicle that didn't fall into the water. Pulled from the wreckage shortly after the accident, Gasper Hinojosa was pronounced dead at Valley Baptist Medical Center in Brownsville.

*   *   *

Stvan Rivas, 22, from Humble, Texas, had been living with an aunt while he took classes at the University of Texas at Brownsville. Born in Mexico City, his parents, Esteban and Mariam, moved the family to Texas and Stvan attended elementary, middle and high schools in Brownsville. When the rest of his family moved to the Houston area, Stvan opted to stay behind and attend the UT-Brownsville. A good student, Rivas was known by teachers and friends as "a humorous yet caring individual." [151] On the early morning of September 15, 2001, instead of staying with his friends at a fast food restaurant after leaving a birthday party on South Padre Island, Rivas instead got in his car and headed for his aunt's home.

"If somehow he was able to eat that hamburger he may still be alive," said his father, Esteban. An engineering student, Rivas was alone heading for Brownsville when, like other motorists, he didn't see the 160-foot gap in the bridge either. "Can you imagine the stress on somebody going down," into the water, the elder Rivas said. "My son tried to use his right hand to protect his head before he hit the water, and then he died [from impact] when he hit the water."[152]

*   *   *

Robert Victor (Bob) Harris spent nearly 30 years as a firefighter with the Port Isabel fire department. Harris' fellow emergency first-responders said he was a "big guy with a gentle heart who wanted to do everything for everybody."[153] He was the first victim to be recovered. Survived by his wife Anita, he was still in his battered red pickup truck, wedged beneath blocks of concrete, shortly before 3:00 p.m. Saturday. Friends said Harris – "very well-respected, hard-working and very dependable" – was returning to the mainland early Saturday from his second job as a security officer at Louie's Backyard, a popular South Padre Island nightspot. Sergeant Mike Brinegar of the Precinct 1 Constable's office in Port Isabel said, "Whenever there was a fire call, you knew he was going to be there. His death is going to be a great loss to the community."[154] Other officers said they understood Harris, the Good Samaritan, had stayed late to allow a co-worker to go home early.[155]

*   *   *

Rene Mata's story is unique among those of the fortunate though injured survivors (the other two being Bridgette Goza and Gustavo Morales, Jr). Mata survived and his passenger did not. Mata was taking twenty-nine-year-old Robin Faye Leavell back to her home in Port Isabel. Sitting in the car's right-hand front seat, she saw the looming disaster before he did and screamed, "The bridge!" It was too late. Mata hit the brakes on the red Ford Mustang coupe but not in time and their car was launched into the depths of darkness.

"It took forever," he remembers about going over the edge. "It was like in slow motion.... We hit [the water], and everything's pitch black. Couldn't see anything. Couldn't wake her [Ms. Leavell] up. Couldn't get the seat belt. I felt something warm running down my head and realized I had a gash on my head." Mata couldn't get the car windows open but he was able to open a door as water flooded into the car and equalized the pressure inside and out, enabling him to swim away. He spent the next week in Valley Baptist Medical Center branch in Harlingen, Texas, passing fitfully in and out of a coma and remembering "fishermen and lights and a helicopter."[156]

*   *   *

As best can be determined, Captain Fowler made the last arc of the "S" curve apparently unaware that the swirling currents were impacting his tow. In a post-accident interview, he said he was "surprised" by the cross-currents and had he recognized them earlier, he "would have set up his approach to the curve differently."[157] Coast Guard expert witness Captain Chadwick was surprised that Fowler was surprised. "In my opinion," Chadwick later testified, "anybody that runs [through the "S" curve] ought to know which way that current's running."

Fowler's sea-going boss aboard *Brown Water V*, Captain Rocky Wilson also was puzzled. He couldn't understand anybody transiting the curve from the Long Island Swing Bridge to the Queen Isabella Causeway Bridge without knowing what the currents were. As he said, "If you didn't set up right, you could lose it in there" [again referring to the "S" curve south of the Queen Isabella Causeway Bridge].[158]

The trouble is, complacency sometimes supersedes common sense among towboat captains and many others. For instance, one survey measured the "complacency potential with respect to the routine and automation of course and speed" of captains with more than 100 transits through the GIWW. It showed "95% of captains often steer the same course and speed through a lock and bridge." Likewise, "95% of captains often encounter the same commercial vessels on subsequent transits on the GIWW" and a full 100% of those captains "often make the same passing arrangements with other commercial vessels on the GIWW." Furthermore, the survey reports that those same towboat captains on the GIWW with more than 100 transits are "seldom" caught by surprise from wind or current.[159]

According to the survey, "one of the best methods of strategic thinking that was mentioned by one of the companies is the solicitation of real-time wind and current information from other captains during passing arrangements. This information gives the captain time to anticipate and adjust course and speed when passing under or through bridges or locks." As best can be determined, Captain Fowler didn't avail himself of that kind of "strategic thinking."[160] It cannot be verified that such "strategic thinking" was available to him for it is not known here if other towboats were in his vicinity.

There are several factors in situational awareness, according to Eric Larsson, director of the Center for Maritime Education for the Seamen's Church Institute in New York (an organization that provides, among other things, a center for research, legal assistance and training on issues relating to seafarers' abuse and exploitation). The above factors include ambiguity, inattention, lack of proper lookout, improper procedures, and not complying with a plan.[161] Life can be complacent, routine, and as repetitive as an automobile production line on towboats traveling along the Gulf Intracoastal Waterway – or any other shipping lane.

Though most certainly not in the case of the *Brown Water V* transiting the slithering "S" curve with all its known difficulties, this reporter has been in the wheelhouse with towboat skippers reading books while underway ("I just steer by feel," one of them said – without looking up from the pages).

In another case, the helmsman was busy watching a wild animal show – all about moose, bears, and snakes, snakes, snakes – on his cockpit commercial television set. Sometimes the FM radio is blaring so loudly with (mostly) country western music, the din could almost drown out a general alarm emergency bell. With waterway bottoms constantly shifting due to tides and silting, the pre-set depth alarms constantly go off, and many times, the helmsman again won't even look up from what he's doing as he automatically reaches over and slams the alarm button off. Complacency can be insidious.

*   *   *

It was God's will he made it out alive, said another survivor, Gustavo Morales. "God didn't want to take me right now. He wants something (from me), I don't know, a mission or something," The following edited story from the *Houston Chronicle* tells much of Morales' story of survival:[162]

> Morales said. "I feel reborn." The manager of Bigo's Restaurant on South Padre Island, Morales, 36, remembered gripping the steering wheel and screaming as his pickup truck flew off the Causeway, plunging toward the dark bay waters below.

"That was the most terrifying moment . . . when I was in the air," Morales said. "I remember I was screaming. I don't remember what I was yelling, but I was screaming."

Bruised from chest to ankle, exhausted and in pain, he said with a smile, "But at least I'm alive." He said the causeway was dark; "...there were no lights on it." Then, the red 2001 model pickup truck his company had given him three weeks earlier was flying off the darkened bridge. "It was like they moved the pavement. I felt my truck fly into the air.... Suddenly, boom, I was going to the water," Morales said. "My first instinct was to hold on the wheel and wait for the impact." As soon as the truck hit the water, it began to sink.

"It was unbelievable. I was already going down," Morales said, adding that he began to panic as the cab began to fill with water within seconds. "In the first two seconds, I was very nervous and scared." He was about to try to break the glass of a side window when a calm came over him. "Suddenly, for three or five seconds, I felt some calm inside of me," he said. "I mean, God helped me. It's a miracle. The Lord helped me – he was with me at that time.

"It took me three to five seconds to think, to take off my seat belt and pull the window down." He went through the open window and swam to the surface. He bobbed up next to the Causeway in time to see more cars hurtling off the span above him....

133

Morales said he swam and floated beneath the Causeway for five or ten minutes, shouting to two other survivors. Then a small fishing boat came along with four fishermen who pulled him and the other survivors to safety. Morales believes that if the causeway had been lighted, "probably it would have saved more cars, but I don't know."

Morales and the other two nearby survivors, Mata and Gosa, were rescued by four McAllen, Texas men who used their 17-foot fishing boat to save them. The rescuers had been on a sports fishing trip and witnessed the collapse. "You hear what happened, but when you see what happened, it's totally different," said one rescuer, Roland Moya, 25, remembering the sound of the tumbling cars and roadway. Almost mournfully, 22-year-old Leroy Moya asked at later ceremonies honoring the rescue crew's hero-Ism: "Could we have done more?"[163]

* * *

That Captain Rocky Wilson previously had no reservations in handing over the command of *Brown Water V* to Captain David Fowler with the "S" Curve looming ahead on that early morning of September 15, 2001, may have been due his acceptance of Fowler's abilities such as Fowler's comments about his experience piloting through that area. In a Coast Guard taped statement almost *immediately* following the allision, the stressed-out Fowler said he had transited the area "maybe 50 times, back and forth."[164]

However, in his Coast Guard *interview* taped two days later, he at one point indicated he had "navigated the ship channel near the bridge three or four times before."[165] And in that same *interview*, Fowler also said "he had been to Brownsville on a tug [sic] eight to ten times and all but one trip was with Brown Water Marine."[166] A review of Brown Water Marine records indicated, "Captain Fowler had been onboard during five trips through the area. Since Captain Fowler took the Fifth Amendment [upon advice of his physician and his legal counselor] at the start of the formal hearing, there was no way to clarify his actual experience through the area during the previous 12 years."[167]

The reason for Fowler's declining to testify at any of the subsequent formal hearings into the tragedy may have come about by the pilot's shock at seeing what happened at the time of the tragedy. In the recorded on-the-spot statement noted above and which was played at subsequent hearings, the horrified towboat pilot, almost tearfully recounted, how after hitting the bridge piling he saw the first parts of the roadway come crashing down on his lead barge. He then frantically "used the boat's horn and fog lights in a desperate attempt to warn motorists of the hole." The failure of his efforts to save some of those lives left Fowler "still psychologically distraught…[and] still under psychiatric care," his attorney Sheldon Wiesfeld said.[168]

Fowler's fellow crew members were jarred from their sleep by the jolt of the tow hitting the piling and the cascade of concrete crashing down on the front of the tow. Captain Wilson, who dashed to the boat's wheelhouse, later verified Fowler's shock. He said Fowler was frantically aiming a spotlight up at cars careening off the gaping hole in the Causeway. Wilson, who also "watched the cars drive off the bridge," later testified Fowler was "flaring spotlights at the cars, saying 'I can't get them to stop! I can't get them to stop'!"[169] Fowler himself said in his immediate post-accident taped interview, "When I see the bridge coming down, I kept blaring my horn and flashing my lights and trying to get the people to stop coming."

Later, Fowler also is heard asking the investigators "has anybody been killed."[170]

Shortly after the accident, all members of the M/V *Brown Water V* crew were chemically tested for drug use. Captain Fowler passed an on-scene field sobriety test, an on-scene Intoximeter alcohol test, as well as a National Transportation Safety Board (NTSB) toxicology screen. All the other crew members tested negative except for deckhand J. W. Blocker, who tested positive for marijuana. Before Blocker could return to work aboard a vessel he had to get a Medical Review Officer back-to-work letter.[171]

*   *   *

The collateral damage – though no way near the personal grief suffered by the victims, their families, and their friends – was economically considerable. The collapse cost nearly five million dollars to repair the bridge connecting Port Isabel to South Padre Island. It cost the local economy an estimated fifty-five million dollars.

The closing of the Causeway – the only link between the 130-mile-long Padre Island and Port Isabel on the mainland – affected twenty-to-thirty percent of the port's traffic. Included were barges carrying fifty percent of the Rio Grande Valley's fuel supply. Thousands of visitors, students and mainland and island residents were stranded on South Padre Island, until a small ferry boat could be put into service. It would be weeks before the state car ferry, sent in from Port Aransas 175 miles up the Gulf Coast, could go into service because loading docks needed to be constructed. Land-line telephones to the island were out of service.

Additionally, in another ironic twist to this story, only forty-eight hours before this tragic episode unfolded, Cameron County Judge Gilberto Hinojosa (no relation to victim Gasper Hinojosa) and South Padre Island Mayor Ed

Cyganiewicz discussed the possibility of a second bridge over the *Laguna Madre*!

Despite the shock of being marooned on the Island and some of the initial difficulties encountered by vacationers wanting to get off, many of them had nothing but praise for their new-found hosts. "I feel that everyone on the island, the government officials and businesses, (has) been very helpful..." said Matt Lauten of Tucson, Arizona. "They've gone out of their way to accommodate us," Lauten said, adding "I haven't seen any price-gouging."[172]

Meanwhile, highway workers were busily constructing the landing to load and unload the ferries being used to shuttle food and supplies to the island, and children to school in Port Isabel. A concerned State Senator Eddie Lucio of nearby Brownsville said, "The thing that worries me the most is our hurricane season right now. Something could form immediately in the gulf," he warned, "come towards us, and cause additional fatalities."[173]

Judge Hinojosa said the situation was "devastating" to the economy. Texas Department of Transportation engineers said repairs to the 240-foot section of causeway that fell would take four to six months to complete by Houston highway contractor Williams Brothers Construction Co. The bridge actually reopened November 21, 2001, a little more than two months after the tragedy occurred. But in the interim, South Padre Island resembled a ghost town.

*   *   *

With prayers and ceremony, Port Isabel and South Padre Island residents marked the one-year anniversary of the Queen Isabella Causeway collapse that killed those eight people and left three survivors with harrowing memories.

A granite memorial was erected via donations from local residents to assure the lives and the tragic deaths of the following would long be remembered:

Robert Victor Harris, 46, Port Isabel, Texas
Gasper Saenz Hinojosa, 52, Alamo, Texas
Robin Faye Leavell, 29, Port Isabel, Texas
Hector Martinez, Jr., 32, Port Isabel, Texas
Julio Mireles, 22, Los Fresnos, Texas
Stvan Francisco Rivas, 22, Humble, Texas
Barry Welch, 53, Port Isabel, Texas
Chealsa Welch, 23, Port Isabel, Texas

A memorial to the eight who died in the Causeway collapse was dedicated on September 15, 2002, one year after the tragic accident.

Those rescued and injured seriously enough to require extended hospitalization were also remembered:

Brigette Marie Goza, 33, Port Isabel, Texas
Rene Francisco Mata, 27, Laguna Vista, Texas
Gustavo Adolfo Morales, 36, Brownsville, Texas

*   *   *

Aftermath

As with most all accidents – whether it's a child falling off a schoolyard swing and getting an "owweee" or a towboat crashing into a bridge piling and killing eight people – there are two sides to every story. The Queen Isabella Causeway-*Brown Water V* story had many sides. Like all good governmental agencies ("we're looking out for you"), the Texas Attorney General's office quickly got into the act. Within five days of the accident, the Attorney General John Cornyn sought to have Brown Water Towing Inc. and Brown Water Service Inc. declared negligent for damages to the Causeway.

Furthermore, Cornyn's suit alleged in the legal language of law suits, "the company failed to maintain lookout and chart a safe course; use global positioning systems [GPS], radar, navigation charts or navigational equipment properly; take appropriate action to assess prevailing conditions to avoid the collision [sic]; and properly train the crew to ensure their safe operation of the tugboat [sic]."[174] Some wondered why the AG didn't also throw in some charges to determine exactly how many Texans crossed Colonel William Travis' famous line in the dirt at the Alamo in 1836. Others later wondered where the AG's follow-up was – or if this was just a typical political grand-standing, headline-grabbing stance?

Counter-charges came from Captain Rocky Wilson and deckhand Levi Old who insisted bridge lights – both streetlights above the span and navigational lights below – were off. Attorneys for Cameron County, the cities of Port Isabel and South Padre Island and the state of Texas were quick to clarify marine navigators are not dependent on bridge lights.[175]

Captain Fowler told the Coast Guard he ran aground briefly after hitting a sandbar or shoals on the right side of the channel. Company lawyers insisted the tow then lost its steering, and strong tidal currents swung the four barges Fowler was pushing into unprotected concrete causeway pilings. That shallow area became the focus of much testimony. There were claims boats owned or staffed by Brown Water Marine Service Inc. had been involved in at least thirty groundings, thirteen collisions and at least seventeen other mishaps in the previous decade.

Those cases prompted a stern warning in 1998 from a top Coast Guard officer. "I wish to express my deepest concern about the alarming number of accidents involving vessels owned or operated by Brown Water Marine Service," wrote Capt. A.D. Guerrero in a letter to the company. Guerrero cited sixteen cases during five years in which he described Brown Water as the responsible party. Several of the accidents, Guerrero wrote, "posed grave danger to the marine environment" and threatened the safety of U.S. waterways. Company officials declined to comment on Brown Water's past safety issues.[176]

Even relief pilot David Fowler got into the suing act. Three years after the deadly incident, Fowler filed a negligence suit, claiming the tow company and the barge line that chartered the vessel knew the tow was unseaworthy. The suit claimed the accident was "due solely to the carelessness, recklessness, and negligence" of the defendants – Brown Water Towing, and American Commercial Barge Line. The claim was filed just under the three-year statute of limitations. Fowler's attorney said his client had been in and out of mental hospitals and only recently found work as a truck driver. Brown Water attorney Will Pierson said the company had contributed a lot of money to Fowler's care and that it was "a little incredulous that he'd turn around and sue us."[177] Fowler ultimately settled for $50,000.

Survivors and relatives of the eight people killed in the causeway collapse would receive about nine million dollars in a settlement tentatively approved on June 29, 2005, attorneys in the case said. The settlement with Brown Water Towing came about a week after U.S. District Judge Hilda Tagle dismissed American Commercial Barge Lines from the lawsuit. There were seventeen plaintiffs in the case: families of the eight who died, three survivors, four fishermen who helped in the rescue, and two children who lost parents.[178]

Defendants in the case included the State of Texas, for allegedly failing to maintain bridge lights; Cameron County, accused of failing to maintain road lights; Brown Water, and American Commercial Barge Line. Ray Marchan, the lead plaintiffs' attorney, said their research found the accident would not have happened if the tow had been adequately powered. His lawsuit blamed the barge company for contracting the tow company.[179]

As the famed, old-time comedian Jimmy Durante so often said, "Everybody wants t'get inta d'act!" But, this was no laughing matter.

It wasn't until April 28, 2005 when the Coast Guard hand-delivered to the surviving families and then publically presented its final report on the Causeway allision. The report concluded several factors – including two strong currents, lack of horsepower, high tides caused by Tropical Storm *Gabrielle*, and a poor tow configuration – contributed to the accident. The report said relief pilot Fowler was solely responsible for the accident because he "failed to exercise good seamanship" coming out of the "S" turn and heading for the bridge. No criminal charges were filed against Fowler but the Coast Guard revoked his twelve-year-old license after the incident.[180]

In a better-late-than-never action, on March 5, 2004, officials unveiled what they said was a first-in-the-nation fiber optic warning system at the Queen Isabella Memorial Causeway. It is designed to spring into action if anything shakes the stability of the bridge. Barriers will come down and lights will flash to warn motorists to stop driving, Texas transportation officials said. As another safeguard, concrete slabs – sixteen feet around – have been placed in front of bridge supports.

The $900,000 warning system consists of two fiber-optic cables about as thick as a fountain pen strung along the bridge's north side. If a portion of the bridge breaks, one or both of the cables will break, sending signals to computers that will activate railroad crossing-type gates to close the bridge. The computers are also programmed to start red lights and illuminate warning signs. Calls will automatically be placed to law-enforcement agencies and the U.S. Coast Guard, according to James Mercier, an Austin, Texas-based TxDOT engineer who designed the system.[181]

*   *   *

For the families of the eight victims in this horrific accident, their losses are unbearable. Not disrespecting those losses, and as tragic as were the events on that dark Saturday morning, those familiar with the events are left with some even more shuddering thoughts:

> What would have happened had barge *NM 315* hit that Causeway piling just twelve hours later – when the Saturday afternoon passages over the bridge would

have been approaching the likes of Houston's "monumental" rush-hour traffic jams with the *Diez y Seis de Septiembre* revelers hitting their stride!

Consider the fact that *thousands* of volunteers were expected later on Saturday to help with an Island beach cleanup project, an Adopt-A-Beach day.

What would have happened had the accident occurred two weeks earlier – during the Labor Day holiday weekend traffic?

And, what would have happened if the Queen Isabella Causeway had come crashing down when South Padre Island – known to many as a Spring Break Mecca, this country's Caribbean water-front resort land, and not unlike Brazil's Ipanema Beach in Rio de Janeiro – would have been host to its usual crowds of up to 200,000 college and high school students who annually make the trek to south Texas for a week-long fun-in-the-sun bacchanal?

*   *   *

Chapter VII
Peace and Tranquility (?) of the Ohio

Seven little girls, between five- and nine-years-old, wearing white dresses and ribbons in their hair, dropped rose petals into the Ohio River at the May 27th annual Blessing of the Ships, a Star of Louisville, Kentucky, ceremony opening the 2001 boating season. The ceremony's emphasis was on safety. "These [rose petals] are symbols of peace and tranquility of the Ohio," Reverend Paul R. Richart of St. Paul Catholic Church in nearby Sellersburg, Indiana said on that day.

Katrina Schnurr, the Blessing of the Ships princess, said, "I think it's very important to bless this water to help increase awareness of boating safety and try to prevent tragedies from occurring." The Blessing event's organizer, Bonnie Meyer, added "The safety message will get out. All the boaters know we're doing it."[182]

Some boaters obviously didn't get the message.

Less than two months into that 2001 boating season, tragic circumstances would make a cruel joke out of "peace and tranquility," and "boating safety" on the Ohio River.

*   *   *

On July 14, 2001, the day before John Beatty, Jr., a printing press operator, went fishing with some of his buddies on the Ohio River about twenty-five miles northeast of Louisville, Kentucky, he warned them: "The river seemed unusually crowded with two-way barge traffic. If you were hit," he said, "it could suck you right under."[183] He never knew how prophetic he was.

Meanwhile, Rob Valentine, who ran an excavating construction company in La Grange, Kentucky, was elated. The engine on a used Wellcraft 180 runabout boat he'd bought four months before and was still paying for was working smoothly during the test run on the Ohio River on Friday, the 13th of July, 2001. Another prophecy?

This Wellcraft 175 SX Excel is similar to the one used by the six fishermen on July 15, 2001.

In any case, everything was set for the Saturday night cat-fishing trip with the thirty-six-year-old Valentine's friends, Bennie Burgan – the youngest at thirty-four – and Joe Lucas Jr., William (Lurch) Young, Terry Hites, and John Beatty – the oldest at forty-five. The entire bunch of "red-necks...in the nicest sort of way" as Hites' wife called them, lived and worked in Louisville and some of the small towns bordering the river in Kentucky and Indiana.

Other than having the right bait, the right equipment, and perfect weather when they set out around eight on Saturday night, July 14, one of the problems the six of them would face was the ever-increasing commercial and recreational traffic on the river. That, according to Brian Hinton, a Jefferson County, Indiana police river patrol officer, led to a commensurate rise in bad boating behavior – such as water-scooterers jumping towboats' wakes or recreational boaters seeing how close they can come to larger, commercial vessels. "People who go near them are playing Russian roulette," Hinton said.

Tony Peveler, a 25-year riverboat captain who operated a commercial cruise boat out of Dayton, Kentucky, agreed with that assessment. He said he recently noticed two young men on personal watercraft who suddenly turned right in front of his large boat and zipped

Pleasure craft operators often put themselves in danger on the waterways. (Patrick Reddy photo)

toward shore – almost like running a red light at rush hour. "That's what I mean," Peveler said. "They just assumed they could clear us. If one of them had stalled out, we would have run right over him."

And, he continued, "I'll pick up some boats on radar sitting in the channel ahead of me, with their lights out. I blow the horn to warn them to move, but when they finally move, they cuss at me and make gestures like I'm the bad guy."[184] Some fisherfolk just don't like it when they have to leave their favorite fishing hole – even when it's right in the middle of the river's commercial channel. On the other hand, Brace Donner, who ran the Boat Docktor dealership in Westport, Kentucky where many fishermen put their boats in the river, said, "You just have to use your head [despite the fact that] accidents are pretty rare when you consider how much traffic is out there."[185]

As Mississippi River towboat captain Gary Cochran put it, "People up north (on the Upper Mississippi River or the Ohio or the Illinois) have such a short season for pleasure boating. So they must have their fun quickly. Sometimes they play 'chicken' with the barges and cut them real close. They get in the wheel wash (turbulence the propellers put out as a tow goes through the water) – especially on water skis and personal water craft – and play around. They just don't realize the danger. They don't realize how long it takes to bring a tow to a stop. It takes 30 seconds just to change engines from full-ahead to full-astern. Down-bound, it takes up to a mile to get stopped – and sometimes more depending on the push of the current. Sometimes," he continued, "if you're on the right boat in the right current, you don't ever get it stopped. I've seen the time where I've been backing down for 30 minutes and still couldn't get it stopped."[186]

Every towboat captain, it seems, has had problems with pleasure boaters on the rivers. Cleve Ward, who's been working towboats on the rivers since 1978, is one who believes "all pleasure boaters should have to go and get a license. They should understand to stay out of the way of these towboats. I guess they think that a towboat can stop like they can. They don't play in front of a train and they shouldn't play in front of one of these towboats. When we're running empties," he said in 2001, "[the pleasure boaters] will go out of sight [due to the height of the lead barge above the water line]. So I think they ought to go to school and get a license to drive a boat. They need to learn the rules and regulations and they need to learn some safety rules and just some basic common sense."[187]

Ward's words about limited visibility out in front of empty towboats would prove clairvoyant at almost the same time as Rob Valentine and some of his friends went fishing on the Ohio River – for the last time.

*   *   *

It was a dark morning on Sunday, July 15, 2001. The moon was fading in its last quarter and the sun wouldn't rise until 6:30. Forty-three-year-old Captain Terry Max Graham and his seven-man crew on board the 151-foot-long uninspected towboat (see "Glossary") *Elaine G* were making their way down the Ohio River pushing fourteen empty barges toward Louisville. It was just another milk run – picking up and dropping off barges at various power plants along the usually uneventful Pittsburgh, Pennsylvania to Louisville, Kentucky trip for the towboat built in 1970. Graham, his crew of four deckhands, a cook, an engineer, and a relief pilot had all stopped the day before with the tow at the homeport of their Cincinnati-based Ohio River Company (a division of Midland Enterprises, a company with a "heritage of excellence"[188]). They weren't there long. They left the same day.

*   *   *

Back in 1669, it also looked as if it was going to be a good day on *La Belle Riviere* – as is was christened by the French explorer with a name almost as long as the river, René-Robert Cavelier, Sieur de La Salle. Like the *Elaine G*, Monsieur LaSalle, too, was headed for Louisville and beyond when he rafted down the 981 miles of that long river. To say the least, traffic on the river had increased greatly since La Salle's time when he and a few Indians in

The *Elaine G* underway (courtesy: Boat Photo Museum)

birch-bark canoes were the river's only occupants. The U. S. Army Corps of Engineers first started keeping records of commercial traffic on the Ohio River in 1917. That year the river carried about five million tons of cargo. The latest figures show commerce is approaching 150 million tons a year.[189]

On that July 15th morning in 2001 at about five o'clock, the summertime temperature was estimated to be a surprising 57 degrees Fahrenheit for July but it was rising and there was fog on the river. How much fog was a matter that never would be resolved to everyone's satisfaction.

Was it a "shut-out" fog where, as the saying goes, "you couldn't see your hand in front of your face"? Or was it just the usual early morning condensation ("radiation fog") caused by cool air settling on the warmer river water and condensing easily? Some witnesses and investigators called it a "dense" fog while others saw it as "light." According to the National Weather Service, which could find no confirmation reports of weather conditions specific to the Westport, Kentucky area, "conditions were right for fog banks to form along area rivers, streams, and other fog-prone places [and it] would have been extremely localized."[190]

However, the U. S. Coast Guard in its Report of Investigation into the incident that wasn't publically released until September 2008, said the *Elaine G* was "in a weather state of restricted visibility due to fog. Witness testimony," the report continued, "from the formal hearing infers that the operators could not see the river banks (approximately 1,000 feet to either side of the tug [sic]), nor any farther than the bow of the lead barge (approximately 1,000 feet from the wheelhouse)." [191]

*   *   *

One thing most everyone did agree on was that Captain Graham, with eighteen years behind the wheels of riverboats and a year-and-one-half in command of the *Elaine G*, one who himself was from another river town, Marietta, Ohio, was steering his tow where it should have been. He was in the middle of the commercial ship channel on the 2,000-foot-wide Ohio River, slightly favoring the Indiana side of the river. Some of the perhaps envious towboat captains on the Mississippi scoff at the job facing their brethren on the Ohio.

Caption Gary Cochran is one of those scoffers. "The pilots on the Ohio river are a different breed. If they had to go to work for a living, they'd go home," he said laughingly. Continuing his put-down, Cochran went on. "The Ohio River, 90% of the time is real easy to run. It has deep water, a wide channel, and them guys up there are running around with 15 barges with 4,000 to 5,000 horsepower-boats and they think they gotta have the whole river to themselves." To top it off, he continued, "They want one-way traffic. If they had to go to work and work in tight situations like they do in the Upper Mississippi, most of them would 'go to the house'."

In many cases, however, it doesn't matter which river you're on. Simmey Brickhouse saw his first light of day in 1964 in Newnan, Georgia, just southeast of Atlanta. Simmey is his formal name. It's a family name he thinks is a derivative of the biblical name Simeon. His father was an assistant port engineer on boats and in 1986 "he got me a summer job out here and I just kinda stuck with it." Fifteen years later, Brickhouse told this writer as we towboated on the Mississippi, "I think just about every towboater out here's been involved in accidents or whatever."

Just like "whatever," there are too many variables, too many unknowns, too many uncontrollables to not end up in the U. S. Coast Guard's "traffic court." You can be coming downstream around a sharp bend in a river on a moonless night only to find another tow with one of its barges "spiked on the hip (attached to the side of the towboat)." It's just sitting there, unlighted for one reason or another, hanging out in the channel. And you have no way to avoid it or the tree-lined shore. There are times when a crew member will simply "walk off" a barge and into the river at night because he isn't paying attention to his surroundings. Then, all you can do is gather up his belongings and ship them home.

You can run aground because a channel buoy is off-station due to a raging river current or it's been dragged there by another boat. A sudden snow squall will blind you and your radar and you can't see the nearest barge, let alone what's out in front of the tow. It isn't unheard of for an empty oil barge to suddenly and inexplicably explode because of an electrical short-circuit or a build up of fumes and then you'll be upwind of a four-alarm inferno blazing right in front of you. And if none of these things get you, wait a short while and a bolt of lightning is sure to find you, no matter where you're hiding. Again, as the poet Elizabeth Barrett Browning so eloquently put it, "Let me count the ways." Accidents can, do, and will happen on the inland waterways.

So it was as Captain Graham proceeded to chug along southbound on the Ohio River at some six miles-per-hour coming up on mile marker 581 near Westport, Kentucky, twenty-five miles northeast of Louisville. His tow was three barges wide and five deep. The barge *OR 2110*, located at the center front, was fairly typical of all the others. The *OR 2110* was a standard 195x35-footer, another of those with a raked (slanted) front end to ease drag through the water.

Since it was still dark, navigation was aided by the helmsman's knowledge of the river and the nautical charts. Two VHF radios were available along with two marine radars, each of them set at three-quarters- to a mile-and-one-half-mile range, the standard setting for the area. They were in use in the pilot house of the *Elaine G*, one on either side of the helm that Captain Graham sat behind that morning on the Ohio.[192]

On the top of the towboat's pilothouse, a green running light on the starboard side and a red running light on the port side were operating as were two amber towing lights on the stern. According to the crew, the tow was lit with a green running light on the forward starboard corner, a red running light on the forward port corner, a special flashing amber on the forward centerline, and a seven-watt white "steering light" on a seven-to-eight-foot pole located all the way forward in the center of the tow.[193] The sides of the tow were also lighted with illuminated panels at each barge coupling.

These then-optional lights were occasionally used on tows on the river system to increase the visibility of the tow's profile between the navigation lights at the head of the tow and the navigation lights on the towboat. These lighted panels were only visible if the tow presented a side aspect to the viewer.[194]

Bridge layout of the *Elaine G*

So far, for Captain Terry Graham, who relieved relief pilot Clinton Pauley of the watch between 0510 and 0515 hours, there was nothing new as he approached mile-marker 568 on the Ohio River that Sunday summer morning.[195] (Somewhat ironically, he was just a little more than exactly 500 miles downriver from the 31.7 mile-marker that located the *Elizabeth M* disaster covered previously in Chapter III, and both towboats were built by Dravo Corporation, Neville Island, Pennsylvania.) With

about 100 miles under the *Elaine G*'s keel since leaving
Cincinnati at mile-marker 471, everything was going fine.
    Until….

                    *   *   *

With a startling suddenness at about 0530 hours, Graham
and his two on-duty deckhands, Richard Isaac Cain and
Christopher Ratcliff, were jarred by the sound of a man's
voice in the river off their starboard side screaming for
help. Cain said he heard the plea as many as seven or eight
times, and that it appeared to come from the same person.
"I just couldn't tell where the voice was coming from," he
said. [196] Without ever realizing it, the *Elaine G* and its
fourteen barges had run right over the top of the seventeen-
foot Wellcraft fishing boat that had so elated Rob Valentine
less than forty-eight hours before. Graham – a vessel
captain for two-and-one-half years and holder of a Master
of Motor Vessels License – immediately sounded his ship's
emergency alarms to get all hands on deck. He snapped on
his searchlights, and as quickly as possible, put his engines
into all stop and then all back in an effort to halt his
forward motion. For a towboat going along at six miles-
per-hour, riding even the modest two-mph current on the
river that morning – with fourteen barges out front – that
was not easy.

    With the tow's fourteen barges strung out front, the
three lead barges were about 1,000 feet in front of the
towboat's pilothouse. The entire mass – including the 151-
foot-long *Elaine G* – was listed as 1,160 feet, close to a
quarter-of-a-mile long. That's the equivalent of almost two
full metropolitan city blocks. With no brakes to apply,
other than full-throttle reversing of the 4,320 horsepower
diesel engines, with no traction to grab, and moving a
towboat along at almost six-mile-per-hour aided by a two-
miles-an-hour current, you can't stop on a dime. This time,

it took something like a full tow length, almost 1,300 feet, investigators said later. Comparatively speaking, tests show that the minimum emergency stopping distance for an automobile going seventy-miles-per-hour is 622 feet.[197]

Another example of the difficulty Captain Graham faced in trying to stop his tow is related in this report:

> ...The real test, as we in the industry know, comes in being able to stop, hold, and maneuver a large tow moving downstream.
>
> My greatest fear occurred when I was pushing just 35 barges at a medium to low river stage. I found that I simply could not stop my tow when fog unexpectedly set in. I backed my 10,500-horsepower vessel full astern at maximum power with all three engines turning at the full 900 rpm for between and *two and three miles* [emphasis added] realizing within the next mile that there was a state ferry docked at St. Francisville, Louisiana, that carried both vehicles and passengers across the river. I backed at full power with the engines screaming and the whole boat shuddering for a *full fifty (50) minutes* [emphasis added]. However, I was unable to stop the tow completely unless and until I dragged the barges to a stop down along the bank or dragged a string down a sand bar to finish stopping it....[198]

Meanwhile in Graham's situation, he attempted to maintain position in the river for approximately twenty minutes while the crew searched for the source of the call for help and checked the tow. Nobody on board ever saw anyone in the water. The captain backed the tow onto the left descending bank on the Kentucky side of the Ohio River at mile 568 for further investigation at approximately 0550 hours. Crewmembers recovered various items

156

consistent with pleasure boating including two seat cushions, from both sides of the center string of barges.

After the fog lifted, Captain Sam Wolfe and his crew aboard the *Pat McBride* that had been approximately one-and-one-half miles up-river of the *Elaine G* at the time of the collision, assisted in breaking the *Elaine G*'s tow apart. All anyone found were two paddles, a plastic bucket, and a baseball cap. As soon as he grounded the tow, Captain Graham contacted Coast Guard Group Ohio Valley by VHF radio and reported that the vessel was stopping to investigate after hearing a yell for help. After the Coast Guard and the Indiana Department of Natural Resources (IDNR) personnel arrived on the scene and the towboat and its barges were disconnected, then they found more seat cushions, seat backs, a bait bucket, another baseball hat, oars, a shoe, and coolers in the water.[199]

The IDNR conservation officers were the first investigators to arrive on-scene at approximately 0800. Coast Guard Marine Safety Office (MSO) Louisville investigators, who arrived there at approximately 1300, and IDNR investigators observed scrape marks on the bow rake of the center lead barge, *OR 2110*. Later, with the barge in dry dock, those marks were also observed by Mr. Jack Deck (retired Commander, USCG), a marine surveyor hired by the barge owner. These marks began at forty-two-and-one-half inches above the waterline and extended down approximately twenty inches. These marks were consistent with the damage that was later found on the fishing boat, indicating collision between the two vessels.[200]

Authorities determined the *Elaine G* had its running lights on and they had "every reason to believe the barge was navigating correctly in the channel," according to Coast Guard spokesman Steven Garcia. The scrape marks later found on the raked bow of barge *OR 2110*, led to speculation the fishing boat was ground under the barges.

Why the fishing boat was in the commercial ship channel and why the fishermen failed to move it with the barges bearing down led to more speculation. And maybe the *Elaine G's* radar units couldn't pick up the fishing boat in the middle of the river because the smaller boat didn't have any radar reflectors on it. The Coast Guard's official report on the accident did, in fact, recommend that, in the future, all recreational vessels have such markings (see "Aftermath" below).

Maybe, said IDNR spokesman Mac Spainhour, it was because of the dense fog that the fishermen didn't see the barge until it was too late. Maybe the Wellcraft's 175-horse-powered engine failed and they couldn't get out of the way of the onrushing barges. Maybe, because the towboat's engines driving the barges are a quarter-of-a-mile away from the front of the tow, the fishermen never heard the mass moving down on them. Maybe, because the fishing boat didn't have a marine radio, its crew had no way of monitoring river traffic other than by eye-balling it.

Maybe, according to Steve Davison, owner of D&E Marine of Louisville, it was because all fourteen of the barges were empty, meaning they rode higher in the water,

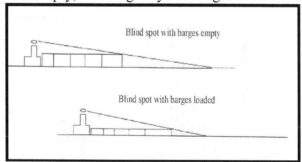

creating a longer "shadow" ahead that the radar couldn't penetrate. Maybe it was because there might not have been any lights lit on the fishing boat (which was not then against the law; boats only have to have their lights on when they're underway).

Maybe, suggested some defense lawyers in subsequent trials, it was because with six grown men sitting in the seventeen-foot-three-inch boat with all their fishing gear, coolers, an anchor and tools, the Wellcraft was fearfully over-loaded at 1,279 pounds. The boat had a rated capacity of seven passengers and 1,050 pounds as it sat in the water almost up to its gunwales, making it even more difficult for the *Elaine G*'s radars to spot.[201]

Or maybe, it was because – according to later testimony from Dr. Barbara Weakley-Jones, a Kentucky state medical examiner – all six victims had cocaine in their bloodstreams and were "all under the influence" at the time of the crash.[202] The cocaine finding was confirmed by Dr. Mike Evans, toxicologist of AIT Laboratories, who stated that the levels of cocaine in the victims indicated that several hours had passed since the drug had been introduced into the bodies.[203] All six fishermen drowned.

The fishing boat's remains are pulled ashore near Bethlehem, Indiana two days after the crash. (Associated Press photo)

The wife of one of the boating victims earlier said that it's typical for some drinking to occur when a group of men fish together, but said the victims never drank to excess. "None of them, under any circumstances, did anything excessively, but if you go fishing, you are going to have a beer," she said. But, she said, she had no knowledge of drug use among any of the victims.[204]

It would be two days before another towboat spotted the wreckage of the fishing boat floating awash in a vertical position with the stern down in the river at mile-marker 571. It wasn't until Wednesday, July 18, that the last of the six bodies was discovered via sonar and underwater cameras and recovered. Thus, the basic causes of the tragedy likely never will be known because, among other things, there would never be any eye-witnesses for the prosecution – the victims.

*   *   *

The fishing expedition started on Saturday, the day before the accident, at approximately 1:00 p.m., when Bennie Burgan, his wife Teresa, and their children along with Rob Valentine launched the unnamed Wellcraft from the Westport Boat Ramp at Ohio River mile 580.5. From there, they proceeded down to Cox's Park at Ohio River Mile 599.7. They were joined there by Cindy Valentine and their children, where they all spent the next several hours engaged in recreational boating activities. At approximately 2000 hours (8:00p.m.), the Burgans and the Valentines were joined by John Beatty and Bill Young. An hour-and-one-half later, Terry Hites and Joe Lucas showed up and, at approximately 2200 hours, the six men departed Cox's Park to go fishing.[205]

What happened following the boaters' departure left many family and friends of the six victims with their own questions. If the *Elaine G* was running with two radar units, why didn't the pilot see the seventeen-foot fishing boat out in front of him? That question was answered by Ohio River Company attorneys who contended that the wooden fishing boat didn't have enough metal on it for the *Elaine G*'s radar to pick up, and radar doesn't reflect back from wood or plastic hulls. Other questions remained. How foggy was it? Was it "shut-out" fog. Was it "dense," as the Indiana DNR spokesman called it? Was it just misty, like the morning dew? Or, was it foggy enough to "restrict visibility," as the Coast Guard contended.

Among still more questions asked by the families in court (and by the Coast Guard in its final report) was why Captain Graham didn't post a deckhand as a lookout at the head of the tow in those foggy conditions. The defense lawyers, noting that such decisions are a captain's prerogative depending on conditions, answered that posting a lookout was not warranted in what they called "patchy" fog.

A number of formal hearings were held by such agencies as the Indiana Department of Natural Resources and the Jefferson County (Indiana) prosecutor's office, with the first being conducted by U. S. Coast Guard, July 25-26, 2001 and officially closing on October 19, 2001. In those investigations, it was shown that an IDNR officer administered a portable breath test to Captain Graham after arriving on-scene (approximately 0800-0900), which was negative for alcohol. Captain Graham also submitted to a drug test following the accident, the results of which were negative, too.[206]

In those hearings it was claimed by the defense that the fishing boat was apparently adrift, overweight, leaking water and improperly lighted. It was also noted the fishing boat was not in motion and fishing lines were reeled in when the accident occurred, according to Tony Stoll, a conservation officer with the Indiana DNR.[207] According to testimony, Mr. Burgan normally drove the boat and was the only non-swimmer aboard.[208]

In its final report, the Coast Guard speculated on some actions by the victims aboard the fishing boat. That portion of the report is presented here:

> The persons onboard the recreational vessel likely had little time to take evasive actions to avoid the collision prior to impact. If the vessel operator was unable to start the engine (due to a weak battery or flooding with fuel), other options were readily available. A spare battery was discovered aboard the vessel; had time permitted, it could easily been connected to the boat's electrical system if the need was present. Additionally, two adequately sized boat oars were on-board the vessel at the time of the collision and could have been used to paddle to the bank. The ignition key was in the "on" position and the throttle was disengaged and pulled all the way back, indicating that someone may have attempted to start the vessel prior to the collision....
>
> During the formal hearing Mr. Allen Zetco testified that he was good friends with all of the victims, except John Beatty, and fished with them on many occasions. He testified that all were experienced fisherman and knew the hazards inherent to navigating on the busy Ohio River. Mr. Zetco stated that they were always well prepared when night fishing and it was their common practice to fish close to the Indiana bank and that they never fished in the middle of the river. Based on the information gathered during the preliminary and formal invest-igations there is no evidence to dispute Mr.

Zetco's testimony. While the actions of the victims cannot be conclusively determined, there is no apparent reason for the vessel to have been in the middle of the river at night and in heavy fog. In keeping with customary practices, it is possible that the vessel was waiting for daylight in order to return to the boat ramp at Westport, Kentucky.

The vessel was not anchored, the only anchor and line was found inside the vessel at the time of recovery, and likely drifted into the middle of the river. As the fog obscured the bank, the victims would have no point of reference and may have been unaware of their position in the river.[209]

The report goes on to ponder the impact of the drugs found during autopsies on the deceased:

The victims may have had severely diminished situational awareness. Cocaine was discovered in all six of the victims' bloodstreams, as were other medications (e.g., prescription painkillers). The toxicologist, Dr. Mike Evans of AIT Laboratories, stated that the levels of cocaine in the victims indicated that several hours had passed since the drug had been introduced into the bodies. This could mean that the typical *affects* of the drug were subsiding at the times of death. While it is impossible to determine the exact mental state of all the victims, the combination of prescription drugs, cocaine, and alcohol could be expected to have aggravated fatigue symptoms. The results could have been anything from extreme fatigue to, in some cases, loss of consciousness. All victims had been out all night and, in the case of Mr. Burgan and Mr. Valentine, had been on the water boating for approximately sixteen hours.[210]

*   *   *

It was later determined by Jefferson County, Indiana prosecutor Nancy Jacobs that it was "very unlikely" that criminal charges would be filed against Captain Terry Graham for the deaths of the six fishermen. It was a decision that affirmed the towboat company's belief that that there was no negligence or misconduct on the part of the barge crew. However, it was "recommended that a Personnel Action Investigation be initiated to determine if suspension and revocation action is warranted against the Coast Guard-issued licenses issued to Terry Max Graham and to Clinton Pauley."

Even though criminal charges were unlikely, heartache was obvious with Graham during the Coast Guard hearings ten days after the accident when a recess had to be called so that a sobbing skipper could compose himself while testifying for two hours. He spoke directly to the victims' relatives, seated a few feet away in the federal courtroom. Graham said he "deeply grieved" for the six victims, but defended his actions at the vessel's helm. "I really feel that I did everything possible that I could," he said. Some family members wiped their eyes as Graham testified.[211]

Those Lost:

John Beatty, Jr., 45, Louisville, Kentucky
Benny Burgan, 34, of Crestwood, Kentucky
Terry Hites, 43, La Grange, Kentucky
Joe Lucas, Jr., 40, Shelbyville, Kentucky
Robert Valentine, 36, LaGrange, Kentucky
William Young, 42, Louisville, Kentucky

Also lost was Terry Hites' dog, Penny, LaGrange,
Kentucky

*   *   *

Aftermath

Some of the actions recommended were as follows in the
U. S. Coast Guard's report on the incident titled:

REPORT OF INVESTIGATION INTO THE
CIRCUMSTANCES SURROUNDING THE
INCIDENT INVOLVING
M/V ELAINE G COLLISION
ON 07/15/2001

MISLE ACTIVITY NUMBER: 1476414
ORIGINATING UNIT: MSO LOUISVILLE
MISLE ACTIVITY OWNER: COMMANDANT
(CG-5453)
MISLE ACTIVITY CONTROLLER: COMMANDANT
(CG-5453)
MISLE CASE NUMBER: 83605

Initiation of legislation/regulations to require uninspected towing vessels to maintain logs. This recommendation was rejected.

Coast Guard should be more aggressive in promoting existing recreational boating safety education programs.... This recommendation was approved.

Coast Guard should continue to aggressively pursue violations of Inland Navigation Rules by commercial towing vessels.... This recommendation was approved – with some objection to the word "aggressively."

Coast Guard should partner with other law enforcement agencies having a presence on the Rivers to ensure towing vessels sound appropriate signals in low visibility [as of September 2008, this recommended action has "amounted to little or nothing," according to the National Mariners Association[212]]....

...and the Coast Guard should encourage owners of recreational fiberglass and wooden vessels to install radar reflective devices on their vessels. This recommendation was also approved.

It took more than eleven pages of that report to reach the obvious recommendations cited above. And because this writer cannot decipher some of the jargon contained in that report – which was made available only after filing a Freedom of Information request – we can only surmise that some of the report was not put in its final, final form until after dates shown therein of September 8, 2008 at 9:37 a.m. – seven years, fifty-five days, four hours, and seven minutes after the approximate time of the incident on July 15, 2001 at 0730 hours.

Following the above recommendations, the report does finally get to matters of greater importance wherein it recommended "that a personal Action Investigation be initiated to determine if suspension and revocation action is warranted against the Coast Guard [licenses issued to the *Elaine G's* captain Terry Graham and its pilot, Clinton Pauley]." Page 13 of the report reads, in part, as follows:

> I strongly believe that the master and the pilot were negligent for failing to maintain a proper lookout as required by Rule #5 of the Inland Navigation Rules. The M/V ELAINE G was transiting the Ohio River with a barge tow of approximately 1000 feet in a weather state of restricted visibility due to fog. Witness testimony from the formal hearing infers that the operators could not see the river banks (approximately 1000 feet to either side of the tug [sic]), nor any farther than the bow of the lead barge (approximately 1000 feet from the wheelhouse).
>
> Despite this extremely restricted visibility, the operators chose to continue underway rather than pull to the side. Also, they chose not to post a lookout on the bow of the lead barge. I have directed MSO Louisville to initiate S&R [Suspension and Revocation] administrative action against the Coast Guard licenses held by both.

This recommendation was approved, and on January 30, 2004 in its case number 1992999, the Coast Guard proposed that *Elaine G* pilot Clinton Pauley receive a twelve-month suspension of his Coast Guard-issued license to pilot uninspected vessels for "failing to post additional lookouts in areas of restricted visibility due to fog." In a Settlement Agreement dated March 15, 2004 and accepted two days later, that suspension sentence was reduced to six months to be followed by a six-month probationary period, both concluding on March 1, 2005. Pauley was also required to successfully complete a Radar Observation Course.

*   *   *

Chapter VIII
Dante's Inferno

"I didn't want to watch them die."

Those were the convulsing words moaned by twenty-year-old Edward Mouton as he looked out over the ghastly sight of the *Sunset Limited* train that had crashed into the swampy waters of the Big Bayou Canot near Mobile, Alabama during the ebony-black early morning of September 22, 1993.[213]

"Them" were the forty-seven hapless and helpless souls who, according to the Alabama State medical examiner's office, all drowned except two who died in the fire and three engineers killed by blunt-force trauma in the murky, snake- and alligator-infested bayou waters. It was the worst accident in the history of National Railroad Passenger Corporation, "Amtrak" – the federal government-owned rail service dedicated to providing modern, efficient, attractive service which began operating the nation's passenger railroads on May 1, 1971.

Almost everything that could have possibly gone wrong that night did go wrong.

- A routine equipment check for the *Sunset Limited* in New Orleans revealed a minor problem that put the train thirty-four minutes off schedule.
- A barge being pushed by the towboat *Mauvilla* hit a railroad bridge piling, dislodging the train tracks.
- The towboat pilot was in a shut-out fog in what he thought was the Mobile River. Actually, he was in a commercially off-

169

limits branch of the river, the Big Bayou Canot.

- There were no waterway mile-markers nor nameplates on the railroad bridge, thereby delaying location of the accident site.
- The towboat helmsman had no formal training in piloting by radar.
- There were no nautical charts of the area on board the boat. The pilot left them home.
- The towboat captain, when first reporting, merely said he was lost, and so he couldn't give specifics as to his location.
- The towboat captain did not mention the allision with the train bridge piling.
- The towboat captain did not mention the burning glow in the skies before him when making some "Mayday" calls.
- The towboat's allision with a bridge support only *moved* the train tracks; it did not break the rails – thereby preventing a warning system to activate and alert the train's engineer.
- The new, modern, "safer" continuous welded rails were in place, thereby allowing the track to bend but not break.
- When a location was finally reported, it was miles away from the actual site.
- An eighty-four-year-old design flaw in the original bridge was never corrected.
- The horrendous accident took place on a moonless night in a dense, jungle-like swampy forest that was totally inaccessible to search-and-rescue operators by road.
- An accurate manifest of the two-hundred-plus passengers and crew members on the

"Train to Hell" was not immediately available following the crash. Thus, the rescue and recovery teams were deprived of vital knowledge about how many survivors and/or victims they needed to look for.

Just about the only thing that didn't go wrong was the extraordinary heroism by some of those scrambling from the train's passenger cars who fought selflessly to save their fellow travelers.

*   *   *

From the time the tiny and tinny *Tom Thumb* pulled its first passenger car across thirteen miles of Maryland narrow-gauge track in 1830, railroads have helped shape America's "Manifest Destiny." Stage coaches, Conestoga wagons, Meriwether Lewis, William Clark and Pony Express riders tied this land together "from sea to shining sea." A century-and-a-half later, souped-up automobiles legally roared at eighty-miles-per-hour across some Interstate highways, jet-planes left fascinating contrails across blues skies, and luxurious cruise ships carried vacationers and business people to "far away places with strange sounding names." Still, as George Pullman, George Westinghouse and the other *Tom Thumb* successors drove in golden spikes, rail travel never gave up its lure of leisure movement in a gentlemanly fashion.

In today's speed-crazed world, there still remains something attractive about relaxing, letting go, and chilling out on an extended train ride. Overcoming the disdain expressed by many about the slow pace of train travel in the heady days after World War II, the Phoenix that was train travel had risen again. Especially when the ride was on board the likes of Amtrak's *Sunset Limited*. A super-liner with double-decked passenger cars, it traveled three times a week from Los Angeles to Miami, covering 3,066 miles across eight states and making fifty-one stops. The trip normally took sixty-eight to seventy-two hours with eastbound passengers, for instance, departing Los Angeles at 10:50 p.m. Sunday and arriving in Miami at 11:10 p.m. Wednesday (time-zone changes included).

It quickly became a favorite of older travelers who didn't like to fly or drive those long distances. It was a very *civilized* way of traveling. The dining car often seemed like a rolling five-star restaurant where passengers sat at linen-covered tables with sterling silverware while white-coated waiters catered to their every beck and call. Businessmen often preferred this mode of travel as it provided more than ample time to prepare for the meeting awaiting them at the end of the line. Cocktails in club cars put a period on the end of each day's clickety-clacking of the rails. West-bound,, there was nothing like riding from the sunrises of the Atlantic coast of Florida to the sunsets over the Pacific Ocean shores of California. And think of the magnificent scenery in between. Either way.

*   *   *

Those were the feelings held by many of the passengers aboard the *Sunset Limited* as they anticipated the end of, for some, a three-day journey from Los Angeles to Miami in September of 1993. With three sleek, 300,000-pound, 6,000-horsepowered diesel-engine locomotives – the lead one, P40 #819, just three weeks old – pulling eight cars on the evening of the 21st, the train made its scheduled stop in New Orleans, Louisiana. The time-table called for the train to take on its last load of supplies, including food and water and 5,800 gallons of diesel fuel.

The *Sunset Limited* was supposed to leave at 11:00 p.m. At the last minute, during one of the usual, routine equipment inspections, a faulty toilet was discovered. By the time repairmen got it fixed, the *Sunset Limited* was

Typical of lead engine on *Sunset Limited*

thirty-four minutes behind schedule. For most people, thirty-four minutes is hardly a lifetime.

For forty-seven people on that train, it was.

At 11:34 on that warm Tuesday evening, September 21, 1993, the *Sunset Limited* left behind the Big Easy's *Vieux Carre* (French Quarter) and whistled out on a one-hundred-forty-mile trip to Mobile, Alabama. The route took the train speeding through Bay St. Louis, Mississippi where seagulls, pelicans and the great blue heron feed on the bay's bounty. Gulfport is the half-way point. Biloxi shows off its Gulf Islands National Seashore, a park stretching over 150 miles east to Santa Rosa Island, Florida. The last stop in Mississippi is Pascagoula, home of the Pascagoula River Swamp, one of the most fertile bird-watching areas in the state.

Just about all the 200-plus passengers on the *Sunset Limited* missed those wonders as the train barreled through the darkness. The seventy-two-seat dining car was empty. After the third dinner seating, a few hangers-on stayed for drinks and conversation. If it was anything like "the good old days" of rail travel, a card game or two followed. Some passengers drifted off to the Vista Car with its floor-to-ceiling windows and panoramic views. But once the sun set, there wasn't too much to see – other than their own reflections in the windows staring back at them.

By the time the train reached Mobile where, twelve years later Amtrak service would cease to be because of another catastrophe, *Hurricane Katrina*, most all the passengers were asleep. The "sky-box crowd" was tucked in their compartment berths and the bleachers crowd curled up uncomfortably in their coach seats. Not many were roused when the train entered and left Mobile, Alabama's port city, on its way to Jacksonville, Florida – some 400 miles east across the Panhandle. It was two-thirty in the morning. The official passenger manifest, as later determined, showed 202 passengers aboard – including three un-ticketed infants.[214] Arrival at Jacksonville was *expected* to be at about 8:30 a.m., September 22nd.

The *expected* turned out to be the tragically unexpected.

*   *   *

Forty-six-year-old Andrew Stabler had been working towboats on the rivers for nineteen years. Conditions on the Mobile River started out quite good that night of Tuesday, September 21, 1993 when he turned the eighty-five-foot-long towboat *Mauvilla's* wheelhouse over to his relief pilot, Willie Corey Odom. They had started their journey ten meandering miles up-river in Chickasaw, Alabama. They were in the early stages of the 365-mile, five-to-six-day river trip to Birmingham. With his second in command of the boat's four-man crew steering the towboat and its string of six barges in three rows of two each, Stabler went below to his bunk. There he propped himself up on his pillow to relax and watch some local TV. There wasn't much on to interest him so the white-bearded Stabler took off his glasses and nodded off to sleep sometime shortly after midnight.

Stabler drifted off being tentatively comfortable for the most part with the forty-five-year-old Odom at the helm. If anything, it was his inexperience that was troubling; the pilot failed a Coast Guard license exam seven times before finally passing it.[215] "Willie does a good job. He's a good pilot, I think" said Stabler defensively.[216]

Interpersonal relationships, reservations about how well a job is being done, and other differences on towboats are not the same as those in your normal work setting. When the boss and the employee have a difference of opinion on the job in an office setting, they discuss it, most times settle it, and then go home and forget about it. On a towboat, those differences take place right there in the "home" and it's sometimes difficult to just "forget about it" because the adversarial problem(s) can continue right down to the dinner table, this time in the ship's mess hall. Sometimes the person you're differing with could be sleeping right there in the cabin next to yours.

Captains do sometimes have to fire people – just like the manager of a local insurance company does. The big difference is, when you fire someone from a towboat, it's like throwing someone out of your living room. If a captain fires what he feels to be an incompetent crew member in mid-trip, the company has to furnish that person with a way back to the home base. Captain Simmey Brickhouse observes, "You always have to talk to people that come out here and don't want to work and stuff. You try to tell 'em what they need to do and you give them the benefit of the doubt. You got some people though, they are just out here to collect a paycheck, figure they don't have to do nothin'."

Likewise, Captain Gary Cochran says he's had occasions where he's had to "throw people off the boat" because of such things as failure to maintain personal cleanliness. He once fired a female cook on her 62d birthday. She insisted on doing things her way and disobeyed his orders to do them otherwise. He had occasion to fire his engineer whom he described as incompetent. He said he's never had to fire a pilot on the spot but he has had to "baby-sit 'em." Continuing, he noted "most of the time there's competent pilots up here. But, there's a lot of pilots out here that aren't competent – young ones, old ones. And when I've got one of those on the boat, they don't stay on very long."

Inexperience of crewmembers, due to turnover, is another cause for many problems. According to Cochran, "there's generally a 70% turnover rate among the new deck personnel in the tow-boating industry. That's because the kids come out here and they get homesick. There's no partying, no drugs, no alcohol, no female companionship. It used to be," explained Brickhouse, "that you had a real old-time mate and he looked after everything for you, and the captain or pilot didn't have to go out there to double-check. But nowadays," he continued, "your Mate's generally about 21-, 22-years-old and they've been out here only a year more than a green deckhand. They try to take shortcuts to save a little time and then end up getting you in trouble later on."

And to compound situations such as this, the U. S. Coast Guard even went so far as "to propose a rule change by slashing from 30 months to 30 days the experience needed to qualify for a federal barge towing endorsement on a master's license. Mariners organized opposition to the change, but so far, few outside of the towing industry have paid attention.... [Expressing industry opposition] Joe

Dady, a New York Harbor tug captain who's been towing barges for 32 years [said] 'you cannot learn how to do it in 30 days'."[217] Dave Gore, another ship master, put it even more succinctly when he said, "If the FAA issued pilots' licenses the way the Coast Guard issues masters' licenses, I would drive."[218]

Troubles also go up and down the chain of command. "There are people out here driving these boats who are prima donnas," observed Cochran. "They're the types that are <u>always</u> right. They don't have patience with the young guys. They think they come into this world always a-hollerin' and a-cussin' and callin' them names. A lot of them on the big boats think the people on the little boats don't know what they're doing. It's sorta like," Cochran explained, "the pilots in the 747s and the pilots in the little regional commuter planes. When you get on a commuter planes, them pilots will say 'Hi' and 'Hello' and all of that whereas them 747 pilots strut in and don't say nothin' to nobody."

Such situations didn't appear to be a problem aboard the *Mauvilla* that dark September night in the Alabama swamp lands. Despite his reservations about his pilot but eased by the weather and the straight-forward routing, the conditions at hand weren't bothersome enough to keep Captain Andy Stabler from falling asleep aboard his towboat that night in 1993. The weather was clear when Willie Odom piloted the string of six 195x35-foot barges, each loaded with 1,400 tons of coal, steel slabs, iron pellets and cement, south from Chickasaw, through the port of Mobile and then on north up the Mobile River at about one in the morning on the 22nd.

But, as often is the case anywhere along the shores of the Gulf of Mexico, fog – as it did in Carl Sandburg's poem – crept in on "little cat feet." It did not, however, as the poet wrote, look "over harbor and city on silent haunches and then move on." The fog grew deeper and heavier and thicker. It soon turned into what mariners call a dreaded "shut-out" fog. That's exactly what Willie Odom called it and Captain Andrew Stabler couldn't agree more when he saw it, too. Except, he saw it too late.

*   *   *

The Mobile River is formed by the confluence of the Tombigbee and Alabama rivers and it flows forty-five miles southerly through Alabama's delta country and on into Mobile Bay and the Gulf of Mexico. Adding in other tributaries, it joins the sixth largest river basin in the United States. The river itself forms part of the Gulf Intracoastal Waterway (GIWW). The marine traffic thereon helped feed Mobile's aerospace, retail, services, construction, medicine, and manufacturing industries with deliveries of coal, wood chips, chemicals, petroleum products. The port easily does four billion dollars a year in export business aided by barges traveling to and from the coal fields of Tuscaloosa and steel factories of Birmingham.

The *Mauvilla* – named after the derivative of an early Native America tribal name that evolved into Mobile – and its barges were just another blip on the waterway with Willie Odom peering into the ever-thickening fog. As many boaters before him have said, it soon became like swimming inside a giant jar of mayonnaise. The eighty-five-foot towboat and its barges were owned by the Warrior & Gulf Navigation Co. (WGN), headquartered in Chickasaw, Alabama. The company came into being when the GIWW was opened in 1945 between New Orleans, Louisiana and Galveston, Texas, allowing river barges to move west from Mobile to the Lone Star State. The company was later acquired by Transtar Inc., a Monroeville, Pa., holding company.

Today, WGN owns and operates twenty-four modern towboats ranging from 1,800- to 2,200-horsepower and has a fleet of over 260 open- and covered-barges. Up until September 22, 1993, Warrior and Gulf had a sterling safety record, Coast Guard officials said. "WGN is very highly respected," said Slade Hooks, the owner of Waterways Towing, a small towboat company based in Mobile. "They are run by very prudent people...."[219] Even so, "the *Mauvilla*, was involved in another rail bridge accident in 1979, according to the *Journal of Commerce*. Both the Warrior and Gulf Navigation Company, and the St. Louis-San Francisco Railway, which owned that bridge over the Tombigbee River at Demopolis, Alabama, were found negligent."[220]

At some point, around 1:30 a.m., Odom – with his thirteen years of experience at WGN on these waterways – made the decision to get out of the fog and tie-up to what he hoped would be a sturdy tree that would hold the towboat and its 8,600-ton laden barges against the river's down-stream current. That was a good decision turned bad. Because of the fog, the pilot couldn't find a tree. He couldn't even find the river's shoreline as he squinted hard out ahead of the 600-feet of barges he was pushing. He was groping along blindly, peering into the haze and trying to get his bearings. The *Mauvilla's* radar was right over Odom's shoulder as he strained his view to the right and left looking for the river bank.

The trouble was Willie Odom's "lack of radar navigation competency."[221] Actually, he had no formal radar training; he had only "received his piloting license only months before, after failing the exam seven times," according to a National Transportation Safety Board (NTSB) seven-month hearing.[222] On the other hand, there are many times when "radar navigation proficiency" is meaningless because weather can blind a radar set as easily as it can a towboat pilot. For instance, a driving rainstorm can obliterate everything on a radar screen – including immediate shorelines, channel buoys, other boats – and even railroad bridges.

While Odom was burning his eyeballs peering into the unending fog, he unknowingly made another decision that turned out even worse than the first. He followed what he could barely see of the left bank of the Mobile River. He should have followed the right bank of the Mobile River because that was the GIWW channel, going past the south side of Twelvemile Island. As he was going up the Mobile on the north side of the island, there was another intersection of waterways, at the entrance to the Big Bayou Canot. By the time he looked at the radar, it no longer showed the intersection of either of the two bodies of water. He and his string were in a narrow tributary "a barely navigable bayou, which leads nowhere and was impassable because the railroad bridge was just seven feet above the surface of the water."[223]

Officially called the "Bayou Canot Bridge," owned and maintained by CSX Transportation, Inc. (CSX), it was a 500-foot-long, single track, steel and timber structure, originally built in 1909. It was designed to be a "swing" bridge that could pivot out of the way of boat traffic but some of the mechanical parts were never installed, leaving some of the tracks on the bridge not fastened properly. However, CSX officials said the track and trestle had been inspected visually earlier that week and had an extensive annual check seven months earlier.

At this point, even an avowed landlubber might ask, "Why didn't the towboat pilot read his navigation chart and follow it?" The sad answer is: There was no Mobile River chart aboard the *Mauvilla*! Odom had left it at home![224] Furthermore, "the NTSB report found that the M/V *Mauvilla* lacked a compass."[225] A lack of radar training, an absence of vital navigation charts, the absence of a ship's compass, and traveling in a "shut-out" fog. And still further, investigators later said "neither a chart nor a compass are required [in 1993] by Coast Guard regulations or the rules of Warrior and Gulf Navigation, and there is no requirement that a pilot be proficient in reading radar."[226] (*Along about here, a writer might not be able to find enough exclamation points to indicate outrage.*) Was there any doubt that death in the swamps was inevitable?

Dotted line is where *Mauvilla* should have gone.

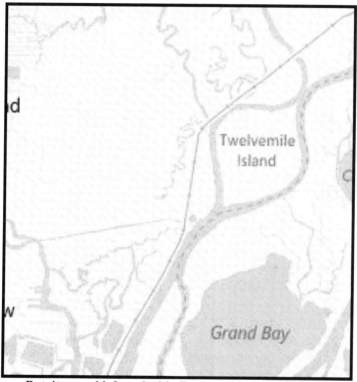

But, it veered left at the big Twelvemile Island instead of staying to the right side of the Mobile River. The accident occurred where railroad crosses Big Bayou Canot, southwest of Nenemoosha.

*   *   *

Odom, the *Mauvilla*, and its six barges were chugging up the Big Bayou Canot at two-to-three knots, barely able to make way against the waterway's down-stream current to the Gulf. "The fog was so thick we couldn't see," Odom remembered later. With his ineffective searchlight trying to stab through the haze, he "sent one of crew [Charles Taylor] out to the forward barge to look for a tree so we could tie off and wait it out.... I called another [boat] up ahead by radio and the other pilot said they were blind and using radar to avoid other river traffic."[227] Jeff Williams, the pilot on the other boat, the *Thomas McCabe*, said the fog wasn't lifting and, as far as he knew, there were no other boats in the area for Odom to tie on to.

With deckhand Taylor out on the barges trying unsuccessfully to lasso a tree, suddenly, the pilot saw something on his radar – a long horizontal image running the full width of the screen. He was only 200- to 300-yards up the bayou. "I seen this object," Odom testified later. "I thought it was a tow. I thought I was still in the Mobile River."[228] Odom headed for it, hoping to raft alongside, tie on to it, and ride out the fog. The long horizontal image turned out instead to be the Bayou Canot Bridge and one of his lead barges banged into it at 2:45 a.m. The pilot said he felt "a thud." When two of the barges broke away at impact, Odom backed off and he and Taylor tried frantically to retrieve them.

Stabler, asleep in his bunk below, called the hit a mere "bump." He said it was just enough to wake him up. To him, it seemed like no big deal; it was kind of like a planned shoreside grounding, something towboats do all the time to get out of adverse conditions.

Sometimes, you can experience the "thrill" of accidently running aground your first time at the helm. Cleve Ward was having his maiden voyage as pilot on the *Elizabeth Lane* and "they turned me loose on the Illinois River and I got aground. It's scary but, after while, you get used to it." He ran aground because there was a red buoy missing. He had to call in and report his grounding but "they (the companies' management) understand that. That happens. You're gonna get aground out here."

Things were somewhat different, somewhat more than routine on towboat *Mauvilla*. After hitting the "bump," deckhand Taylor, however, almost burst into the captain's cabin and told him he'd better get topside fast. When Stabler got there, he found Odom badly shaken mentally. The pilot was "confused," said the captain. "I don't think he realized what was happening. He was just in shock." Now, Stabler was also confused. "I asked Willie, 'Where are we?' He said, 'I think we're somewhere around 13-mile Marsh'."[229]

That would have placed them a mile up-stream on the south side of Twelvemile Island – where they were supposed to be – when actually, they were actually in the Bayou. "Somewhere in there, I seen [a] fire," said Stabler. "That just added to the confusion. Where Willie said we were at, couldn't nothing be burning but the woods."[230] Later, Odom recalled saying, "Oh, my Lord, I made a wrong turn.... "I hope I didn't hit this bridge." He said he too "felt a bump." He thought he had hit a sandbar, he said, and found he had lost two barges.[231]

Stabler grabbed the wheel from the confused pilot and with both deckhands now out on those still-attached barges, he started maneuvering to try to round up the barges drifting down-stream, away from the bridge. The current was winning the battle. After twenty minutes of struggling, the captain grabbed his ship-to-shore VHF radio mike and called the Coast Guard at 3:06 a.m. "Mayday, mayday," he shouted. "I've lost my tow. There's too much fog. Don't know exact location. Just around Twelvemile Island."[232]

Obviously, Stabler too thought they were still on the Mobile River. When he saw the trestle that Odom had hit, he thought it was the Sara Bayou. When the Coast Guard asked for more information about imminent danger, location, number of persons on board, etc., all the captain could say was, "We have four people on board. There's a lot of fog. I don't have time to talk to you. Let me go see what is going on. I'll get right back with you. Out."[233]

The U. S. Coast Guard faulted Stabler. "The fact is he was lost," said Captain Mike Perkins, commander of the Mobile Coast Guard station. Captain Perkins later said the boat's crew did not follow proper procedures when [it] failed to stop after becoming lost in the fog. "Once he knew where he wasn't, he was incumbent to stop and find out where he was," Captain Perkins told reporters. "He should certainly know where he is at all times."[234]

Meanwhile at the scene and almost immediately, Stabler radioed back: "Coast Guard, this is *Mauvilla*. There's a train that ran off the track into the water, and there's lots of people that need help. And there's a fire. I'm going to try to help some of them, and I'll get back with you." [235] The strange part about these recollected and sometimes recorded calls is Odom testified he heard the noises of the train crashing into the Bayou just shortly after he hit the trestle at 2:45 a.m.

There was a huge explosion and a fireball as the three engines' diesel fuel tanks erupted into an inferno. Experts calculated the *Sunset Limited* crashed at approximately 2:53 a.m. Could Captain Stabler be totally unaware of the disaster spewing skyward and lighting the black night with a bright orange glow for miles around? Could the residents of Chinatown not know an earthquake hit San Francisco in 1906?

In later testimony, Stabler said, "We seen the train in the water. I don't know if Willie told me of the fire before I seen the fire with my own eyes." [236] A radio transmission from the *Mauvilla* mentioned the train for the first time at 3:08 a.m., but Stabler said he still had not seen a train. He said he assumed that the fire was a train wreck only because a nearby drawbridge operator radioed him that one had occurred. Stabler called the Coast Guard again: "I believe we're right below the train, uh, uh, they's a hell of a fire up here in the middle of the river, and there ain't supposed to be no fire up here and, like I say, I don't know exactly where we at. It's so foggy I can't tell by looking on the radar, so there's something bad wrong up there."[237]

As was famously said in another national affair twenty-years earlier, "What did he know and when did he know it?"

*   *   *

As usual in circumstances such as these, there were more questions than answers.

- If the *Mauvilla* hit the Bayou Canot Bridge at 2:45 a.m. and backed away to roundup the loose barges, and...
- If Captain Stabler took the helm from Willie Odom almost immediately after the *Mauvilla's* allision with the bridge, and...
- If, as later determined, the *Sunset Limited* flew off the trestle at 2:53 a.m., and...
- If Odom, as he said, heard the crash at that time, and...
- If, within seconds, a large orange fireball was seen to engulf the area – a fire that the captain himself later described "a hell of a fire, a huge fire and the smoke was blowing right into my wheelhouse; I couldn't see and I couldn't breathe," then...
- Why did Captain Stabler
- not mention the *Mauvilla's* encounter with the bridge,

- not mention the fire, the smoke, the glowing sky, the smoke in his Wheelhouse, and
- then wait more than twenty minutes to report he was lost when a captain is required to do that immediately so that other vessels in the area can be warned?

*   *   *

A repeat of this tragedy with another *Sunset Limited* train carrying 147 passengers and fifteen crew members was narrowly avoided just four months later on January 18, 1994. An empty barge broke away from its moorings and hit a swing bridge near Amelia, Louisiana, sixty-miles west-southwest of New Orleans. The allision knocked the tracks out of alignment by six inches. Another disaster was averted in this case when the swing bridge operator notified the Coast Guard, which in turn was able to notify the engineer on the oncoming super-liner – with ten minutes to spare.

*   *   *

Odom and his tow crept up the fog-bound bayou, which in normal times of the day would be filled with local fishermen in their Pirogues bobbing for catfish, crappie, redfish and flounder while long-necked white egrets stalked the banks looking for prey. At the same time, John Turk, On-Board Services (OBS) supervisor on the *Sunset Limited* – one of the twelve service crew members – was busy in the train's crew dormitory car trying to resolve some questions about the *Sunset Limited*'s passenger manifest.

There are always such problems with long-distance, multi-stop trips involving several crew changes. For instance, here he had those three infants he knew were aboard even though they weren't ticketed. (In the days after the accident, at least ten people showed up at various hearings to say they, too, were on board the train at the time of the accident; a not unexpected happening because some passengers board and buy their tickets on the train. And it would also not be unheard of if some other people with nefarious tendencies actually claimed they were also aboard.) Therefore, concluded the NTSB, an accurate passenger account would have improved emergency responses. The train, having just left the Azalea City station at 2:30 in the morning, was heading north into the big thickets of the desolate swamp country and was picking up speed over the first of its initial fourteen miles of the 240 en route to Tallahassee.

Driving the train in that three-week-old forward locomotive as it left Mobile was forty-seven-year-old Billy Rex (B. R.) Hall, engineer-in-charge, from Birmingham. Peering into the misty gloom were assistant engineers Ernie Russ, forty-six, from Gulf Shores, Alabama, and Mike Vinet, thirty-nine, from Kenner, Louisiana – all three fresh from a coffee-and-doughnuts break during the Mobile stop. Hall, one of the six operating crew members, had to feel like he needed all the eyes he could muster in the off-shore fog as the train started to barrel down the silvery rails heading for the Florida Panhandle. Those tracks went almost due north out of Mobile.

About six miles out of the city, the tracks angled off to the northeast where they crossed a trestle seven feet above the Big Bayou Canot, that non-navigable channel branching north of Twelvemile Island. Billy Rex Hall may still have been trying to make up for the time lost with the toilet repairs in New Orleans as he pushed the throttle forward and the speedometer on the *Sunset Limited* crept past seventy-miles-per-hour for that area. At 2:51 a.m., the *Sunset Limited* passed an all-clear, green light.

Billy Rex Hall, Ernie Russ, Mike Vinet, two other crew members and forty-two passengers on the *Sunset*

Limited were a mile-and-one-half away from meeting their Maker.

*   *   *

The conductor on the *Sunset Limited*, Dwight (D. K.) Thompson, and his assistant, Gary Farmer, were at the rear of the train, in the dining car. The rest of the conductor's crew at that hour was asleep forward in the dormitory car. Engineer Hall had just called on the train's crew intercom to say thanks for the coffee they were enjoying up forward in the cab. While "D. K." was doing some paperwork, Farmer commented to him, ironically, about how smooth the ride had been "so far." Almost immediately thereafter and with a suddenness no one could have ever expected, the two then were hurtled forward from their seats with an impact that Farmer said felt like "flying into the side of a mountain." The force was horrendous, even to the extent that Thompson, Farmer said, went "sailing over my head."[238]

The three engines roared over the Bayou Canot Bridge at seventy-two-miles an hour – two-miles-an-hour faster, some lawyers were to contend later, than the regulated speed for that area (not that it would have made the least bit of difference) – and seven-miles-an-hour faster than the then national highway speed limit. One subsequent court ruling contended the train was "traveling between 72-74 mph when the Casualty occurred, [putting it] below the 79 mph speed limit for that class of tracks and that type of train."[239] Again, neither of those differences in speed would have made any difference in the final outcome of the tragedy.

The *Mauvilla* allision had knocked the tracks out of line by thirty-eight inches to their left and moved the east steel girder of the span into the path of the speeding engines. When they smashed into the girder, the engines went cart-wheeling 240 feet into the bayou and its east bank.

Most of the eighty-four-year-old bridge went with them. The crash was so devastating that the brand-new lead engine was totally buried in the muddy shore on the river's far side. The three-man crew in that engine – Billy Rex Hall, Ernie Russ, and Mike Vinet – never had a chance. It would be more than two days before their bodies could be excavated.

The Aftermath: Notice the coach in the middle of the picture, sitting on a section of bridge trestle – which prevented it from sinking in the Bayou. Other lucky passengers were those in the car hanging off the end of the bridge (lower right)

Also in the bayou's waters – usually infested with alligators and snakes that this time were obviously scared off by the commotion – were the baggage car, the crew's dorm car, both ablaze, and two of the double-decked passenger coaches, fast filling with murky water. Remaining on what was left on the west bank of the bridge and the rails behind were one coach, the sleeper car, the Vista car, and the dining car. Those cars were kept from joining the others in that slimey, watery cemetery by a newly installed automatic braking system, activated when engines are separated from the rest of the train.

When the lead-engine plowed into the bayou's bank, the two engines following it cork-screwed in behind and into a scrap-yard of twisted steel. The impact of engines set off a huge fireball as the remnants of the 5,800 gallons of diesel fuel taken on in New Orleans exploded into what survivor Julie Dicks said, "looked like 'Dante's Inferno' with the heads bobbing around in the dark and the flames."[240] The ignited fuel then spilled into the bayou, turning it into a fiery, oily ribbon through which some of the gagging survivors escaping from the water-logged cars had to swim.

When the passengers in those two forward coaches ended up in the bayou, they were on their own, without any crew personnel to help them. And, unlike airline passengers, the railroads at that time had no pre-departure safety instructions for passengers prior to leaving the station. Most of those passengers were, literally and figuratively, in the dark, on their own, and, as it turned out for some, in their tomb.

The lead double-decked coach (#34068) began to sink fast in the murky waters as it filled in seconds, That left the passengers on the lower level – most of whom didn't know which was up, which way to safety, which way to the emergency doors, or how to open the emergency windows – groping blindly and unsuccessfully. The second coach (#34083) had the good fortune to land on top of some of the bridge timbers that preceded it into the bayou, thereby keeping it from immediate submersion. With only the light from the blazing diesel flames illuminating the inside of the car, those passengers were able to find their way to safety as they frantically kicked out the emergency exit windows.

*   *   *

James Altosino, a 72-year-old passenger who had boarded in San Antonio, Texas, was "asleep, and a jolt knocked me from my seat. By the time I awoke, water was coming into the car." When he saw a woman literally floating toward him in the upended coach, he helped her get out a window. Then he climbed out next and swam for what remained of the trestle, where he hung on for about an hour, watching the engines burn. "The only light was from the fire," Mr. Altosino said, "and it was so hot that I had to splash water on my back to cool off. The stench of the diesel fuel was terrible."

Bill Crosson of Tallahassee, Florida, and his wife, Vivian, passengers in another car, said they barely escaped drowning. "The water just rose immediately up to the top, and I mean there was just room for air," he said. "Everybody just kind of floated together and went out the back of the car. There were a few times when I wondered if we were going to make it."[241]

Some called her a "miracle child." Now she's an orphan. Eleven-year-old Andrea Chancey, wheelchair-bound with cerebral palsy, took the cross-country trip with her parents, Geary and Mary Jane. They wanted her to have the experience of the train ride. "Andy," as she was known, believes it was her forty-five-year-old parents who pushed her through an open window after their passenger coach submerged in the bayou. Her mother and father didn't make it out.

Michelle Dotting, returning to Fort Lauderdale from a family visit to Houston, took the train because, she thought, it was cheaper and it would be more enjoyable. She was on the upper level of the double-decked lead coach when, without any warning, the bridge collapsed. "I just knew I was dead when the train was going somewhere off the tracks," she said. "When it stopped and I realized I was alive, I just kept saying, 'Oh my God! Oh my God! Oh my

God!' It was chaos, lots of panic and confusion" as the water rose rapidly, leaving only about a foot of air between the water level and the roof of the car.[242]

"Everybody started screaming," Dotting said, "because the water was gushing in." The fight for survival was less than civil, she said. "Somebody pulled on my shoulder, and I lost my grip and went under. People were kicking and screaming." The injured, weak and slow were left behind. After she got out of the car, she grabbed a piece of driftwood and paddled her way to shore.

Also in the slimy waters were Sheila Summers, from Alachua, Florida and Ann McKee from Houston, as they clung to a steel girder to keep the bayou's current from sweeping them away. Despite their dire circumstances, they actually were very fortunate. Because they were on one of the longer legs of the trip, they were moved from the lead coach car that ended up being completely submerged into the next one – that wasn't. The two of them managed to get out a window and grab that girder. The car next to them was ablaze and the fire was spreading. "Everybody was screaming. I felt," said Ms. McKee, "like it wasn't my time to go. Thank the good Lord!"[243]

Ken Ivory was another of those whose luck alternated between good and bad. When he missed his airplane flight out of Houston for Miami, he decided to take the leisurely way out of town. He had never been on a train ride before so, he decided to hop aboard the *Sunset Limited* and watch the 1,000-plus miles go by. Like most people on the train, he didn't get to see all of those miles. But, he'll never forget the last few feet. The crash "wasn't but a few seconds but it seemed like a lifetime."

When his coach went airborne, "it did like a 360," Ivory said. "I thought I was going to die. I thought all of us was going to die. It was a pretty rough impact. I heard screams. I heard people just yelling. Just all kinds of chaos." And seconds later, "you could hear people gurgling. People drowning."[244] People pinned under debris as the water in the car rose. People too old or infirm to extricate themselves. People too injured to move.

Passenger Edward Mouton, the UCLA student from Los Angeles who had to turn his back on the sight of death in the waters, also said, "We were throwing sheets and blankets out of the cars that were still on the track to the people who were wet from being in the water.... Some people were hysterical. There were a lot of old people on the train." And, he remembered, "You could smell the smoke from the fires burning in the engine cars and see ash falling from the sky. But it was so foggy you really couldn't see the water."[245]

*   *   *

Most of the Onboard Service crewmembers – the cooks, waiters, cabin attendants, etc. – asleep in the dormitory car at the time of the crash, were ultimately brought to safety as they clamored into or clung onto a skiff (a small, aluminum row boat) Captain Stabler sent out from the *Mauvilla*. In all, seventeen victims were rescued by the skiff shuttling back and forth from the accident scene to the towboat. The *Scott Pride*, another towboat plying the Mobile River, and personnel from the *Sunset Limited* aided in hauling dozens of other people from the oil-slicked water.

When emergency responders were finally able to make it to the scene, more than an hour after the initial crash, they began the grim task of body recovery, firefighting, and triage. At this point, had an accurate manifest been available, it would have been of little use in saving the lives of passengers identified as missing and presumed trapped in the submerged cars.[246] Thus, emergency responders did not know when to discontinue operations because the count changed frequently. At that time, Amtrak's printed manifest provided the names of first class and sleeper passengers holding reservations. However, it only had a count (without names) of coach reservations and was not checked against the number and names of passengers actually on board, including those onboard ticket-buyers from nearby Mobile. Thus, it was not a comprehensive passenger accounting system, according to NTSB.

*   *   *

Amtrak assistant conductor Farmer described the scene aboard the coach remaining on the trestle as "sheer chaos." When he got to the car's doorway that opened out on the scene of total devastation, Farmer radioed "D. K." and told him the obvious: "We're in serious trouble, D.K. The bridge is gone. We've got cars in the water." Then, the assistant conductor bellowed his most sage advice to the confused passengers in that precariously-positioned car: "Ladies and gentlemen," he said, "remember your high school days. We're going to conduct this like a high school fire drill."[247]

With Farmer blocking the car's exit on his end of the car and herding the passengers toward the far door and with Thompson guiding the passengers out of that other end, their two-fold mission was accomplished. They got the weight in the car shifted from the end leaning over the bayou, and they got their passengers out to safety. According to a Department of Transportation (DOT) report, Farmer then set up a relay system with passengers in the water who could swim. He instructed them to space themselves "about 20 yards apart and to swim out and meet these elderly people [who were evacuating the submerged cars] and swim them to the next guy and so forth, on up to the bank."[248] The relay passed people from the middle of the waterway to the bayou bank. Thompson and Farmer handed out blankets and pillows to the survivors brought ashore.

Later, the autopsy reports showed that all forty-two passengers who perished in the wreck died from drowning. Some with non-life-threatening injuries were temporarily bound with strips torn from dining car table cloths into make-shift bandages. There were 103 injured people taken to local hospitals, most of them were what one local doctor called "the walking wounded." Bodies were taken to a makeshift morgue at Port Chickasaw.

*   *   *

It in the midst of that twenty-six-minute time frame between the crash and the *Mauvilla*'s confirmation of it, the area airwaves and land-lines were crackling with other communications – sometimes tripping over each other. Assistant conductor Gary Farmer said that after his supervisor, Dwight Thompson went flying over his head, he immediately got on his portable phone and all but screamed: "Mayday! We are in serious trouble. Please clear this channel. We need all the help we can get." Even that presented a problem because with the mobile phone technology of 1993 being somewhat primitive compared to today's multi-featured cellular phones, Farmer was not even sure that his limited-range transmission was reaching anyone. For about 18 minutes – from 3:02 to 3:20 a.m. – confusion ensued as the Mobile, Saraland, and Chickasaw 9/11 operators tried to locate the accident site. Exactly where the *Sunset Limited* had derailed was unclear, and no roads lead into the heavily wooded swampland.

When communications were finally established and the actual location of the wreck was pin-pointed, the Coast Guard diverted its H-60 helicopters from Search and Rescue operations in the Gulf to the accident scene. But when they got there at about 5:20 a.m., there was no place to land. The chopper crews had to winch survivors out of the water and into their aircraft. Coast Guard Lieutenant

Robin Stearrett reported "smoke and fire everywhere," that "it was devastating," the "most catastrophic wreck I have ever seen."[249] It took more than an hour for the City of Mobile's fireboat to arrive on scene. More than an hour-and-one-half elapsed before the Coast Guard's rigid-hull inflatable boat got there.

Many of the survivors were still in the water, clinging to large pieces of debris. Others helped each other by forming human chains and passing people, hand-to-hand like an old-time bucket-brigade, to the shore. As the night skies showed their first steaks of daylight, divers were brought in. Mark Lampkin and John Barnett, volunteer firefighters from Orange Grove, Mississippi, dove into Big Bayou Canot, groping through one of the sunken coaches, searching for the dead. "It's 'groper' diving, as we call it, when you have to feel for what you find," said Lampkin, "There is no visibility at all."

He pulled the tiny body of six-month-old Sean Galvan out of the submerged coach where the baby died along with his mother, Sheila. Later, Lampkin and Barnett spotted the body of three-year-old Jennifer Camarena floating a few hundred yards away. Her mother, Nedra, also perished. Barnett said, the little girl "looked like a doll floating in the water." Lampkin said, "This is probably one of the worst ones we've worked before. Dealing with children is what bothers me. Dealing with children this small has to bother you."[250]

*   *   *

On board the *Mauvilla* and in many other areas, confusion still ran rampant following the crash. Communications were garbled. Some of those sending distress calls weren't sure if those calls were being received. Some sending "Mayday" calls continued in panic to keep pressing down the send button on their hand-held radios and thus were unable to hear calls coming back asking for clarification. Almost all calls from the accident scene were wrong in trying to pinpoint the exact location of the crash. They were unanimous in believing the accident occurred on the Mobile River.

As previously noted herein, the river splits itself to surround Twelvemile Island with the GIWW course taking the leg flowing south of the Island (see map on page 181). Odom had steered the *Mauvilla* into the north leg around the island and then turned from it into the Big Bayou Canot, a place where he had never been before. When the initial emergency calls came in, recipients immediately assumed the *Mauvilla* was on the south side of the island, in the Intracoastal, not too far from the small town of Saraland.

The first emergency call, at 3:01 A.M. (eight minutes after the crash), came from Warren Carr, a CSX assistant terminal train master in Mobile. He may have been alerted by local bridge tenders in the area who saw the fire glow coming from Big Bayou Canot. Or maybe the now-functioning train track alarm system which, because the rails were totally fractured during the accident, was doing its intended (though cruelly too-late) job of sending out warning signals. Carr, who thought the crash was at Bayou Sara, several miles from Big Bayou Canot, told emergency first-responders, "I got people in the water. I got cars on fire. You're going to have to get some helicopters and boats and Coast Guard and all those people" out there he told the dispatcher.[251]

The second call, from Ronnie Seymour, another CSX employee, came nine minutes after Carr's. He at least pin-pointed Saraland as the closest town when he told the operator, "It's going to be Saraland, but it's a passenger train that's derailed," adding, "crew in water, the train's on fire." The last call, at 3:16 A.M., was placed by an Amtrak supervisor aboard the train. He mistakenly said that "we're on the Mobile River," but added: "The bridge has gone out. We got cars burning, people in the river, can't swim. We need help. Any kind of help you can get down here."[252] That any help got there at all is, by some, still considered a miracle because of the inaccessibility of the crash scene. In all, it took more than five-and-one-half hours to get all the survivors treated and transported to local hospitals or hotels.

*   *   *

When Willie Odom was steering the *Mauvilla* that morning, he wasn't the first towboat helmsman to plow into the Bayou Canot Bridge. Officials from the National Transportation Safety Board said at the conclusion of a nine-month investigation into the tragedy that the trestle was also hit in 1979. Furthermore, said the NTSB, there were at least thirteen other cases of barges hitting bridges in the first eight months of 1993 alone. Barges bumping bridges was not an oddity.

What was odd was the seeming unwillingness of the *Mauvilla* crew to face the problem they had created. Maybe they were in a state of denial. Maybe, just as in the case of the *Elizabeth M* tragedy described in Chapter III in this book, the *Mauvilla* crew was too occupied chasing their loose barges. Captain Stabler and his crew took drug and alcohol tests nine hours after the crash. A Warrior and Gulf spokesman said the crew passed both tests. There was a question about the effectiveness of the tests, administered nine hours after the crash. Maybe only a "Philadelphia Lawyer" could make their case.

They hit the bridge at 2:45 a.m. Even if Odom thought the bridge was another barge when he approached it, he must have known immediately after that it wasn't. Eight minutes later, the explosive crash of the *Sunset Limited* lit up the area like London during The Blitz.

According to a DOT account of the tragedy, "at approximately 3:19 a.m. (twenty-six minutes after the accident), the captain of the *Mauvilla* called and advised the Coast Guard that he had his barges under control [and he] further related that he would try to render assistance to the survivors."[253]

(Later, Dennis Sullivan, Amtrak's executive vice president and chief operating officer, said that had anyone on the *Mauvilla* reported the accident immediately, there would have been enough time to send an electronic signal to stop the train, or make radio contact with engineer Billy Rex Hall in time for him to halt it.) It was only after Stabler's 3:19 call that he ordered the *Mauvilla's* skiff into the water. A deckhand rowed it back and forth to the accident site four or five times and he was credited with rescuing seventeen survivors, including those six OBS crewmembers who had evacuated the blazing dorm-coach.

One of the train's crewmembers who did not make it was forty-four-year-old Roland Quaintance, from Jackson, Mississippi. Charley Jones was a bartender on the train who – along with most of the OBS crew – was asleep in the dormitory car as it crashed into the bayou. He heard Quaintance, his friend and co-worker, scream from the next compartment, "Help me, help me! I can't get out!"[254] He was trapped by a door that opened inward and he died in the partly submerged but burning car. As Jones struggled to get the jammed door open, the last he heard from his friend was him reciting "The Lord's Prayer" and the "Twenty-third Psalm" as the flames consumed the car.

*   *   *

Unfortunately, it takes tragedies to create heroes. Think about the Medal of Honor winners on the battlefield. Think about the firemen and police officers racing up the stairwells of the Twin Towers on 9/11. Think about

Michael Dopheide in the burning swamps of Big Bayou Canot. *Sunset Limited* passenger Adele Massaro, no doubt, thought about him a lot. Unable to swim, when she found herself in the oily, diesel waters of Big Bayou Canot following the wreck, "The only thing that kept me going was his calm voice. I just followed his voice to safety." As did some twenty-nine other passengers Dopheide was credited with saving.

Sheila Summers was one of those. "He just took charge," she said. He told those non-swimmers to just jump from the train car into the water where the twenty-six year-old former life guard awaited them. He told Ms. Summer to jump in and he'd be there to bring her back up. Then, as with many others – including a two-year-old baby girl and an eleven-year-old cerebral palsy patient Andrea Chancey, who lost both her parents, Mary Jane and Geary, in the crash – he had them clasp their arms around his neck and he swam them ten feet or more to some of the trestle girders protruding from the bayou which they clambered on and held on to until rescue boats reached them.

Donnie Hughes was another of those who said she owed her life to Michael Dopheide. Looking down at the dark oily water six feet below the passenger car window frame, she hesitated, knowing she couldn't swim. More escaping passengers were lined up impatiently behind her. It was like being in the doorway of an airplane wondering if your parachute would open. But, Ms. Hughes said she couldn't move. Then, she said, "I look below and I see this boy, this beautiful boy, with his arms up-stretched, and he's saying, 'It's okay, I'm here, come on, I've got ya.' And so," she continued, "I jumped and went down under the water. And then I felt that boy's arms pulling me back up. I am covered with diesel, and my eyes are on fire, and this boy is holding me, telling me I'm okay. I don't even know his name—but I'll never forget him."[255]

Just like many of the passengers on the Sunset Limited, Dopheide (pronounced DUP-hide) was grabbing some uncomfortable zees when the train went barreling into the abyss. A recent graduate from DePaul University's law school in Chicago, he was ending his cross-country train ride, taking a bit of a vacation before he would have to stand for his bar exam. Having removed his glasses and put them in his shoes for safe keeping before nodding off, Dopheide then was "practically blind throughout the whole ordeal" after the train plunged into the bayou.

With water rushing into the coach, people screaming wildly that "we're all going to die," the flash of flames from the exploding engines bursting about them, the husky Dopheide managed to break open one of the car's windows. Calling to other passengers to follow him, he leapt into the bayou where he stationed himself amid the debris to rescue those thirty survivors. Dopheide, who as a young lad attended the famed Boys Town institution of Father Edward Flanagan's in Omaha, Nebraska, said the school's motto flashed through his mind throughout the ordeal. "He ain't heavy, Father. He's my brother."[256]

*   *   *

Aftermath

The National Transportation Safety Board (NTSB), which investigates major transportation accidents and issues recommendations, said [on June 21, 1994] the probable cause of the accident was displacement of the bridge "when it was struck by the *Mauvilla* tow as a result of the *Mauvilla*'s pilot becoming lost and disoriented in dense fog." But the board spread the blame, saying barge owner Warrior & Gulf Navigation Company had failed "to ensure that their towboat operator was competent to use radar to navigate his tow during periods of reduced visibility." The board also cited the U.S. Coast Guard for failure to establish higher standards for operator licensing.[257]

Subsequently and almost one year to the day after the September 22, 1993 calamity at Big Bayou Canot, the NTSB issued its "Railroad-Marine Accident Report RAR-94-01, Adopted September 19, 1994." In it, the Board made a number of specific recommendations it hoped would prevent future catastrophes. Among those recommend-dations were:

To the U.S. Coast Guard:

Amend [its regulations] to specify the time limits, not to exceed 8 hours, within which employers must conduct post-accident alcohol testing.

In consultation with the inland towing industry, develop radar training course curricula standards for river towboat operations that emphasize navigational use of radar on rivers and inland waters.

Upgrade licensing standards to require that persons licensed as Operators of Uninspected Towing Vessels hold valid river-inland waters radar observer certification if they stand navigation watch on radar-equipped towing vessels and to require that employers provide more specific evidence of training.

Require that all uninspected towing vessels carry appropriate navigational devices, including charts, in the wheelhouse.

Promote, in cooperation with the U.S. Army Corps of Engineers, the development and application of low-cost electronic charting navigation devices for inland rivers.

Require that radar be installed on board all uninspected towing vessels except those that operate within very limited areas.

Require that all bridges vulnerable to impact by commercial marine traffic bear unique, readily visible markings so that waterway and bridge users are better able to identify bridges involved in an accident when they report such accidents to emergency responders.

Periodically publish a list of bridge identification markings in a national register of bridges.

To the National Railroad Passenger Corporation (Amtrak):

Develop and implement a uniform system to effectively apprise passengers of information pertaining to safety features.

Develop and implement procedures to provide adequate passenger and crew lists to local authorities with minimum delay in emergencies.

Equip cars with portable lighting for use by passengers in an emergency.

To the American Waterways Operators, Inc.:

Recommend that member companies equip their tugs and towboats with suitable navigation devices, including charts.

Assist the Coast Guard in developing a curriculum for a training course on river radar navigation.

Recommend that member companies incorporate into towboat operator evaluations a practical method of assessing proficiency in navigation, including the use of radar.

To the Warrior & Gulf
Navigation Company:

Require that company towboat operators complete a recognized training course on river radar navigation after the curriculum for such a course has been developed.

Establish a training protocol that requires company towboat operators to demonstrate proficiency in use of radar, compasses, and charts and incorporate into towboat operator evaluations a practical method of assessing proficiency in river navigation techniques, including use of radar.

Equip all company towboats with a suitable compass, a complete, up-to-date set of navigation charts for the waters over which the vessel is intended to operate, and other appropriate navigational devices.

Establish procedures that encourage towboat operators to inform management when they are taking medication, to determine whether such medication may affect performance of their duties, and to arrange for a qualified relief, if necessary.

*   *   *

Should anyone want to hear some knee-slappers and high hilarity, gather around towboaters discussing the compass requirements so prominently mentioned in the above set of recommendations. Towboat pilots say they are just another one of those feel-good regulations passed by uninformed, desk-bound pencil pushers, and shore-bound legislators whose only maritime experience is attending lobbyists' cocktail parties on expensive yachts on the Potomac River. Those people seek to solve sometimes non-existent problems with non-working, supercilious requirements.

A compass is now "mandated" as required navigational equipment on all towboats. But what in the world does a towboat skipper need a compass for when he's driving a boat up a sliver of a river that has more twists and turns than a bowl full of overcooked linguini? The wheelhouse of one $1.5 million dollar boat this writer sailed on had a $14.95 compass right out of a Pep Boys auto parts store, meeting its mandated compass requirement.

*　　*　　*

Time Line of Events

(all times CDT)

12:55 a.m. – *Mauvilla* departs Mobile.
1:53 a.m. – heavy freight train crosses Bayou Canot
            Bridge, reports no problems.
2:30 a.m. – *Sunset Limited* departs Mobile.
2:45 a.m. – (approximately) barges pushed by *Mauvilla*
            strike and displace Big Bayou Canot
            railroad bridge
2:53 a.m. – Amtrak Train 2, *Sunset Limited*, with 220
            persons on board, strike displaced bridge
            and derail.
2:56 a.m. – (approximately) train assistant conductor makes
            "Mayday, Mayday" transmission over rail-
            road-designated radio; heard by CSXT train
            579, with crew repeating it to yardmaster at
            Sibert Yard, Mobile.

2:56 a.m.   – (approximately) bridge tender at Mobile River Bridge and train engineer of Train 579 also radios train dispatcher in Jacksonville that train No. 2 is transmitting a "Mayday" call.

2:56 a.m.   – (approximately) assistant terminal trainmaster at Sibert Yard hears train No. 2 transmitting "Mayday" over radio and at

2:57 a.m.   – notifies train dispatcher in Jacksonville, Florida, and at

3:00 a.m.   – (approximately) notifies Mobile Police Department's 9/11 operator that Train 2 has derailed.

3:02-
3:05 a.m.   – Mobile Police Department 9/11 operator contacts Mobile Fire Department and Coast Guard. Police, fire, and Coast Guard begins notifying other emergency responders.

3:05 a.m.   – (approximately) Train's OBS supervisor, using cellular telephone, calls Mobile 9/11

3:02-
3:20 a.m.   – confusion ensues as Mobile, Saraland, and Chickasaw 9/11 operators try to locate accident site.

3:19 a.m.   – (approximately twenty-six minutes after accident), captain of *Mauvilla* advises Coast Guard he has barges under control and will try to render assistance to Amtrak survivors.

3:59 a.m.   – (over one hour after the accident) towboat *Scott Pride*, approaches accident site.

4:00 a.m.   – Mobile fireboat *Ramona Doyle* arrives on scene.

4:25 a.m.   – (approximately) Coast Guard's rigid-hull inflatable boat arrives on scene.

5:20 a.m.   – (approximately) Coast Guard helicopters arrive.

8:30 a.m.   – Last survivors treated and transported to local hospitals or hotels.

*   *   *

The following, without the ages of some, is the complete list of the forty-seven people who died in the crash:

Anderson, Shirley, 55, Portland, Oregon
Ball, Maxine, 69, Gibsonton, Florida
Camarena, Nedra, 20, Los Angeles
Camarena, Jennifer, 3, Los Angeles
Caspolich, Martha, 40, Long Beach, Mississippi
Chancey, Mary Jane, 45, Orange Park, Florida
Chancey, Geary Lee, 45, Orange Park, Florida
Childs, Marianne, 36, Las Vegas, Nevada
Crenshaw, Lilly Ruth, 63, Tampa, Florida
Diener, Robert J., 54, San Diego
Dixon, Patrick, 78, Apopka, Florida
Dixon, Doris, Apopka, Florida
Furano, Patricia, 57, Winter Haven, Florida
Galvan, Sean Scott, 3 Months, Bainbridge, Georgia
Galvan, Sheila, 21, Bainbridge, Georgia
Hall, Billy Rex, 47, Birmingham, Alabama (Engineer)
Hampton, Penny, 47, Hammond, Indiana
Haystead, Suzanne, 22, Britain
208de-Becellar, Claudia Nicola, Brazil
Hernandez, Esteban R., 65, Los Angeles
Holtzworth, Geraldine, 63, Tallahassee, Florida
Holtzworth, William John, 73, Tallahassee, Florida
Leonard, Mary Ellen, 84, St. Petersburg, Florida
Lester, Marsha, 50, Los Angeles
Main, Lorna, 50, Britain
McMahon, David, New Orleans
McNab, James, 57, Long Beach, California
McNab, Janice, 55, Long Beach, California
Newton, Eric, 44, Kissimmee, Florida
Pearce, Billie Patricia, 62, Reynoldsville, Pennsylvania
Poole, Dorothy, Tallahassee, Florida
Poole, Harold, 68, Tallahassee, Florida
Powell, Olga, Tampa, Florida

Quaintance, Ronald, 44, Jackson, Mississippi
    (OBS Crew Member)
Renz, Alan C., 71, Bradenton, Florida
Renz, Catherine, Bradenton, Florida
Russ, Ernest Lamar, 46, Gulf Shores, Alabama
    (Assistant Engineer)
Skelton, Betty, 64, Pensacola, Florida
Skelton, Oscar, 65, Pensacola, Florida
Taube, James, 31, Loxahatchee, Florida
Taube, Ruth, 28, Loxahatchee, Florida
Veite, Christina E., 72, Eldred, Pennsylvania.
Vinet, Michael, 39, Kenner, Louisiana
    (Assistant Engineer)
Walker, Dorothy, 62, Novato, California
Walks, George, 56, West Palm Beach, Florida
Williams, Julia, 22, Britain
Wilson, John, 62, Lyon, Mississippi

*   *   *

Chapter IX
An Exercise in Poor Judgment

At about 2:00 p.m. on Friday, May 28, 1993, the towboat *Chris* departed the Bergeron Marine ship repair yard on the east side of New Orleans, Louisiana on the Gulf Intracoastal Waterway (GIWW) to pick up an empty hopper barge, DM 3021, at a cement plant near the Big Easy's Florida Avenue wharf. It was the start of a long holiday weekend celebrating Memorial Day. The *Chris* was to move the barge through the Industrial Canal to the Huey P. Long barge fleet yard on the lower Mississippi River.

Most waterway traffic moving between Lake Pontchartrain or the Gulf Intracoastal Waterway and the Mississippi River transits the five-and-one-half-mile Industrial Canal and its narrow, 600-foot long lock running north-south about a quarter-of-a-mile below the Claiborne Avenue Bridge in New Orleans. The Canal was described as a "major link in the U. S. Inland Waterway System" and the lock accommodated 48,021 vessels during the previous year (1992).[258] The lock within the Canal has also been described as a "major bottleneck," damned by many a boatman, as shall be seen.

Empty, the 195x35-foot barge DM 3021 weighed 202 long tons and had a draft of about eighteen inches. The *Chris*, a small, conventional twin-engine towboat weighing eighty-three tons, was typical of the river vessels that move empty barges through the inland waterways of the United States. The towboat had a three-man operating crew: a licensed operator and two deckhands – Tom DuBois and Larry Demen. The operator in charge of the tow, forty-six-year-old Andrew Long, had twenty years' experience

209

transiting the inland waterways of Louisiana, including the Industrial Canal.

The two deckhands, hired by Bergeron Marine earlier that week, had not served aboard the *Chris* before, but each had more than two years' experience as a deckhand on tow or crew boats. Neither deckhand had worked with Captain Long before. The deckhands alternated standing six-hour watches. When the *Chris* tow left the Florida Avenue wharf, the off-duty deckhand, Larry Demen, went to the towboat's crew quarters, one deck below the wheelhouse.

Demen testified the *Chris'* captain told him to drain the engine's fuel traps "on every watch" because they had "picked up some dirty fuel....." According to DuBois, the then on-duty deckhand, the towboat engine seemed to be "in perfect running order" when it left Bergeron Marine. But then, he said, "the performance of the [starboard] engine went down [i.e., diminished]" shortly after 2:00 p.m. while they were moving the barge toward an area local mariners refer to as Saucer Marine. There, they would stand by and wait for access to the lock.

Gladys Duplessis, the Claiborne Avenue Bridge tender on duty that day, said towboats often idle in front of the bridge while waiting clearance to go through the locks. They are supposed to wait in front of a large concrete bumper in front of one of the bridge's two main supports, she said. The bumper, a barrier to keep towboats from hitting the bridge support, also is supposed to be a reminder to boats that they are not supposed to go between the bumper and the canal's embankment, said Leroy Farve, another bridge tender.[259]

Standard Operating Procedure (SOP) for boats using the lock was: call the lockmaster, get on a waiting list along with, at times, ten other tows seeking an estimated time of lock entry, and then just sit and wait – for even up to thirty-eight hours – while listening to be called on the ship's marine radio, Channel 14. Saucer Marine was a small marine repair firm, under contract with the Board of Commissioners of the Port of New Orleans, which owned the bank area, to provide such service to boats waiting to transit the Industrial Canal's lock.

Known officially as the Inner Harbor Navigation

The Claiborne vertical lift-bridge (foreground) and the Industrial Canal lock (background)

Canal (IHNC), the waterway is five-and-one-half miles long, intersecting the Mississippi River and the Gulf Intracoastal Waterway, and it also leads to New Orleans' famed Lake Pontchartrain. The lock is and was notorious throughout the commercial and even recreational boating world for its long delays on the waterways caused by its small size and the high volume of traffic exiting and entering the basically north-south oriented Mississippi River and the east-west Gulf Intracoastal Waterway. The Canal, a major waterway for coal, jet fuel and other bulk cargoes, would if closed, force ships to make a 130-mile, twenty-hour detour into the Gulf of Mexico and back up the Mississippi River to the Intracoastal Waterway.[260]

*   *   *

At about 2:30 p.m., Captain Long pushed the empty barge's bow aground and onto Saucer Marine's bank about 350 feet – little more than a football field's length – north of the Claiborne Avenue Bridge, a common practice. The bridge, opened to vehicular traffic in 1957 and one of seven over the five-plus-mile length of the canal, is officially named the Judge William Seeber Bridge, although many locals who regularly used it were unaware of that name. The Claiborne name came from William C. Claiborne, the first United States governor of Louisiana, after President Thomas Jefferson executed the Louisiana Purchase which ended France's control of the Pelican State in 1803. The bridge – carrying 38,000 vehicles a day in four traffic lanes, two in each direction on Louisiana Highway 39 – is a major thoroughfare in New Orleans.

After the push in, the *Chris'* starboard main engine continued to run rough. So, Captain Long told deckhand DuBois to go below and change the primary filter for that engine. With the towboat engines engaged ahead at one-fourth throttle to hold the tow to the bank, DuBois went to the engine room, shut down the starboard engine, and changed the primary filter "in about 5 minutes." After restarting the engine, he said "the captain pushed the throttle forward ...to see if the performance was better. The barge slid up onto the bank a little more, and he told me that he was still having problems with it...[and] I needed to change the secondary (filter)."

Meanwhile, another south-bound towboat, the *A.B. Barr*, with an empty tank barge, pushed in at Saucer Marine about 150 to 200 feet north of the *Chris*. The *A.B. Barr's* operator testified that the U.S. Army Corps of Engineers

(USACE, owner and operator of the lock) lockmaster instructed him to also move his tow up to the Saucer Marine site "between the bridges (Florida Avenue and Claiborne Avenue)." The *Barr* skipper could see the propeller wash coming from the *Chris'* stern, showing him that the latter boat was still in gear and pushing against the canal bank.

The *Chris* deckhand who was changing the secondary filter was "surprised" to see Captain Long come down to the engine room and say "he was going to give me a hand" because DuBois felt it was a simple, one-man job. While the deckhand was changing the secondary filter, the captain handed him a ratchet socket. When finished, they both went to the galley to wash up. All the while they were in the engine room, DuBois said the port engine was "engaged at low-idle speed."

(Because Captain Long, on advice of counsel, later refused to talk with Safety Board investigators, there is speculation that Long wanted to make sure his new crewman, DuBois, was doing the job right. The complacency factor – the captain had been through the Canal lock so many times under similar circumstances without incident that he felt perfectly secure in leaving the wheelhouse unattended – was also considered by investigators.)

While awaiting his turn to go through the Industrial Canal lock, the skipper of the *Barr* noticed that his tow was beginning to be pushed down along the bank by the gusting winds. Official weather records for the area at that time showed winds out of the east at nine- to twelve-knots per hour (10-14 miles-per-hour) with gusts up to seventeen (almost 20 mph) – hitting both south-facing boats on the port beam. The *Barr's* captain was able to maintain his position by adding engine speed to keep the barge and his boat wedged to the shoreline. But, he also noticed the *Chris* was starting to slide down towards the Claiborne Avenue

Bridge. When that boat's prop wash did not change, which would have indicated Long was taking the same action as he was to hold his position, he tried to call the other captain on the loud hailer (an exterior public speaker). Getting no response from the *Chris*, he sounded the *Barr's* whistle. By that time, he said, the *Chris'* tow swung around until it was parallel to the bank and started to drift down-stream toward the bridge at "less than a knot (1.15 miles per hour)."

Shortly after Captain Long and deckhand DuBois got to the *Chris'* galley to wash their hands, the skipper looked out a window and yelled that the boat was moving. He bolted out of the galley and ran for the wheelhouse where he put the engines in reverse. He was too late. DuBois said he felt "three hard bumps" that weren't, however, hard enough to affect his equilibrium. A watch-stander on the Coast Guard cutter *White Holly*, docked across the canal from the *Chris* and the *Barr*, said he heard "a loud rumble towards the bridge," about 3:30 p.m. "and saw a barge with a push tug [towboat] drifting toward the bridge near the opposite bank of the Industrial Canal." He next heard a loud bang that "sounded like a sledge hammer striking a piece of metal." The bridge began shaking, and a section of it collapsed. He said he then heard the towboat's engines revving in reverse at a high revolutions-per-minute. At the same time, the *Barr's* skipper was "very surprised" when the bridge collapsed because the *Chris* was moving so slowly and "barely bumped the bridge."[261]

The DM 3021 barge, with the towboat riding behind it in a 285-ton total load and no effective pier protection measures to block its path, drifted down-stream and ran into one of the columns supporting the Claiborne Avenue Bridge. The column twisted and broke, leading to the bridge's collapse along with a 145-foot section of the four-lane highway it supported. Ironically, Coast Guard spokes-man Tony Tangeman said he the tragedy might have been avoided if the barge had not been empty. The weight of cargo likely would have caused it to run aground before it reached the bridge, he said. "If [the barge had] have been full, he'd never have gotten that far."[262]

DuBois, who had been with the captain in the engine room and the galley, immediately ran forward to the front of the barge where he discovered a steel I-beam and huge chunks of the concrete roadway. He also found two cars that had dropped forty-five-feet. One was an upside-down stationwagon lying atop some of the concrete debris keeping it out of the water. In it he found fifty-two-year-old Alan Gonzales, and the one-year older Elton "T-Boy" Dinet, mechanic and forklift operator, respectively, who regularly drove to work and back together. One was injured and asking not to be removed because of the pain, and the other was alert though pinned in the car.

By now, off-duty deckhand Demen told local television station WDSU-TV, he had also come forward on the barge, jumped into the shallow water where he checked the other car, a sedan sitting on its side in about three feet of water. There, he found Cynthia Martin, a thirty-six-year-old New Orleans woman, also pinned in the wreckage. Her car lay on the driver's side in shallow water. Demen yelled to DuBois for help in getting Ms. Martin out. The two deckhands, with help from local tow-truck driver Thomas Moore who joined in and twisted his ankle in the rescue attempt, got her out and to the shore. There, Demen administered mouth-to-mouth resuscitation, but to no avail. She died at the scene.[263]

Ms. Martin, five months pregnant, was on her way to pick up her 18-month-old daughter, Shelby, from a baby sitter when she was killed. She was less than a mile from home and her husband, Larry. She bled to death after the crash impact severed her abdominal aorta, the body's main blood vessel, said Orleans Parish Coroner Dr. Frank Minyard. She probably died within two minutes and was not conscious. Marland Atkins, manager of an auto parts store where Ms. Martin worked, said she was scheduled to go on maternity leave the following Tuesday. She was off that Thursday and Friday because, Atkins said, "I just gave her two days off back to back so she could get some rest."[264]

As bad luck had taken Cynthia Martin, good luck was sitting on the shoulders of a number of regular bridge users. Warren Bourgeois had just sat down to get his hair cut by his cousin when he heard the bridge had collapsed. He had crossed it minutes earlier. "I couldn't believe it. I just couldn't believe it," Bourgeois said. He felt a last-minute decision to go directly to his cousin's house and not stop at the bank might have saved him. "I'm just glad I didn't go to the bank first, because I would have been a little later and I could have been on the bridge [when it collapsed]," he said.[265]

Lester Triche, Jr. was driving across the Claiborne Avenue Bridge and when he looked back, he saw two cars – one directly behind him and another headed in the opposite direction – "disappear." Triche is believed to have been the last person to make it across the bridge before the *Chris* and its barge struck it, sending the 145-foot section of four-lane roadway plummeting. "I just praise the Lord. I'm so happy to be here," a shaken Triche said.[266]

The Coast Guard crew and civilians who had seen what happened had already called 9/11 and first-responders from ten agencies were on scene in a matter of minutes. Tyrone Thornton, who lives nearby, said he "saw a big cloud of smoke and saw the bridge collapse. It vibrated the whole neighborhood." Then, Thornton said drivers slammed on their brakes, leaped out of their cars and ran back to warn people behind them on the bridge. Traffic on the bridge was halted almost immediately, unlike the other tragedies outlined in these pages – the Queen Isabella Causeway in Texas and the Interstate-40 highway in Oklahoma – where cars continued to run off the ends of bridges because the rising highways in front of the drivers didn't let them see the yawning gaps until it was too late to stop.

One witness said the allision with the bridge happened at 3:30 p.m. Official records show the Coast Guard had search and rescue (SAR) personnel with emergency medical kits on site shortly after 3:31 p.m. Some ambulances got stuck in the muddy ground along the canal, but rescue workers and bystanders pushed them free. Three Coast Guard cutters moored nearby sent boats to help people in the water. Dive teams searched the Industrial Canal for possible missing persons, and the Coast Guard dispatched two H-65 helicopters from its Air Station New Orleans to aid in the search effort. No other victims were found.

Two Emergency Medical Technician (EMT) units from the New Orleans Health Department were on scene by 3:41 p.m. Rescue efforts were hampered by the ever-building rush-hour and Memorial Day-weekend traffic backed up on Claiborne Avenue leading to the bridge. However, by 4:14 p.m., the EMT units had removed the two injured men in the station-wagon and had taken them down Route 39 to nearby Chalmette Memorial Hospital, where they arrived at 4:28 p.m.

*   *   *

All this quick response by emergency personnel was almost overshadowed by the botched job done in the toxicological testing required of a towboat's crew after such an event. Captain Long radioed the crew's employer, Bergeron Marine, within ten to fifteen minutes of the accident. Bergeron arranged for the crew to take the mandatory toxicological testing at the nearby Pendleton Memorial Methodist Hospital. Coast Guard investigating officers reported Captain Long showed "no signs of impairment" and he appeared to be "totally sober" immediately following the allision.

However, testing procedural misunderstandings arose. The Bergeron officials thought the Coast Guard would take drug and alcohol samples for marijuana, cocaine, opiates, phencyclidines (PCDs), and amphetamines; the Coast Guard thought the company would do it. One clinic's early closing hours and another being swamped with other emergency calls, resulted in the testing not being done until 11:00 p.m., seven-and-one-half hours after the incident – far too late to be conclusive.

Nonetheless, the investigating Safety Board said – in its June 7, 1994 report – the immediate cause was the "poor judgment" of Captain Long for leaving the wheelhouse of his unsecured towboat *Chris* for three to five minutes, allowing the barge to crash into the bridge.

"What" asked Lieutenant Chris Palmer, one of several Coast Guard investigators, "would a prudent mariner do under these same circumstances? Is it prudent for an individual to leave the wheelhouse unattended while either engine was still engaged? The clear answer is no," Palmer said.

Lieutenant John Manganaro, assistant chief of port operations for the Coast Guard, said towboat captains, with few exceptions, are supposed to be on the bridge when a vessel's engine is engaged.[267] "The captain had an excellent record," Carl Vogt, chairman of the safety board, said. "He was very well experienced and this was an apparent aberration kind of action on his part. In the context, (three to five minutes) didn't seem like much, but it's indicative of the kind of thing that can cause accidents."[268]

*   *   *

The board didn't stop its criticism there. Federal, state and local government agencies with jurisdiction over bridges were also chastised for failure "to institute an effective program for assessing and managing the risks to the bridge." Board members expressed surprise that the government agencies with responsibility for the 14,000 bridges in Louisiana apparently had not met since the accident to develop a strategy to improve safety. Chairman Vogt called that "unfortunate."

The Louisiana Department of Transportation and Development (LADOTD) was further singled out after some surprising testimony during the NTSB's investigation. When asked about LADOTD procedures to determine if bridges were vulnerable to vessel collisions and should be protected, the bridge maintenance officer testified: "We repair what is damaged. We do not enhance what's there," and he added, "If we know who damaged the bridge, then we bill them for it…." But when LADOTD has "a serious problem" and it can't identify who caused it, the agency doesn't always have funds of its own to fix the problem.

In the case of the Claiborne Avenue bridge, although inspection photographs show prior damage to the substructure and the bridge protection systems, the collisions were never reported. Consequently, that previous damage caused by marine vessels *was not repaired* [emphasis added].[269] In other words, if the LADOTD can't find someone to pay for damages to the bridges, then the bridges may not get repaired – at least not by using funds from the LADOTD – and then, apparently, only if another agency does have the funds to pay for the job! It should be noted that after the accident, the state did build a protective barrier, or "dolphin," around the column that was knocked out.

Further testimony revealed that when bridge inspectors see something they believe is critical, they notify their supervisors and then inform the maintenance foreman. If district maintenance crews cannot do the work, the maintenance foreman reports the condition to State maintenance headquarters in Baton Rouge. Headquarters then either schedules State crews to perform the repair or bid the project to independent contractors. (And this time-consuming bureaucratic process is for "critical" repairs.)

The Safety Board examined documents that showed from 1983 until 1992, the year before the *Chris* accident, the Claiborne Avenue Bridge fendering (barrier) system "was not performing the function for which it was intended and requires maintenance." This appears to refute the statement made by LADOTD Andrea Populus who said after the bridge's collapse that it was free of structural defects when it was inspected in December 1992.[270] Dennis Burke, district maintenance engineer for the LADOTD, said the rating given during the bridge's last bi-annual inspection "was not a bad one." He would not be more specific.[271] Good thing – otherwise, he may have had to explain how "bad" it was.

For some, it was no surprise that the bridge support failed when the *Chris* hit it while drifting down-stream at "less than one-knot-per-hour." Several spectators discussed the safety of the bridge. Leroy Garrison, who fishes in the canal, said he had been alarmed the day before the accident when he saw cracks in the bridge as he walked across it.[272]

Despite the fact that the NTSB report concluded "the bridge did not fail from a pre-existing structural problem," the report also stated the bridge "was vulnerable to vessel collisions because the approach piers were inadequately protected." Furthermore, vulnerability to vessel allisions was shown by the NTSB report to be not limited to the Claiborne Avenue Bridge nor to those other 14,000 bridges then in Louisiana. It was a nationwide problem, enhanced by the variety of then 576,000 bridge structures (up to 600,000 in 2007) and the ever-increasing amount of marine traffic on the nation's inland waterways.

The proof of this dilemma was catastrophically emphasized almost exactly four months later when the towboat *Mauvilla* "bumped" into the Big Bayou Canot railroad bridge near Mobile, Alabama, which led to a misalignment of the train tracks and sent forty-seven passengers and train crewmembers to their deaths – as discussed in the preceding chapter in this book.

*   *   *

Back a few paragraphs here, Coast Guard investigators suggested Captain Andrew Long was not being a prudent mariner when he left his wheelhouse unattended. Many mariners would completely agree with Lieutenant Palmer's assessment. It is amazing how quickly so many things can go wrong. For instance and just one case in a million: While tied up on an August mid-afternoon at a Mississippi River loading dock bringing product into some barges, a big "salty" came rumbling upriver. With this writer as a witness, he was going so fast and creating so much wake he nearly tore the tow loose from its moorings. An irate relief captain called the blue-water boat on the radiotelephone and told it to slow down because it had broken one steel mooring cable and another rope line. As ultimately harmless as this incident turned out, it also shows one of the many reasons a captain or a pilot has to be in the pilothouse at all times because in this case, for instance, suppose <u>all</u> the mooring lines had snapped?

Chapter X
For Some, "The Big Easy" Wasn't

In the early 1970s, the U. S. Coast Guard conducted an exhaustive study of vessel traffic service (VTS) needs for the nation's ports and waterways. According to this report (U. S. Coast Guard, 1973), the port of New Orleans in particular and the lower Mississippi River area in general, ranked first among the nation's ports in deaths and injuries and second in dollar loss resulting from vessel accidents.[273]

The following pages show a few reasons why.

*   *   *

When officially opening the world's then longest bridge – the twenty-four mile span across Lake Pontchartrain north of New Orleans, Louisiana – instead of merely cutting a ceremonial ribbon, the Greater New Orleans Expressway Commission should have painted a big, red bull's-eye on both sides of it. As a matter of fact, the good city fathers maybe shouldn't have waited for opening day in 1956 for the paint job. Marine collisions with the bridge began even before construction was complete. In October 1955, a towboat struck a piling and caused several sections of the bridge deck to collapse into the lake. Since then, fifteen other marine vessels have struck various parts of the bridge, according to Debbie Lopreore, Supervisor of Operations for the Greater New Orleans Expressway Authority.

"However, this does not mean that portions of the 24-mile twin roadways were knocked down that number of times," she cautioned.[274] In two of the collisions, nine persons died; six on June 16, 1964, and three on August 1,

1974. It got to the point where one editorial writer was comparing a trip across the bridge to Russian Roulette.[275] Another compared it to making a driver "feel like he's placing a $1 bet with the toll taker, gambling that he'll reach the other side alive."[276]

Lake Pontchartrain (and therefore, the Causeway) was named for the Count de Pontchartrain who served as minister of finance during the 18th Century reign of "*Le Roi Soleil*" (the "Sun King"), Louis XIV of France, for whom the entire state of Louisiana is named. The twin spans of the Causeway are made of pre-stressed panels supported by over 9,000 concrete pilings. The first span opened to the public in 1956, the second in 1969. Since the first bridge was opened in 1956, traffic volume has grown from approximately 3,000 vehicles each day, to over 3,500 vehicles during just one peak <u>hour</u>.

Two bridges – the North Pass Bascule at the sixteen-mile marker and the South Pass Fixed at the eight-mile marker – permit commercial and recreational marine traffic to pass. The mile-markers begin at the south end of the Causeway. For most people, the opening of the Causeway was a boon and a blessing as it cut the drive-time north and south into and out of the Big Easy by up to fifty minutes.

*   *   *

Clifford Milley wasn't looking to cut his travel time across Lake Pontchartrain on Thursday morning, June 16, 1964. But then again, Milley wasn't driving a car north or south across the Lake. He was driving a towboat – the *Rebel, Jr.* – westerly, pushing a derrick barge out in front and an empty shell barge lashed to the *Rebel*'s port side ("on the hip," in the vernacular). First Mate Milley took over the watch at 0030 hours from Captain Ned Palmer after they had pushed the boat, owned by the Ace Towing Company, and its two barges through the Industrial Canal and into the big lake (see "An Exercise in Poor Judgment" in Chapter IX).

It was such a clear night that there was no need to even use a $14.95 compass. The beacon at the bridge opening was guiding them on, a view unimpeded by the derrick on the barge looming forward. It was what every sailor hopes for: a night of "fair winds and a calm sea." It isn't always that way on the wide-open expanse of Lake Pontchartrain or other wide-water openings along the Intracoastal Canal.

"When you're driving a towboat and its barges east-west on the [GIWW] and the wind is blowing up from the Gulf of Mexico out of the south at 25-30 miles per hour, it can, according to towboat captain Simmey Brickhouse, "make it real rough and choppy. Your tow won't stay together. Weather's really not that bad when you're in protected water but when you get out there in that open water, it'll break your tow up." And when you throw a driving rainstorm into the mix, "it shuts the radar out," he advised. "You can't see. Then, it's just a case of stoppin' and landin' your tow on the bank 'til the weather clears up. I once had to stay on the bank for three days, which was mostly just waitin' for the weather to clear."

Such ugly conditions didn't exist for the *Rebel, Jr.*, as First Mate Milley pointed the bow of his barges left for that South Pass fixed bridge while Captain Palmer went below to get some sleep. Fifty-one-year-old deckhand Harold Robin had already found a napping place in an area just aft of the wheelhouse. The float plan was an easy trip through the Industrial Canal after leaving Louisiana Material Company and into the lake. About two miles west of the Causeway, the *Rebel, Jr.*'s three-man crew would drop off the empty barge, pick up a full one, and return home through the Industrial Canal. Normally, it was a two-hour trip or less.

There was only one problem. Just before reaching the Lake Pontchartrain Causeway, First Mate Clifford Milley fell sound asleep at the wheel!

*   *   *

For fifteen minutes or so after Palmer turned the wheel over to Milley, things went as planned. Milley made a routine ship-to-shore radio call to the Louisiana Material Company. He reported he was on course and headed straight for the Causeway in the direction of its South Pass Bridge.

At the same time, a Continental Trailways bus with thirty-eight-year-old Ernest N. Vaughn from Jackson, Mississippi at the wheel and seven mostly sleeping passengers on board was roaring north toward Jackson, on the Lake Pontchartrain Causeway. Vaughn and his bus were headed in the same direction as was the *Rebel, Jr.* Of the eleven people whose lives – and even deaths – were about to be entwined, Vaughn may have been the only one awake at that time on that morning.

That radio call to Louisiana Material was the last thing Milley said he remembered. According to the first mate's later testimony, he simply "passed out." He "didn't even feel the crash." [277] He said he didn't regain consciousness until he picked himself off the wheelhouse deck where he had fallen. It wasn't until after the lead barge – now three-quarters-of-a-mile north of the bridge opening – slammed into one of those 9,000 piers holding up the twenty-four-mile long Causeway. The impact tore out 224 feet of the north-bound roadway – the same roadway bus driver Vaughn was barreling north on – at the same unfortunate time.

At a subsequent hearing, Captain Palmer, with nineteen years in the towboat industry, theorized the tow was sixty-two degrees off course and had been traveling out of control for about forty-five minutes at the time of the accident. Assuming the controls had been left alone, Palmer said, the tow took a sweeping turn to the right, away from the South Pass opening, over a distance of several miles at an estimated speed of about eight knots. Speculation also said the tow's speed may have been increased by Milley's body falling across the throttle when he passed out. He himself similarly guessed his fall may have altered the tow's direction when he blacked out.[278]

*   *   *

On the bridge and above the water and the *Rebel, Jr.*, were bus-driver Vaughn and his seven sleeping passengers. At 1:30 on the morning of July 16, 1964, there was no highway traffic around him; just a towboat and two barges under him. As he drove north at what he called "normal" speed, his bright headlights were stabbing ahead into the darkness hovering over the 600-square-mile Lake Pontchartrain. Just as suddenly and unexpectedly as the towboat and its barges hit the piling, the highway beneath Vaughn and his bus dropped out from under them. As they went crashing into the black waters below, the driver felt the tow "hit the bridge just the same time as I was on it. I believe it did, because I remember seeing those big pillars twisting up and turning over."

What he also remembered was "the nose of the bus heading right into one of those big pillars. It must have hit something else because it threw me out of the bus. Undoubtedly," Vaughn continued, "that bridge was breaking in behind the bus all the time." The Trailways bus, its driver and his seven passengers were beyond the point of no return.[279] "The [towboat] and the barge," Vaughn recalled, "must have hit the bridge just at the time I got on it. It just fell out from under me all of a sudden. I never slowed, never touched the brakes or nothing. Just suddenly there wasn't any bridge."[280]

The impact of the bus smashing into the crumbled concrete sent Vaughn flying through the wide-screen front windows of his bus. "I went through the windshield before the bus ever hit the water," he said. "I tried to climb back up onto the bus but couldn't, because it was rolling the other way in the water." He also remembered (as folks put it back in 1964), "one boy – one man – came up [out of the water] the same time I did." That "one boy – one man" was long-time Army Staff Sergeant William Cockerham, who was headed to his home in Baton Rouge, Louisiana, from his base at Fort Benning, Georgia.

*   *   *

Back on the towboat, Captain Palmer was jolted from his bunk to the floor of his cabin, awakened by the boat's sudden stop, and the screams of Milley in the wheelhouse yelling to the captain, "For God's sake, get up here." The captain was in the wheelhouse in seconds where he found the first mate to be dazed at first and unresponsive to the captain's orders. Palmer immediately radioed the Coast Guard and nearby towboats *Patty H* and *Donald Roth*, seeking assistance. He called the draw bridge operator to halt traffic on the Causeway. That warning came in time but much too late for the Trailways bus. It was already in the water. He could hear some of the bus passengers in the water fighting for their lives and screaming for help.

Vaughn and Cockerham made it because of the heroics of the *Rebel, Jr.*'s deckhand Robin. Immediately after the crash, he grabbed the towboat's full complement of six life preservers and went forward on the lead barge, hoping to spot survivors. Jack Church of Mandeville, Louisiana – the northern terminus of the Lake Pontchartrain Causeway – and Bernard E. Gautreau of nearby

Abita Springs, were driving south along the roadway when they came upon the accident.

With little regard for their own safety, they both jumped into the water trying to save some of the bus passengers. Deckhand Robin was already in there trying to get some life preservers to those scrambling for safety. Milley wasn't with him because he couldn't swim. Gautreau said he too could hear the people in the water screaming. Church swam out to one of the men calling for help, but by the time he reached the man, it was too late. He was dead. Church and Gautreau did manage to reach bus driver Vaughn and Sergeant Cockerham and get life preservers to them. The four clung together until Coast Guard helicopters hovered overhead and lifted them out of the dark waters. Church and Gautreau were subsequently recommended for the Carnegie Medal Hero Award.

Another one of Vaughn's passengers on the bus was also heading home, this one to Lakewood, Ohio, to begin a new life. His name was George W. Broa, who had had his scrapes with the law, dating back a couple of years. He ended up in jail in the Louisiana State capital of Baton Rouge, where he was ultimately being held as a material witness in an inmate murder case. On Monday evening, June 15, 1964, Broa was finally released from prison. A kindly municipal clerk worked overtime just to get his papers cleared so he could catch the 9:30 p.m. bus out of Baton Rouge and connect with a 1:00 a.m. bus out of New Orleans. He made the connection in plenty of time as he contemplated returning home to his wife and daughter in Ohio. The last thing he did before climbing aboard the bus was to telephone his wife and joyfully tell her that he was finally on his way back. That bus out of the Big Easy was the one being driven by Ernest Vaughn.

The bus driver and the army sergeant escaped.

These poor souls did not:
George W. Broa, 54, Lakewood, Ohio
Willie C. Matthews Jr., Negro,[8] 20, Bogalusa, Louisiana
Charles Perrone, 54, Chicago, Illinois
Michael Clayton Schultz, 22, Manchester, New Hampshire
William Ellis Wilson, 20, Prentiss, Mississippi
(One other victim, was a Negro woman, who still had not
been identified by state police late the night of the crash.)[281]

*   *   *

In the words of author Lewis Carroll, things got "curiouser
and curiouser" and it seemed more and more like "Alice in
Wonderland" at a future investigative hearing. But this,
however, was no tea party. Despite First Mate Milley's
claim that he "blacked-out" prior to crashing into the
Causeway, Captain Ned Palmer said he had never known
the first mate to suffer black-out or fainting spells.
Conversely, the captain said Milley always appeared to be
in good physical health. Even the third member of the crew,
Harold Robin, testified that Milley appeared to be "a very
healthy man." With the man at the wheel apparently having
had a good seven-and-one-half hour sleep before returning
to duty on June 15, the possibility of him blacking out
because of sleep deprivation was dismissed.

Yet, equally as curious were some of the revelations
about Captain Palmer. Despite his nineteen years as a
boatman and four years on the *Rebel, Jr.*, Palmer told
investigators that he never was licensed to captain
Uninspected Towing Vessels – certification needed to show
he was capable of commanding a towboat![282] Or even a
rowboat. Not only that, but he also said he didn't know

---

[8] This is how racial identities were reported in 1964 in Louisiana – as
well as in much of the rest of the country at that time.

230

how to plot a course and he couldn't give a definition for something as basic in navigation as magnetic north!

In defense of Palmer's position, many towboat pilots scoff at having to "plot a course." Some of them, when talking about the requirement that they attend a Radar Certification School where one of the necessities for classroom passage is the need to "plot a course," sneeringly agree that none of them has ever plotted a course on "brown water." As one of them said of course plotting, "that's totally useless to us." They just "go from Point A to Point B and stay between the lines (channel markers)."

Another revelation came to light in an alarming bit of prescience just three months before the *Rebel, Jr.* plowed into the Lake Pontchartrain Causeway. Herman Nebel, chairman of the American Waterways Operators' Regional Bridge and Lock Committee, noted that "the causeway was a modern day marvel in rapid construction, but because of the type of construction, it will always be vulnerable to marine accidents. Constructed as it is, in separate concrete slab sections sitting atop un-braced concrete piles, the structure has a match stick effect that could prove disastrous any time a vessel comes into contact with it."

This was immediately rebutted by the Great New Orleans Expressway Commission via a letter written by Maurice N. Quade, senior partner for the Causeway's consulting engineers' firm. Quade said, "Nebel's charge that the bridge was 'constructed in separate concrete slab sections sitting atop un-braced concrete piles,' is completely without foundation fact and completely misleading to the public. Of course," Quade contended, "it is constructed in sections. Anyone who attempted to build a continuous bridge 24 miles long would find himself confronted with a bridge that grew 50 feet in the summer and shrunk 50 feet in the winter. The 'match stick effect' is completely absent and an erroneous analogy."[283]

*   *   *

Another of those incidents giving the New Orleans' waterways their dubious first-place ranking among the nation's ports in marine deaths, in addition to the towboat *Chris'* crash into the Claiborne Street Bridge (covered in Chapter IX herein), was the allision involving the towboat *Miss Andy*. In what could be called another "Sleeping Beauty" accident, the captain of that tow fell asleep at the wheel and his barges crashed into the Lake Pontchartrain Causeway a mere 300 feet from the exact spot hit by the *Rebel, Jr.* ten years previously. The circumstances were eerily similar.

On the morning of August 1, 1974, forty-seven-year-old Captain Ronald Duet took the wheel from crewman Larry Stelly at 0230 and the towboat *Miss Andy* headed west on the Lake, just as was First Mate Milley on the *Rebel, Jr.* Both boats followed the same track; through the Industrial Canal, out into the Lake, and a left-turn toward a bridge opening. Both pilots had excellent weather conditions in the dark of night. Both towboats were pushing two barges. Duet had his tow lined up to pass under one the Causeway's "humps" (rises in the roadway surface above the water to let low-profile boats pass under without the need of a draw- or a bascule-opening). And then, about a mile-and-one-half away from the Causeway opening, Duet also went unconscious.

Just like Milley, he did not wake up until the impact of his tow with the Causeway jolted him from his pilot's seat to the floor of the wheelhouse. Both boats had the same crew complement with Captain Duet, mate Stelly, and deckhand David Knott, being aboard the *Miss Andy*. These two allisions were almost carbon copies. The most important difference between the two accidents a decade apart was, although six people died in the *Rebel, Jr.*

incident, the fatality count was three in that of the *Miss Andy*.

The three who died were motorists Tazille Charles Madison, Edgar E. Dillon, and his brother Wallace. All three were from New Orleans and their two vehicles – the brothers in a pickup truck and Madison in his car – crashed fifty-five feet to the lake through the 252-foot hole in the road after the bridge was rammed. Further devastation was halted when a southbound motorist who had passed the north-bound scene told the next toll-taker who was able to get the Causeway closed. It was also fortunate that traffic was light during those early morning hours.

It was later surmised that Madison's car drove into the abyss first, followed right behind by Dillon's truck. Madison's and Edgar Dillon's bodies were recovered from the wreckage shortly after daybreak by divers. Wallace Dillon's body was not found until two days later when cleanup crews found the nineteen-year-old pinned under concrete slabs.

*   *   *

Another big difference between the two situations came during Coast Guard hearings to consider the revocation of Captain Duet's operator's license. Testimony by both Stelly and Knott characterized the company owning the *Miss Andy*, American Tugs, Inc., as "a loosely-run outfit lacking clearly defined lines of communication and duties for crewmembers and with no set work or watch schedules.

Both said that when they were hired (Knott was hired only a week earlier) they were not told of any specific duties they were to perform or at what time of day they were to perform duties.... Stelly said watch duties for him and the captain ran as much as twelve hours at a stretch....with no accounting for the number of hours worked in a given day. Knott testified his workday averaged thirteen to fourteen hours.... Asked if a crew of three was sufficient to handle the boat's work load, Knott said three was "not enough."[284]

Such assertions may have been one of the reasons why both Captain Duet and the American Tug's company president – on the advice of counsel – took the Fifth Amendment at that Coast Guard investigation. The hearing examiner, Lieutenant Junior Grade Richard C. Wigger, informed both Duet and Autry J. Dufrene, president of American Tugs, Inc., that the Coast Guard would take future action to make them testify.

The Coast Guard's investigating officer at the accident scene, Lieutenant Junior Grade Terry L. Rice, was there within ninety minutes. Accompanied by a sheriff's deputy, he boarded the *Miss Andy*. While questioning the towboat's skipper, Rice felt Duet looked "very nervous" and "like he had been up a while."[285] The Coast Guardsman then read the captain his Miranda Act rights, and arrested him. Duet was charged and released later that day after posting bond on two counts of negligent homicide and one count of reckless operation of a motor vehicle.

Conversely, shipmate Stelly had nothing but praise for the captain's actions following the crash. After being knocked out of his bunk by the force of the early morning crash and rushing to the wheelhouse, he testified that Duet "knew what he was doing" in securing his vessel, informing authorities and setting up methods of signaling causeway motorists of the danger in their path. "He did a lot more than I would," said Stelly, with five years' experience on the water, and five months as a licensed pilot.

He continued, saying "I would have panicked. The captain was nervous, but I was shocked." The mate further said of his captain, "He's the first man (superior) I ever got along with on a boat"[286] The hearings and subsequent criminal trial evolved into not only charges against Duet, but also about seamen's working conditions at American Tug, Inc. At times, it got ugly.

On September 19, 1964, U. S. Coast Guard Administrative Law Judge Archie Boggs – based on the previous hearings conducted by hearing examiner, Lieutenant Junior Grade Wigger – revoked Captain Duet's license to command towboats. The towboat skipper had previously sought to stop that hearing, claiming he had not been administered his Miranda rights, that when questioned at the scene of the accident he was still in a state of shock, and that he was coerced into signing a statement saying he had "fallen asleep" at the wheel.

The judge said the captain failed to navigate his vessel cautiously, leading *Miss Andy* and tow into a collision with the Pontchartrain Causeway. Duet's attorneys immediately announced they would appeal the ruling. Two weeks later, a New Orleans district attorney brought charges of negligent homicide in the death of Tazille Charles Madison only against Duet, even though a local grand jury failed to agree on such an indictment.

A trial was held in New Orleans. It lasted only one day and was heard by a five-man jury on December 12, 1974. Duet's attorneys argued their client didn't "fall asleep" at the wheel; they said he "passed out" from overwork and exhaustion, brought on by the demands of his employer, the America Tug company. The prosecutors counter-claimed that immediately following the accident, Duet stated orally and signed a document admitting he had "fallen asleep." The defense's rebuttal was the captain was a native-born Cajun who had difficulty understanding and expressing himself in English. They also claimed a "black out" cannot be prevented while blame can be attached to merely "falling asleep."

Duet's claim of overwork was seconded by defense witnesses, Duet's fellow crewmembers Stelly and Knott. Prosecutors shot back saying he could have resisted such demands. The captain then stated and his crewmen agreed; if they did reduce their work schedules, they felt they would be "fired and blackballed" by their employer from further towboat employment. When asked why the *Miss Andy* was operating with only a three-man crew when Coast Guard regulations said four crewmen were the minimum for such boats, Duet answered that American Tug hired his crews and he had to live with its decisions.

The prosecution's summation said Duet "wasn't fit to handle that boat..." and his actions were those of a "grossly negligent" towboat captain. The five-man jury took just two hours to reach a decision. It was unlike that of its predecessor grand jury. Captain Roland J. Duet was found guilty of negligent homicide in the death of Tazille Charles Madison.

One week later, on December 19, 1974, Duet's sentence for negligent homicide was handed down. He was sentenced to the maximum, five years in jail. However, the judge then suspended the sentence and fined the former skipper of the *Miss Andy* $500 and court costs.

Case closed.

*   *   *

Ten years after Clifford Milley and the *Rebel, Jr.* crashed into the Lake Pontchartrain Causeway in 1964, an editorial writer stated, "the Greater New Orleans Expressway Commission, [was] considering an alarm system designed to activate and warn motorists instantly of any break in the twenty-four-mile bridge. To our knowledge, this system of battery-powered amber and red lights was never installed.

236

Though such a device may not have saved the motorists in [the *Miss Andy* disaster] it was conceivable that other drivers, unaware of the circumstances, could have plunged into the hole in the causeway before authorities had time to seal off the danger area." The writer continued by saying, "The commission may claim economic considerations preclude further expenditures, but safety must be given priority and cannot be compromised."[287] It might behoove any concerned Causeway driver to see if that priority has yet – almost forty years later – been addressed.

In its infinite bureaucratic wisdom, another Pelican State government agency developed a plan to "prevent causeway rammings" by putting a Coast Guard patrol boat out on a 24/7-basis to ward-off would-be causeway crashers. Evidently, nobody told those deep-thinkers the Lake Pontchartrain Causeway is twenty-four miles across nor had they figured out how to get that patrol boat from the north end of the Lake to south end to ward-off a vessel there on a collision course. Furthermore, local officialdom had still another "solution." A general phone number was issued to be used by the public if and when anyone saw a boat off course.[288]

Still another collision-avoidance proposal was discussed in April of 1969. In authorizing a future meeting but failing to set a date for it, the New Orleans Dock Board took note of a system of radar or fog towers that were installed in some parts of Europe. These devices would take over ships as soon as they approached the Crescent City and control them until they leave. This apparently turned out to be another proposal still awaiting further consideration forty-years later.

The Louisiana Legislature did finally take some steps – fourteen years after the *Miss Andy* became the second towboat to ram the Causeway causing fatalities. Effective July 14, 1988, it passed and the Governor signed into law Louisiana Act (1988) No. 552, regulating navigational safety near the Lake Pontchartrain Causeway Bridges.

Key features of this Act:

1. Require all tugs, towboats, self-propelled dredges, jack-up barges, jack-up rigs and all self-propelled vessels of one hundred net tons or greater, or one hundred feet in overall length or greater, and all vessel flotillas of one hundred aggregate net tons or greater operating on Lake Pontchartrain to be equipped with Loran C Equipment suitable for use with the Lake Pontchartrain Collision Avoidance Warning System (CAWS); [Author: Loran C has since been superseded in maritime circles and elsewhere by the Global Positioning System.]

2. Establish a "prohibited zone" paralleling each side of the entire length of the Lake Pontchartrain Causeway Bridge and extending outward for a distance of one mile from the easterly and westerly outboard sides of the causeway bridge twin spans;

3. Prohibit [with certain exceptions] all privately-owned vessels within the classes listed in paragraph (1), above, from entering, navigating, mooring, or anchoring in any manner within the "prohibited zone;"

4. Provides for the assessment of a civil penalty in the amount of up to $1,000 per vessel per violation against the owner, operator, or charterer of any vessel within the classes listed in paragraph (1), above, which impermissibly enters the "prohibited zone," or which enters the "prohibited zone"

without the Loran C equipment required by
the Act....

At its regular meeting on October 4, 1988, the
Greater New Orleans Expressway Commission adopted
rules and guidelines for the administration and enforcement
of Act No. 552.[289]

[Author's note: As far as our research has shown,
there have not been any *deadly* towboat allisions with the
Lake Pontchartrain Causeway since the enactment of Act
No. 552. Still, in that typical act of "legislation by
tombstones," many wonder what any of Act No. 552 would
do to have stopped Captain Duet – or any of the other pilots
in similar situations noted in these pages – from "blacking
out" and ramming bridges.]

*   *   *

Chapter XI
A Classic Failure to Communicate

To many people, Kenneth H. Scarbrough was known as a "perfect gentleman" and a "prince of a man." Those who knew him saw him as one who "always did more than his own share." They called him a "perfect gentleman who never used profanity [and a] devoted religious and family man." Others saw him as "the kind of guy you lived to work with. He was soft-spoken, and very calm in hazardous situations," He was well-liked and skillful, "a wonderful man, very neat, and a man who lived for his family." And, remembered one co-worker, even on the hottest days in the sultry confines of New Orleans and the lower Mississippi River, he always wore a suit and tie.[290]

But what he ultimately became most remembered for showed up in an extreme act of heroism that saved "The Big Easy" from a fate rivaling that of the Great Chicago Fire of 1871. This time, it wasn't Mrs. O'Leary's cow kicking over an oil lantern and setting a whole city ablaze. It was a horrendous collision between a Chinese Nationalist freighter and a towboat pushing three barges containing 27,000 barrels of crude oil on April 6, 1969. It turned the Mississippi River into a spectacular towering inferno with flames leaping more than 150 feet in the air and threatening to do the same to New Orleans as that old cow did to the Windy City. And it turned Kenneth H. Scarbrough into an undeniable hero. Unfortunately, his heroism had to be recognized posthumously. And with some questions.

*   *   *

Terms in the marine world get confusing, just as they do in many other occupations. For instance, there's a "pilot" and then, there's a "pilot." Both have different meanings. The first definition of a "pilot" in the towboat world is the person who shares command and control of a towboat with the "captain" during its normal working conditions. This "pilot" backs up and relieves the captain on a shift basis, keeping in mind, of course, that the captain never relinquishes his overall command of the boat. Willie Odom on the *Mauvilla* and David Fowler on the *Brown Water V* – whose stories appear elsewhere in these pages – were towboat pilots.

Then, there's another kind of nautical "pilot" (not to be confused with the airplane pilot) whose job it is to bring the big "blue water" vessels from their deep-ocean surroundings into the ever-changing, narrow channels of "brown water." In the Greater New Orleans shipping area, these pilots are ferried 100 miles or so down to the mouth of the Mississippi River and into the Gulf of Mexico. There they climb aboard the big ocean-going freighters and tankers and take over the helm. Then, with their local knowledge of the waterway's conditions, these pilots are better able to steer those ships up the twisting, turning, shoaling channels of the Big Muddy to the Port of New Orleans and even further on to Baton Rouge, Louisiana. These pilots also make the same trips in reverse. Captain Kenneth H. Scarbrough was such a pilot.

*   *   *

As noted elsewhere in these pages, it is believed by some towboat captains that bridges over rivers are placed in some of the "ungodliest" places. When pressed for specifics, they will often cite the Eads Bridge over the Mississippi River at St. Louis, Missouri which, one said, should be marked as "a hazard to navigation." Records show that just about every

242

bridge over the Lower Mississippi has been hit by water traffic at one time or another. Those bridges crossing the river in the vicinity of its many sharp bends – such as at Baton Rouge, Louisiana – where the upper bridge is considered one of the worst because it's so close to a sharp bend – and those at Greenville and Vicksburg, Mississippi – are particularly hazardous because of obstructed views and swift current forced by a bending river.

And there's no place where the Mighty Mississippi bends more, it seems, than when it flows past New Orleans, Louisiana. In the course of just a few short miles, that river will cover every single one of the 360 points on a compass. If you can imagine a horizontal roller-coaster, you can see the Mississippi as it flows by The Big Easy.

(The down-bound river flow here is from left to right.)

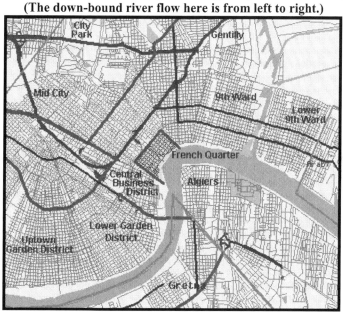

Just above the Greater New Orleans Bridge (lower center) is where the freighter *Union Faith* and the towboat *Doucet* met.

In the first day of 1969's Daylight Saving Time and in fading twilight of Easter Sunday on April 6 at about 1915 hours, Captain Scarbrough piloted the freighter *Union Faith* up the Mississippi River heading for a berth at the Public Commodity Warehouse Wharf in the Port of New Orleans. His destination was about three miles up-river from the Greater New Orleans Bridge. The ship – 503 feet long, 64 feet wide and weighing 9,391 tons – moved along under 6,300 diesel-engine horsepower. Owned by the China Union Lines, Ltd. in New York City, the ship had Taiwanese registration out of Keelong, Formosa. It's cargo hold was filled with high-density baled cotton, paper rolls, rubber footwear, plastic flowers, plywood sheets, sodium chloride, toys, handbags, and other household goods – all destined for American markets.

At that very same time, the sixty-five-foot towboat *Warren J. Doucet* (owned by Warren J. Doucet, Inc., headquartered in New Orleans' neighbor city Galliano) assisted by the tug *Cay & Mitch*, came down-river pushing three tank-barges. The tow's initial destination had been up-river to Baton Rouge but even with an assist from the *Cay & Mitch*, the *Warren J. Doucet* and its barges, with each barge loaded with 9,000 gallons of crude oil, was barely able to gain ground to the river's current. So the company ordered the *Doucet* to reverse course and head back down-river where it could, via the Intracoastal Waterway, take a lengthy but quicker detour to Baton Rouge.

Thus the tow was preceding down-river along its right bank and going past New Orleans on the Algiers side of the river, headed northerly for the next bend. Just as it passed under the Greater New Orleans Bridge, the tow was angled across to the left side of the river, positioned to take the bend ahead close to the French Quarter shore side. The twenty-seven-year-old *Union Faith* was going up the right side of the river hugging Algiers Point, one of the deepest parts of the Mississippi. Both ships were in keeping to local maritime "points and bends" custom. (The winding river through New Orleans almost makes all directions confusing, as shown vividly on the map on page 243.)

As darkness approached on that clear evening – one hour later than the previous day because of the inaugural of DST – and with at least a ten-mile visibility range, the *Doucet* skipper – his radar on but not needed nor monitored – visually spotted the running lights on the *Union Faith* as it came around Algiers Point. It is unknown if the *Union Faith* was using its radar, but the fully-loaded barges being pushed by the *Doucet* would have been an extremely tough target for a radar to pick up because they were riding only a foot or so above the water. What is known is that what happened next was a lesson-learning example of a classic failure to communicate.

The towboat industry, like all commercial interests on the waterways, does a good job in keeping up with technology – especially navigational regulations and gadgetry. Sometimes it does seem like overkill when the federal authorities hand down rules "from on high." A couple of captains this writer sailed with were talking about "asinine" rules that mandate attendance at a Radar Certification School where one of the requirements there for passage is the need to "plot a course."

As noted earlier herein, their gripe was that course-plotting is only done on "blue water" and no one has ever plotted a course on "brown water." As one of them said, "That's totally useless to us." Another case in point is the previously-cited requirement that all commercial vessels have a compass in the wheelhouse. Why is a compass needed to transit, for instance, the Illinois River? Thus, it also seemed "asinine" to be on a multi-million-dollar towboat with its Coast Guard-mandated compass in the wheelhouse – that infamous $14.95 compass purchased in an auto parts store mentioned in Chapter VIII herein – just to be in compliance.

On the other hand, most boats on the Inland Waterways today have upgraded equipment, such as day-display radars, color radars, better depth sounders, better swing indicators, and electronic navigational charts. Because of these electronic charts, steersmen no longer have to depend solely on eye-balling channel-marking buoys (or picking them up with their searchlights in the dead of night). The charts tell them exactly where the buoys are supposed to be – even if they have been washed off station by a storm or an allision with a boat.

The charts come with overlays that show the waterways in almost all conceivable stages. There's hardly a towboater out there today who doesn't have his own cell-phone with personal communications account such as Facebook, Twitter, LinkedIn and other means of keeping in touch with the home-front. Global Positioning Systems (GPS) are almost as common. FAX communication between ships and the home office are in abundance. The industry has come a long way since Samuel Langhorne Clements came downstream on a paddle-wheeler calling, "By the mark, Twain" – an old boatman's cry for measuring a safe depth (twelve feet) of a river.

Unfortunately, back in 1969 and without many of these present-day navigational advancements, it was a total failure of communication between two ships' wheelhouses – even by the most rudimentary means (a VHF radio, a bullhorn, or even a manual loud-hailer of the type used by cheerleaders at football games) – that led to the disaster near the Greater New Orleans I-90 high bridge in plain sight of New Orleans' *Vieux Carre*.

*   *   *

With the *Doucet* and its three-man crew making its way down-river and approaching the blind big bend at Algiers Point, normal procedure required a radio call on the marine working Channel 16 to alert all vessels in the area saying it was coming around the bend on the "two-whistle" (left/port) side of the river. The master of the *Doucet*, using voice radio, made such a call on Channel 16 at 2738 kilohertz (kHz) radio frequency just before starting his cross from the starboard side to the port side of the river. It was the same channel and frequency that was heard on both the *Doucet* and the *Cay & Mitch* as the *Union Faith* contacted other towboats further up-river.

For some unknown reason, Captain Scarbrough on the *Union Faith* at some point evidently switched transmitting – and receiving – channels. Using his portable transceiver, he then broadcast his vessel's required intentions on Channel 13, operating on the 156.65 megahertz (Mhz) frequency, as he had previously done on Channel 16 with the other down-bound vessels that had just passed him on his starboard side, such as the *SS President* and the towboat *Mama Lear*. [291] As a consequence, with the *Doucet* calling on Channel 16 and the *Union Faith* now operating on Channel 13, neither ship's advance warning of intentions was heard in either pilothouse.

The *Union Faith* swung southward around Algiers Point and the *Warren J. Doucet* proceeded northerly beyond the vast Greater New Orleans Bridge (now known as the Crescent City Connection and the fifth longest cantilevered bridge in the world) that tied the city's business district to the lower Algiers community. The freighter was just three miles, only twenty minutes, away from its destination at the Warehouse Wharf. At that point, even without knowing it, both boats were in the clear. But, for some still unknown reason, the *Union Faith* altered its course to starboard, to the opposite side of the river, where the *Doucet* was.

The two boats were then clearly on that most dreaded of all maritime situations – a collision course. They were only about one-and-one-half miles apart and closing fast with the *Faith* barreling up-stream at a reported ten-knots-per-hour (11.5 mph). Very quickly, the *Doucet* skipper blew two rapid blasts on his ship's whistle, again proposing a starboard-to-starboard passing but he received no reply.

Unfortunately, the wind was blowing out of the north at seven-miles-per-hour against the *Doucet* and may have impeded the whistle's effectiveness. What did happen next is quoted directly from the U. S. Coast Guard's Marine Casualty Report of the incident:

> When the vessel had closed to approximately one-half mile, personnel aboard the *Warren J. Doucet* noted, by the changing aspect of the *Union Faith*'s navigation lights, that the freighter was altering her course to her starboard and her bearing remained constant. The master of the *Doucet* sounded another two-blast signal and again received no reply. Following the second signal, the rate of change of the *Union Faith*'s course to her right increased. Realizing that collision was imminent, the master of the *Warren J. Doucet* turned his searchlight on the lead barge, sounded four blasts of the whistle, and placed his vessel's engines full astern. The *Union Faith* also sounded a danger signal and put her engines full astern. The speed of the *Union Faith* had been reduced to about 5.5 knots about 5 minutes before the order for dead slow (about 3 knots) which was in effect approximately 2 minutes before the danger signal was sounded. The stem of the *Union Faith*

penetrated the starboard side of *I.O.C. 7* [the lead barge in the *Doucet's* tow] at an angle of about 45° at a point about one-third the length from the bow of the barge.[292]

In its analysis of the collision, the U. S. Department of Transportation said it was "likely that the collision would have been avoided had the pilot of the *Union Faith* ordered full astern in lieu of dead slow; however, he did not do so until collision was imminent."[293] Just as the <u>*Doucet*</u> did in reversing its engine, so too did its assisting towboat, the *Cay & Mitch.* Even with their combined 1,400 horsepower, they couldn't back out of harm's way.

Thus, there was only one good thing to come out of the above narrative. Of the three tank barges – the *I.O.C. 7,* the *TM 113,* and *LB 19,* all properly displaying their navigational running lights – the *I.O.C. No.7* was the only one of the three barges, each filled with 9,000-gallons of crude oil being pushed by the *Doucet,* to explode. The ensuing mixture of tragedy and triumph was immense. The U. S. Coast Guard Marine Board of Investigation that convened in New Orleans on April 10, 1969 and is cited above, concluded that bridge personnel on the *Union Faith* did not detect the tow until the collision was unavoidable.

The acknowledged problem with that analysis was that there could be no rebuttal from the bridge personnel on the *Union Faith.* Every one of them was lost – including river pilot Scarbrough – in the conflagration that consumed the *I.O.C. 7* and the freighter.

The freighter impaled the tank barge just after the *Cay & Mitch,* sensing the impending disaster, cut loose from the tow. In so doing, the Cat's engines were fouled by hawsers hanging over the side, leaving it inoperative and unavailable to help as it had to be beached on the bank. Meanwhile, the highly volatile 9,000 gallons of crude oil in the *I.O.C. 7*, ignited by sparks produced by the shearing of the deck and side of the barge, burst skyward like the end of a Fourth of July fireworks program with cannon booming to close Tchaikovsky's "1812 Overture."

Within two minutes, there was a small explosion, immediately followed by several larger ones and flames immediately enveloped both the forward end of the freighter and the barge completely. The ensuing fire lit up the New Orleans sky for the next seven hours.

Exploding and spraying flaming crude oil all over the bow of the *Union Faith* and turning the river into the fires from Hell, the struck barge immediately broke in two

**The *Union Faith* is a blazing inferno before sinking
in the Mississippi River at New Orleans with the
World Trade Center looming in the background.**

and, most fortunately, separated itself from the rest of the tow.

Burning furiously, the two parts of the *I.O.C. 7* and the *Union Faith* drifted down-river and back under the Greater New Orleans Bridge where an heroic crew aboard a city fire boat kept encircling and containing the burning barge pieces despite dense smoke and encompassing flames until they sank in ninety feet of river water. The freighter, now nothing but a floating, flaming hulk abetted by its highly combustible cargo and its wooden deck hatches and tarpaulins, started drifting toward the shorelines of New Orleans.

There, citizens by the hundreds clambered almost on each others' back for a better view of what could have been their very own doom. They were in the direct path of the ship, covered in crude oil and now nothing but a roaring inferno, as it drifted toward the wharfs lining the river.

It was under these dire conditions that Captain Kenneth H. Scarbrough saved the lives of untold hundreds but lost his own in the effort. Known as a prudent skipper, Scarbrough, as usual, had his ship's anchors "on the brake," ready to drop. The captain, probably still "very calm in a hazardous situation" and still at the helm of the *Union Faith*, surely recognized what could have been a shore side conflagration of immense magnitude.

His final order, given shortly after the last explosion, was for the *Union Faith* to drop its anchors. The two anchors went down, slowing the flaming vessel somewhat in its path toward possibly even greater destruction. And Captain Scarbrough was never seen alive again. The people of New Orleans may well remember the late Captain Kenneth H. Scarbrough as the brave and solitary man who saved the city's wharves from fiery destruction.[294]

Captain Kenneth Davis, another river pilot and a friend of Scarbrough, said he heard him calling for help over the radio shortly after the collision. "He probably had a good chance to get off that ship," said Davis and he added that Scarbrough probably would not have left the ship until it and all the men were safe. "He was that kind of a person," Davis said.[295]

Another hero – and there were many in the saving of the city – was Captain Douglas Grubbs, skipper of the tug boat *Cappy Bisso*. His action in hooking one of his ship's hawsers to one of those chains from an anchor dropped by Scarbrough helped keep the *Union Faith* from dragging and drifting into the waterfront areas. New Orleans fireboats extinguished the two burning sections of tank barge *I.O.C. 7* before they sank and before they could spread the fire ashore.

Other towing vessels and pilots moved thirteen moored vessels along the downstream docks, in a precautionary measure to keep the crude oil burning on the water from reaching the facilities on the shore. Thus, according to the Coast Guard report, prior emergency planning, fortuitous circumstances, and timely coordinated action by many waterfront personnel averted a potential major fire on-shore.[296]

Such good planning and good luck was not, however, to be the fate for twenty-five of the fifty-one seamen aboard the freighter. The intense flames and pungent smoke blocked the usual routes of escape from some in the crews' quarters where many were changing their clothes and getting ready for shore leave at the time of the collision. Several sailors escaped through portholes to the deck, and jumped overboard into flaming waters seventy-five feet in circumference around the *Faith*. The tremendous loss of life was attributed to the victims, one who was just visiting from another ship, being trapped by the fire and smoke in their quarters, as well as in the engine room and on the bridge. Even more would have been lost but for the rescue efforts of the crews of the towing vessels *McGrath II* and *Cappy Bisso*.

With the *Union Faith* adrift and burning like a prairie wild fire, those seamen who weren't trapped on the bridge or below decks, found their way to the ship's fantail where they dove overboard. Others climbed down ropes and slipped into the flaming cauldron. It was a classic out-of-the-frying-pan-into-the-fire as the exit from the burning ship was an entrance into the burning river. Moving through some gaps in a river ablaze with oil, two tug boats rescued at least twenty of the twenty-six Chinese seamen known to have survived the fiery collision.

Chris A. Rieder, captain of the tug *McGrath II*, and his deckhand, Bill Arbuckle, rescued four of those men. In the intense heat, they moved to the side of the burning ship three times to assist the tug *Cappy Bisso* as Captain Douglas Grubbs and his six crewmen maneuvered their ship in the rescue effort. Rieder got the *McGrath II* under way as soon as he heard the whistle blasts from the *Union Faith* and the *Doucet* signaling danger. Even though he could hear the men screaming aboard the freighter, the smoke and flames prevented Grubbs aboard the *Cappy Bisso* "from seeing any part of the ship except a part that had turned cherry red from the flames," he said. "You could almost see through the steel plates." Rieder went on to say, "I prayed and I prayed, not only for myself and my crewman but for the screaming seamen aboard that burning ship."[297]

One of the *Union Faith's* Chinese crewmen, Yu Fang Fan, escaped from the electricians' room by breaking windows and crawling through the window frames. "There was no air. We just sat down and waited to die," was the way Yu said he felt before he discovered an escape route.[298] The *Faith* continued to burn furiously. It began taking on a port list and started sinking by the bow. At approximately 0145, on April 7, 1969, with the main decks forward awash, the *Union Faith* rolled over on her port side and remained in that position, still burning, until 0200 when she sank in a position approximately mid-stream in 110 feet of water.[299]

As rescue operations speeded frantically on the river, motorists also continued their flow across the Greater New Orleans Bridge as it quickly became engulfed in smoke billowing upwards from the burning ship and from the flaming crude oil on the water's surface. According to a *New Orleans Times-Picayune* newspaper story, a twenty-seven-year-old woman, her husband and their three-year-old child outdrove a fiery gauntlet to safety that night. As they approached the bridge while returning home from a family dinner in Algiers, they "could see smoke and the sky was lit up but," said Mrs. Arnold Regouffre, "we didn't think much of it."

However, by the time they got to the section of the bridge above the fire, flames were coming up both sides of the span. Mrs. Regouffre said her husband was driving at about forty-miles-an-hour before hitting that fiery stretch but he speeded up to sixty and roared through the danger area. "All I can say was that I was scared," Mrs. Regouffre continued. "We could feel intense heat, but we rolled up the windows and kept going. Now I know what it would be like going through Hell," said Mrs. Regouffre.[300] So too, did the twenty-five seaman who went down with the *Union Faith* that Easter Sunday Night of 1969.

*   *   *

Aftermath

The failure to communicate was strongly recognized in the U. S. Coast Guard report on the *Warren J. Doucet/I.O.C. No. 7/Union Faith* collision when it commented thusly on conditions prevailing at that time:

> This collision demonstrates the practical limitations of the visual and audible methods of communicating intentions of passing prescribed by the Inland Rules of the Road. The pilot of the *Warren J. Doucet* was unaware that the *Union Faith* apparently did not see the tow's lights, or hear his

initial two-blast signal, until he observed the change of course of the freighter. Performance standards for navigation lights and whistles required by the rules are vague, or nonexistent. The pilot of one vessel has no way of knowing whether his whistle signal is heard by another vessel, unless a responding whistle signal is received. He has no specific way of knowing the range of audibility of his whistle. Similarly, he does not know how far his navigation lights can be seen. When he receives no response to his whistle signal, he does not know whether his proposal is heard, or is not acceptable to the other vessel. Uncertainty exists, and under the Inland Rules, he should sound the danger signal, but again he is not sure this signal will be heard.

Prudent seamanship requires his slowing or stopping his vessel until agreement for passing is achieved. The decision on how far from the other vessel he should slow or stop when no whistle reply is heard requires accurate judgment by the person in charge of the vessel. Relative speed, wind current, maneuvering characteristics of both vessels, restrictions of navigable waters, local customs, traffic pattern, and a number of other factors must be considered in his decision-making process....[301]

Clearly, as the *Union Faith/Doucet/I.O.C. 7* collision has so graphically and dreadfully demonstrated, the most amazing thing about it was and is that such collisions are, fortunately, so infrequent, no matter how busy the flow of nautical traffic gets.

*   *   *

The Greater New Orleans Mississippi River Bridge was declared to be structurally sound, though it suffered some warping of a maintenance walkway and considerable paint damage. But, the bridge itself had "no structural member which shows evidence of failure." It was reopened to all traffic the next afternoon. This seems to be a rather amaz-

Commercial boat traffic, near the end of the Mississippi River at New Orleans, often needs a nautical traffic cop.

ing development in light of the fact that Easter tourists visiting the observation deck on the 29th floor of the nearby International Trade Mart building (now known as the World Trade Center of New Orleans) reported the whole conflagration seemed to be covered by what looked like a dense fog.

Deep-draft ship movement in and out of the port was little affected, except that large draft vessels had to pass along the west bank (the New Orleans business district side of the river because of the submerged hull of the

Union Faith. The ship sank shortly before 2:00 a.m. on April 7, mid-stream in the river about three-tenths of a mile down-stream from the bridge. It was in about 110 feet of water, with parts of the hull fifty-seven feet below the surface. At the time it sank, tug boats were pulling the still-burning hulk down-river where it was to have been beached.

In August of 1999, thirty years after its sinking, the hulk of the *Union Faith* was found to still be seeping fuel oil from its engine room into the Mississippi River. After the sinking, the U.S. Army Corps of Engineers had hired contractors to dispose of the ship lying on the river's bottom by sliding it into a 600-feet long, 100-foot wide, and 50-foot deep trench dug next to the ship. On October 31, 1970, the ship slid into the trench and rolled onto its port side to give a safe navigational depth of 65 feet over the vessel. Years later, after spotting the mysterious oil sheen surfacing on the river, the Coast Guard contracted Bisso Marine Company of New Orleans, parent company for the tug boat *Cappy Bisso* that was so heroically involved in saving the lives of the *Faith's* crewmen at the time of the collision, to locate and identify the source of the oil.

Bisso Marine divers identified the ship resting on its port side in 110 feet to 128 feet of water. The ship's superstructure was missing two decks above the main deck and approximately half of the ship was buried in mud. Recognizing that the hull of the *Union Faith* was, indeed, a burial vault for Captain Kenneth H. Scarbrough and others of the ship's crew on that Easter night in 1969, the Coast Guard held a memorial ceremony on the river for the family of the heroic pilot. In all, 500 barrels of bunker fuel oil was recovered from the *Union Faith*, most of it free-floating in the engine room. To date, no additional oil has been observed leaking from the wreck.[302]

*   *   *

In April of 1969, the country was deeply engaged in the war in Vietnam and trying to find a way to get out. The Cold War was hot. And its tentacles reached all the way to New Orleans in the aftermath of the *Union Faith-Warren J. Doucet* tragedy. Upon their discharge from local area hospitals, the released *Union Faith* crewmen, none of whom spoke English, were immediately taken to New Orleans's Jung Hotel. Reporters were barred from entering their suite by an armed detective. Victor Gregori of Leon Detective Agency said, "The ship company (Chinese Union Line) has ordered that no one talk to these men." An attorney for the shipping line said the survivors would not be allowed to comment on the accident until after a full investigation has been conducted by the Coast Guard.[303]

A four-million dollar law suit was filed in the United States District Court in New Orleans on April 23, 1969 by the *Union Faith's* owner, China Lines, Ltd. The company claimed its boat "had reversed its engines and was dead in the water" when it became involved in the accident. The suit also claimed that the *Warren J. Doucet* and the *Cay & Mitch* were manned by "improper and incompetent crews who were inattentive"[304] to their duties. Defendants in the case were Warren J. Doucet, Inc., and B. and B. Towing Company of Galliano, Louisiana.

Primarily because the captain of the *Warren J. Doucet* was not licensed to operate such a vessel (a not uncommon practice at the time), the National Mariners Association (nee Gulf Coast Mariners Association) stated that this incident led to the licensing of towing vessel "operators." Such action was recommended on October 15, 1970 by the National Transportation Safety Board based on the Coast Guard report referenced herein. In less than two years, the Towing Vessel Operator Licensing Act (Public Law 92-339), RS 4427, as amended 46 U.S.C. 405(b) (July

7, 1972) established that U.S. uninspected towboats would be under the command and control of persons licensed by the Coast Guard. While the law allowed the employment of traditionally licensed masters, mates and pilots, it also created a new class of licensee, the towboat "operator".

*   *   *

One other result of the failures to communicate in this tragic episode was the realization that standards were needed for large-boat whistles' effectiveness.

As documented in the Coast Guard's final report, "the failure of the *Union Faith* personnel to hear the towing vessel's two-blast whistle signals may have been affected by the wind which was blowing against the *Doucet*." The Rules of the Road require mechanically propelled vessels to be equipped with "an efficient whistle or siren." The Motorboat Act requires a range of one mile for whistles on Classes 2 and 3 motorboats, but no performance standards are prescribed for larger vessels. (In other words, if you were operating a sixteen-foot runabout on a river, you had to have "an efficient whistle or siren." But, if you were driving a 1,000-foot, ocean-going oil tanker, you didn't!) Range of audibility, it was contended, was difficult to determine due to such variables as wind, atmospheric conditions, obstructions, wave condition, noise level on the receiving vessel, frequency, and directional properties of the whistle. The need for specifying a minimum audible range for ships' whistles was declared "obvious." A rating system, such as that developed by the International Association of Lighthouse Authorities, seemed, according to the report, to be desirable."[305]

*   *   *

Once again, as it was then and is now, it would be fruitless to delve into any type of speculation, psychoanalytic, forensic or otherwise, as to what was happening on the bridge of the *Union Faith* on April 6, 1969. There were no survivors from among the freighter's officers and its river pilot in command and control from the bridge at the time. All that can be asked are unanswerable questions, such as:

- Who was at the helm when the *Union Faith* rounded Algiers Point and headed south toward the *Warren J. Doucet* and its tow? Was it river pilot Kenneth Scarbrough?
-

As in several other incidents recounted within these pages, was it another case of –

- a pilot fainting or momentarily blacking out at the helm?
- Why did whoever was at the helm – or anyone one else joining him on the freighter's bridge – not see nor hear the towboat's position announcements via radio and/or ship's foghorn?
- Why did anyone on the bridge of the *Union Faith* not see the running lights of the towboat *Doucet* and its lead barge – and – of the towboat *Cay & Mitch* assisting in the tow?
- Why did they not see the head of the tow after the *Doucet's* skipper illuminated it with his searchlight? Despite the fact that the ship was crewed entirely by Chinese Nationalists from Formosa, some of them – especially among the officer cadre – could speak and understand English, as was shown at the investigative hearing held after the crash.

These questions led even the Coast Guard investigators to wonder fruitlessly about "the state of attentiveness on the bridge of the *Union Faith.*"[306]

- Why, when a collision was clearly evident but still avoidable, did Scarbrough order his ship's engine merely into dead slow instead of the necessary full astern?

Even forty years after this tragedy, as investigators were then, those with interest today are also left only with many questions that have no answers.

*   *   *

In a rear-view mirror look at some tragically unintended consequences, the *Warren J. Doucet* cleared the Inner Harbor Navigation Canal Locks at approximately 1630 hours that Easter Sunday afternoon. Her tow was made up with *I.O.C. 7* as the lead barge and tank barge *TM 113* was the face barge (closest to the *Doucet*) with barge *LB 19* between the other two. The *Cay & Mitch* was lashed to the port side of *TM 113*, assisting the *Doucet*. The tow, with two towboats providing forward motion, was barely able to make three-and-one-half to four miles per hour against the river's current.

In one of those mind-boggling twists of fate that can have completely unexpected and sometimes disastrous consequences, the *Cay and Mitch* cut loose from the tow as ordered at about 1730 hours leaving the *Doucet* unassisted. The latter's 800-hp diesel engine was quickly proven to be under-powered and unable to move the heavily-laden tank barges against the river's current. The *Doucet's* owner was informed of this situation and ordered the tow to turn around, go back down-river to the Algiers Locks with the *Cay & Mitch* assisting, and then take an alternate route to

Baton Rouge, using the Gulf Intracoastal Waterway. Had the *Doucet* had enough power to make it up-river alone, it wouldn't have had to go back down-stream – where it met the *Union Faith*.

And this story would never have had to be written.

*   *   *

Chapter XII
One Last Brush with Disaster

Those who have spent any time at all on our nation's waterways can probably empathize with some of the accounts within these pages as they read about the fear and panic that can overtake the crew when facing imminent life-and-death situations. This writer shares those feelings through personal experience. There's a spot along the Gulf Intracoastal Waterway near the 132-mile marker, close to Cypremort, Louisiana, where the Louisa swing bridge used to cross the GIWW. Three times within three months in 2001, towboats and their barges have rammed it. This writer almost did, too.

This is what could have happened to this writer – or worse!
(Photo from the Collection of John R. Miller)

*   *   *

Offered here, as an excerpt from another book we've written entitled *We Three: Fred, the Ferry Boat, and Me*, is an account of our personal face-to-face with death and destruction along the nation's inland waterways. It was one that for us – my crewmate Fred Ebdon and me – ended far less seriously than any of those reported previously in these pages. But, having been in "the vicinity" of their situations, we know a little of what it was like for them.

This scene from *We Three* was the last day of a three-week, 2,400-mile odyssey bringing my forty-seven-foot sail-less sailboat from Lake Superior to the Gulf of

Harper's Ferry II **makes it safely to the end of its voyage in Freeport, Texas.**

Mexico via the Great Lakes and down through the Illinois and Mississippi rivers, along the Atchafalaya and Gulf Intracoastal waterways:

...[Along the way, w]e then ran into the most excruciating moments of raging excitement and deadly fear when we approached a (since replaced) swing bridge at Cypremort, Louisiana.

It was in the closed position straddling the Waterway and there was no bridge-tender answering our call for passage through. A passerby on the bridge shouted to us that the bridge swings to the closed position for water traffic once in the morning and again in the afternoon for a school bus crossing. There's no boat traffic going through then. No big deal. It was about 1430 and we could wait for the afternoon school bus, even if it did delay us a bit. Besides, we had no other choice.

We tied up near the waterway's right bank against some filthy creosote-encrusted pilings paralleling the roadway with our boat [*Harper's Ferry II*] facing south, perpendicular to the GIWW's east-west flow. We were about twenty yards from the bridge's opening span. After ninety minutes or so, we decided the school bus was running late or maybe it was a school holiday or the bridge-tender got sick and stayed home. Maybe the damned bridge just wasn't going to open that afternoon until some barge traffic came along. Maybe, we thought, it would be better for us to go back up-river for a couple of miles to a place called Port of Saint Mary and spend the night there. Making that decision was almost fatal for – *We Three: Fred, the Ferry Boat, and Me.*

The waterway's channel opening through and under the bridge was quite narrow; hardly more than thirty yards – just enough to let a small, two-wide tow through. It was the narrowest opening on the entire GIWW. In effect, that narrowness created a vortex where the water was compressed through the opening at a brief but outrageous speed [because of severe flooding earlier in the year], estimated at about ten knots! It's the same principle as the compacted wind howling through the narrow concrete canyons of New York City. The backed up water on the up-bound side of the bridge had the *Ferry* boat pretty much pinned against those filthy creosoted pilings.

265

Finally, I had Fred let go all lines on our starboard side, except the stern line. I was hoping I could swing the bow of the boat to port and head back up stream. The relentless water pressure broadside against the portside of our hull was stronger than our 130-hp diesel engine. We couldn't get up enough rpms to start our swing. As a matter of fact, the only thing we accomplished was to break our man-overboard pole lashed to the starboard side of the surging but restrained boat.

That's when I made that almost fatal decision. We could have stayed right there and waited longer for the school bus. Or, possibly a towboat might come upon the scene to radio the bridge-tender. Or, we could have stayed for the night hoping to catch the next morning's school bus bridge opening. Nevertheless, sooner or later, we were going have to try to get out of there somehow.

That's hindsight, of course. (Of course, British Prime Minister Neville Chamberlain could have also used a little hindsight in 1938 after Adolph Hitler promised him, "peace in our time".) I decided to head back east to the Port of Saint Mary. I put the engine in forward gear, revved it up pretty good, and then told Fred to let go the aft line which was the only thing holding us to the pilings. At that point, I gunned the engine throttle full ahead and drove the boat straight at the torrent roaring under the bridge. I figured we had just one chance. We had to get up "a full head of steam" with enough forward thrust to bring the bow up-river before the torrent overcame us and drove us into and under the bridge, which was no more than four feet above the water.

We had about sixty feet, less than one-and-one-half boat lengths [*Harper's Ferry* was a 47-footer], to power up before hitting the full force of the vortex. Then we had about two more boat lengths to make the turn up-river before plowing into the opposite shoreline. Whatever the maximum rpms that engine could make were turning even before we had gone half that distance. I had the engine throttle rammed full forward and was even holding it down with my right hand. The bow was coming around – ever, ever so slowly. Would the *Ferry* boat come all the way around? I began to doubt we would make it, I warned Fred to be ready to jump for his life.

I held the steering wheel hard over to port with my left hand. I could not get the rudder over another inch. If that pointed end of the boat didn't point upstream before the rushing waters grabbed it, we would be slammed with uncontrolled force into the unopened bridge. "Come on, Baby," I screamed. "Come on, Baby!" Inch by maddening inch the bow started coming around as diesel smoke poured from our stern exhaust pipe. I don't know what Fred was yelling and I don't know if he was yelling at me or the boat. But it sure was loud. Since it wasn't his boat, he may have had a slightly less affectionate name for it other than "Baby."

Then too, we had the opposite bank of the river dead ahead and rapidly approaching. "Come on, Baby. Get up there! For God's sake, Baby, get up there!" Slowly, oh so awfully slowly, the *Ferry* boat got "up there." We made it! Even without falling into that raging river, I was soaking wet. And both Fred and I needed an immediate trip to the head below after we cleared the danger.

Somewhere around the 132-milemarker on the GIWW, at the end of an eight-plus-hour harrowing day, was where we gladly, with huge sighs of relief and still-knocking knees, tied up to some pilings at about 1630 and anticipated another sparkling, moonlit night. Neither Fred nor I were much interested in a big dinner that night. We honestly felt like we had cheated the Devil. What we were soon to learn was that the Devil still had plans for us further down the GIWW.

(It should be noted here that the near-miss "Bridge of Death" was replaced by another span – one that is *seventy-three feet* above the water line – on April 10, 2005….)

*   *   *

Chapter XIII
Is the Fox Guarding the Henhouse?

Obviously, from these pages and other sources, all was – and in many cases, still is – not well in the towboat industry. There are several bones of contention within the industry with some of them, such as "over-worked" crews and "under-powered" towboats, being noted in these pages. In light of the disasters highlighted herein, the circumstances behind them, and the sometimes difficulty in assigning responsibility for them, presented below are extracted comments made by the Gulf Coast Mariners Association (GCMA – later named the National Mariners Association, NMA) following the release of the U. S. Coast Guard's final report on the Queen Isabella Causeway calamity on September 15, 2001. The GCMA comments, presented as part of the apparent on-going feud between it, the American Waterways Operators organization, and the U. S. Coast Guard, are based primarily on an Associated Press story dated May 6, 2005. Most of the details of that AP story are covered elsewhere in this book. First, however, what are the GCMA and its counterpart, the American Waterways Operators (AWO)?

Calling itself "The Voice for Mariners" in its membership solicitation brochure, the National Mariners Association (nee the Gulf Coast Mariners Association) represents 126,000 credentialed mariners.[307] The "GCMA was founded in April 1999 with the help of four maritime labor unions that recognized 'lower-level' mariners in this industry need just as effective a voice as the deep-sea mariners have. Our mariners' voices must be heard in Washington and in many other places to protect mariner interests [and keep them from being] exploited by many employers.[308]

The American Waterways Operators (AWO) is "the national trade association representing the owners and operators of tugboats, towboats, and barges serving the waterborne commerce of the United States. Its mission is to promote the long term economic soundness of the industry, and to enhance the industry's ability to provide safe, efficient, and environmentally responsible transportation, through advocacy, public information, and the establishment of safety standards."[309]

[In layman's terms – that both organizations may dispute – this is a classic union-management situation with the AWO representing the boat owners and the GCMA/NMA speaking for the "lower-level" workers on those boats. The GCMA/NMA statement regarding the Queen Isabella Causeway allision in Texas follows:]

QUEEN ISABELLA CAUSEWAY ACCIDENT:[310]
Coast Guard blames Captain for bridge collapse

"The Coast Guard investigated the Queen Isabella Causeway disaster while the National Transportation Safety Board investigated the Interstate-40 bridge allision at Webbers Falls that occurred nine months later. [Author's Note: These incidents are covered elsewhere in this book.] Both reports were 'bad news' for the towing industry.

"...As [an Associated Press article] indicates, there are several ongoing lawsuits. One of these lawsuits involves the owner of the barges – a large corporation that was supposed to be a poster child for the American Waterways Operators' 'Responsible Carrier Program' (RCP).

"For the past 10 years, the Coast Guard allowed the towing industry to 'self-regulate.' During much of this period, our mariners watched it self-destruct. It is not that the RCP is not a step in the right direction, as GCMA believes it is, but that some of the executives who agreed to abide by it took unconscionable shortcuts to make a fast buck.

"Part of a lawsuit developed outside the Coast Guard's purview and well outside the recently released accident report [on the Queen Isabella Causeway incident] included videotaped depositions taken from senior executives of that corporation and the small operating company they hired to push their heavily-laden barges. These depositions show how the larger company nullified many of the safeguards built into the industry's 'Responsible Carrier Program' in an attempt to maximize their own corporate profits. The result cost eight lives, severe injuries to three more people, heartbreak to countless family members, and shock to a south Texas community. There was also huge expense and tremendous inconvenience with the destruction of public facilities and other losses to the public at large.

"The accident also alerted the [U. S. Coast Guard's] Eighth District to the question of towing vessel horsepower and overloaded tows and gave them a good reason to think about this problem.... [T]he Eighth District to this day continues to appease the industry. How many more lives will it take before the Coast Guard regulates tow size and horsepower?

"A GCMA forensic investigator gave us a copy of portions of the video deposition that became part of the court record. It revealed the shortcomings and demonstrated the ease with which senior corporate executives could bypass many of the safeguards built into the Responsible Carrier Program.

"If a 'picture is worth a thousand words,' these were damning pictures and included the spoken words that made it clear beyond a shadow of a doubt that the towing industry should no longer be allowed to regulate itself with a <u>voluntary</u> safety management system like the RCP.

"We brought the video to a Towing Safety Advisory Committee (TSAC) meeting in Washington. However, we never were allowed to show it. In fact, it appeared that most TSAC members – many of them also AWO members – did not want to see it. Hear no evil, see no evil, so you will speak no evil – and there was much 'evil' (as well as ignorance and downright stupidity) revealed in the business practices and disregard for the risks involved. The company threatened GCMA with an injunction to prevent us from displaying the video. We documented all this activity.

"The Responsible Carrier Program (RCP) represents years of efforts by many corporate executives and dedicated AWO staff members who worked hard to clean up the towing industry and polish its image in the nation's capital. Yet, one of AWO's own member companies sold all this work and the public images it spent years in creating down the river.

"It is clear that, in its place, a strict regulatory regime without regulatory loopholes must emerge. The Coast Guard must prove to the public that it is capable of <u>enforcing</u> its new regulations on its 'partners' in industry. That may be a tall order for some Coast Guard officers who find it politically correct to appease industry and go with the flow.

"The RCP, known by the broader generic term of a 'Safety Management System,' must expand to <u>support</u> the new regulations that the Coast Guard is now drafting. In barnyard terms, this should put the horse in front of the cart where it belongs and remove the fox from guarding the hen house (as he has done for the past decade) where there is clearly a conflict of interest."

(Author's Note: The American Waterways Operators organization was offered the opportunity to comment on the above position of GCMA/NMA. AWO did not respond to that invitation – nor to any other offered by this writer. The readers hereof may have to make their own judgments, based on just this one-half of the story.)

*   *   *

Epilogue
A Pocketful of Miracles

In reading about all these tragic episodes between this book's covers, it's hard to imagine that they don't contain slightly more than a pocketful of miracles.

Think about Max Alley being able to stop his truck after Interstate-40 dropped out from under him and his wife Goldie on May 26, 2002, keeping them from sliding into the Arkansas River and meeting the same violent deaths that claimed the lives of fourteen other unsuspecting souls after the towboat *Robert Y. Love* knocked that Oklahoma Interstate highway down?

Think about truck-drivers James Bilyeu and Rodney Tidwell who took an involuntary swim that morning, only to find themselves in the middle of a tournament full of anglers who fished them out of that river's cold waters and saved their lives?

Think about Brigette Marie Goza, Rene Francisco Mata, and Gustavo Adolfo Morales who were also scooped out of the *Laguna Madre* waters in Texas on September 15, 2001 by local anglers after the *Brown Water V* towboat knocked the Queen Isabella Causeway out from under them?

Think about what the magnitude of that tragedy might have been if the towboat had hit that bridge a mere twelve hours later on that Saturday – during the height of the closing of Padre Island's vacation season. Or, if it had happened two weeks earlier during a boisterous Labor Day weekend.

Think about deckhand Jacob Wilds who survived the *Elizabeth M* tragedy in the icy waters of the Ohio River on January 9, 2005 after being plucked out of a hypothermic death bed by crewmen from another towboat who saw only his head bobbing among the churning waters in the black of that night?

Think about the forty-seven people who died in the Amtrak train's dive into the Big Bayou Canot on September 22, 1993 when the towboat *Mauvilla* dislodged the train's tracks? Then think about what the toll might have been had not championship swimmer Michael Dopheide ("He ain't heavy, Father. He's my brother.") been there as a passenger on the *Sunset Limited* to save another thirty passengers?

Think about calamity caused by the towboat *Chris* and its empty barge when they drifted into one of the supports holding up the Claiborne Avenue Bridge over the Industrial Canal in New Orleans on the late afternoon of May 28th, 1993? Why were there only two cars to go down with the bridge on that very heavily-traveled thoroughfare at that Friday afternoon?

*   *   *

It goes almost without saying: Most towboaters can spend their entire career never being involved in a serious, life-threatening situation. Joe Waller started working on towboats when he was thirteen years old (it was during World War II and there was a massive shortage of river-working personnel; most towboat pilots were steering LSTs onto the beaches at Normandy, Iwo Jima, and Anzio). "The most serious accident I ever had," he told this writer as a sneaky smile crossed his already well-creased face, "was when I was southbound down the Mississippi at Port Allen, just above Baton Rouge. I was piloting a 110x30-foot towboat with a 2,400 horse engine," he said. It was a good handling boat but the river was "running."

Waller got talking to an up-bounder "who was down beyond a turn in the river and he told me he was going to stay where he was until I made the turn. What he done," according to Waller, "was that he had a barge "spiked" [on the hip] on the channel side. And when I came around that bend, he was sticking out into the channel with no lights on the spiked barge and he was comin'. I tried to stop. I tried backing up and backing up but with the current, there was no stopping." Waller said he "ended up just climbin' on top of that barge and I put a hole in it big enough to drive a Volkswagen through. There was no physical damage to anyone but a lot to that barge," said Waller with a grin. "The Coast Guard tied us up for a long time." Fortunately for Waller, the other pilot did not have any license; it was expired.

In times of tragedies such as the basic stories told in these pages, whether we are personally involved or merely detached observers, we're often told consolingly that "bad things do happen to good people." As we have seen here, sometimes good things happen to good people, too.

*   *   *

GLOSSARY

After Watch – sometimes called a "back watch," is the period when the vessel's Relief Pilot is at the ship's helm, generally speaking, between Noon and 6:00 p.m. and Midnight to 6:00 a.m. Crew personnel assigned to the shift serve the same hours. Watches are basically limited to no more than six hours during a shift. (See "Captain's Watch")

Allision (n) – a vessel striking a fixed object, (v) allided. (See "Collision")

American Waterways Operators (AWO) – is "the national trade association representing the owners and operators of tugboats, towboats, and barges serving the waterborne commerce of the United States.

"Blue water" – a nautical term used to differentiate ocean waters from inland rivers and streams.

"Brown water" – a nautical term used to differentiate inland rivers and streams from ocean waters.

"Break-up a tow" – When a tow has too many barges to fit all into a waterway lock, the towboat crew has to break-up the tow into as many barges as will fit into the lock at one time. This may result in several "break-ups."

Captain's Watch – sometimes called a "front watch," is the period when the vessel's Captain is at the ship's helm, generally speaking, between 6:00 a.m. and Noon and between 6:00 p.m. and Midnight. Crew personnel assigned to the shift serve the same hours. Watches are basically limited to no more than six hours during a shift. (See "After Watch")

Collision – a vessel striking another moving object, (v) collided. (See "Allision")

Inland Rules of the Road – a set of rules of navigation (most of which are mere "common sense" in nature) developed by the U. S. Coast Guard in conjunction with the maritime industry that apply to all vessels operating on the inland waters of the United States with a primary objection of making passage on those waters safe.

Joy stick - actually, "steering wheels" on towboats are pretty much of an anomaly these days as steering is done with a "joy stick," much like the ones used by computer gamers.

Locking through – The "locking" process means that a boat going up-stream, for instance, goes through a massive steel gate on the down-river side and enters a lock where it ties up to cleats or bollards on the lock walls. Traffic in a lock can be up-stream or down-stream – but only one direction at a time. The lock is sort of a huge rectangular concrete bathtub (chamber) with its duplicate gate on the up-river side closed to keep the "tub" relatively empty.

When the down-river gate is closed behind the boat(s), a lockmaster fills the "tub" with water through a series of valves. The then-rising water level in the lock lifts the vessel(s) to the level of the up-river side where that opposite gate is then opened allowing the traffic to proceed. The process is reversed on a down-river trip with a boat entering a full chamber which is then closed and emptied, lowering the boat(s) to the next lower level of the river on the down-bound side of the lock.

MPH/KPH - A river's or a vessel's flow measured at "mph" (miles per hour) differs from those nautical reports that list speed in knot per hour (kph) because one kph is the equivalent of 1.15 mph. Therefore, in *The Rivers Always Win* segment herein, for instance, where the Ohio River's reported speed of thirteen kph, that speed is actually about fifteen mph (1.15 x 13).

National Mariners Association (NMA – nee, Gulf Coast Mariners Association, GCMA) – an association of "lower-level" mariners in the towboat industry declaring itself "The Voice of Mariners" and "completely independent, self-governing and managing its own affairs."

One-Whistle – A blast on a ship's whistle or horn or a verbal statement via radio that a vessel is proceeding along and to the right (starboard) side of a waterway's channel or that it wants to pass an oncoming vessel on its left side (see "Two-Whistle").

Pilot – in the towboat world is the person who shares command and control of a towboat with the "captain" during its normal working conditions. The pilot (sometimes called "relief pilot") backs up and relieves the captain on a shift basis, keeping in mind, of course, that the captain never relinquishes his ultimate responsibilities and command of the boat.

Pilot, river – is one whose job it is to bring the big "blue water" vessels from their deep-water surroundings into the ever-changing, narrow channels of "brown water" rivers and on to their port destination. They perform the same service in reverse on out-bound vessels.

Port – always to the left side of a boat (when facing forward) no matter which way the boat is going.

Special Circumstances – When imminent danger makes it prudent to break the nautical "Rules of the Road."

Starboard – always to the right side (when facing forward) of a boat no matter which way the boat is going.

String – a line of barges in a tow.

Tow - the combination of a towboat and its barges.

Towboat – a compact, shallow-draft boat with a squared bow designed and fitted for pushing tows of barges on island waterways.

Tugboat – a powerful small boat, generally with a pointed bow, designed to pull or push larger ships, generally in harbor operations.

Two-Whistle – A blast on a ship's whistle or horn or a verbal statement made via radio that a vessel is proceeding along and to the left (port) side of a waterway's channel or that it wants to pass an oncoming vessel on its right side (see "One-Whistle").

Uninspected Towing Vessels – An uninspected vessel does not have a Coast Guard certificate of inspection under 46 *United States Code* (U.S.C.).

Wire – Any kind of steel cable ("Facewires," "Jockey wires," "Backing Wire," etc.) used to attach barges to each other and to a towboat.

About the Author

William T. (Bill) Harper spent 50-odd (and we do mean "odd") years as a newspaper and magazine reporter, writer, editor, and natural gas industry executive before retiring to what he thought was going to be a new life on the high seas aboard his sailboat, *Harper's Ferry II*.

Didn't work out that way.

Instead, he ended up in College Station, Texas where there's no room for a forty-seven-foot sailboat. So, he tearfully sold the boat and returned to his roots as a

With his sailboat on automatic pilot on a trip across Lake Superior, all seems right with the world (for the moment) for author William T. (Bill) Harper.

writer. He became an award-winning author (*Eleven Days in Hell: The 1974 Carrasco Prison Siege in Huntsville,*

Texas – honored by the Writers League of Texas as "the best in Texas non-fiction for 2005").

In addition to *The Rivers of Life – and Death*, Bill has also written the above *Eleven Days in Hell*, and
An Eye for an Eye: In Defense of the Death Penalty,
We Three: Fred the "Ferry" Boat, and Me,
Second Thoughts: Presidential Regrets with Their Supreme Court Nominations
and
How Come: 96 Unanswerable Questions

He is the father of six and grandfather to twelve and great-grandfather to five. He now writes and broadcasts on public radio in Bryan, Texas, where he lives with his wife, Joyce (Juntune, PhD, teaching at Texas A&M University).

Bill's e-mail address is harperhere@LIVE.com

INDEX

Claiborne Avenue
  Bridge, **209-10, 212-14,
216-17, 219-20, 276**
Claiborne, William C.,
212
Clark Bridge, **16**
Clark, William J., **107-11**
Clark, William, **171**
Clarksville, AR, **78**
Clements, Alexandra, **72**
Clements, Andrew D., **72**
Clements, Andrew F., **71-
72, 82, 101, 103, 108**
Clements, Christina, **72**
Clements, Ronald, **104**
Clements, Samuel L., **246**
clinical evaluation, **92**
Coast Guard Group
  Lower Mississippi, **90**
Coast Guard Group Ohio
  Valley, 157
Coast Guard Marine
  Safety Office (MSO),
157
Coast Guard, U. S., **33-
34, 36, 42-44, 46-47, 50,
54, 56, 62, 64-66, 68, 77,
81, 90, 105, 118-19, 125-
27, 130, 134, 140-42,
151-52, 157-58, 161-62,
164-68, 175-77, 179-80,
183-86, 195-97, 199, 201,
203, 205-06, 214, 216-18,
221, 223, 228-29, 233-37,
245, 248-49, 252, 254,**

**257-60, 269-73, 277, 280,
282**
Cochran, Gary, **80-81,
148, 152, 176-77**
Cockerham, William,
228-29
Colorado, **76**
complacency, **131, 213**
Congress, U. S., **119**
Conklin, Rick, **36, 41, 43-
44, 53, 57, 65**
Corman, Robert, **50**
Cornyn, John, **139**
Corpus Christi, TX, **31,
125**
Covert, Justin, **47**
Cox's Park, **160**
Crall, Michael, **66**
Crenshaw, Lilly Ruth,
207
Crescent City
  Connection, **247**
Crosson, Bill, **182**
Crosson, Vivian, **191**
Crucible, PA, **57**
CSX Transportation, Inc.,
180, 197
Culver, Patrick, **119**
Cumberland River, **20**
Currituck County, NC
125
D&E Marine of
  Louisville, **158**
Daniel MacMillan, **29**
Dante's Inferno, **169, 190**
Davis, Kenneth, **251**

Davison, Steve, **158**
Dayton, KY, **147**
Deadman's Alarm, **104-05**
Deck, Jack, **157**
Dedmon, William Joe, **72-73, 75, 78-79, 81-83, 87-88, 91-92, 94, 105, 109-10**
Demen, Larry, **209-10, 215**
Department of Transportation (DOT), **194, 249**
DePaul University, law school, **201**
Diener, Robert J., **207**
Diez y Seis de Septiembre **116, 143**
Dillon, Edgar,
Dillon, Wallace,
Dinet, Elton, **215**
Dive-Recovery Team, **118**
Dixon, Doris, **207**
Dixon, Lynn, **118**
Dixon, Patrick, **207**
DM 3021, **209, 214**
Donald Roth, **228**
Donner, Brace, **148**
Dopheide, Michael, **200-01, 276**
Dotting, Michelle, **191-92**
Doucet, Warren J. **10, 243-49, 253-55, 258-61**

Doucet, Warren J., Inc., **244, 258, 261**
Downer, Bill, **66**
Dravo Corporation, **46, 154**
Drugs, **14, 163, 176**
DuBois, Tom, **209-10, 212, 214-15**
Duet, Ronald, **232-36, 239**
Dufrene, Autry J., **234**
Duplessis, Gladys, **210**
East Liverpool, OH, **30**
Easter Sunday, **13, 243, 254, 256-57, 261**
Elaine G, **10, 21, 149-51, 153-55, 157, 161-67, 165, 167**
Elizabeth M, **10, 33-36, 38, 41-44, 46-50, 52-53, 55-56, 62-69, 126, 154, 198, 275**
EMT units, **217**
environment, **57, 124, 140, 270**
environmentalists, **117**
Ergon, Inc., **72**
Evans, Mike, **159, 163**
face-up, **43**
fairness disclaimer, **109**
Farmer, Gary, **184, 194-95**
Farve, Leroy, **210**
Federal Bureau of Investigation (FBI), **107, 110**

Notes

1 http://news.minnesota.publicradio.org/features/200009/29_newsroom_mississippi-m/barge.shtml

2 Captain David Whitehurst, "The Voice for Mariners," GCMA News, #44, November/December 2006

3 Virginia Linn, "Winter proves the most dangerous season for those working on the rivers," *Pittsburgh Post-Gazette*, January 10, 2005

4 "Memorandum for Waterways Association of Pittsburgh," U.S. Army Corps of Engineers, Pittsburgh Operations Division, February 8, 2006

5 Waterways Journal, "Study Predicts Costs of Lock Failures," Weekly News Summary for November 19-25, 2007

6 Middleton, Pat, *Discover! America's Great River Road*, Volume 2, Heritage Press, Stoddard, WI, June 2005

7 "Crash closes Mississippi River indefinitely," USA Today, February 22, 2004

8 Barry, John, Rising Tide: The great Mississippi Flood of 1927 and How It Changed America, Simon and Schuster, 1998, 21

9 Edward M Brady, "Tugs, Towboats and Towing," Cornell Maritime Press, Inc, Centerville MD, 1967, 6

10 http://mainland.cctt.org/istf2006/towboats.asp

11 http://imaginagrapher.com/transportation/parsonage.jpg

12 Ibid, Brady, 5

13 http://en.wikipedia.org/wiki/Tugboat#Gallery]

14 Ibid, Waterways Journal

15 National Oceanic & Atmospheric Administration (NOAA), NOAA Central Library

16 Ibid, Whitehurst

17 *Gwin v. American River Transportation Company*, United States District Court for the Southern District of Illinois, No. 03-C-862, April 10, 2007

18 Reid R. Frazier, "Towboat pilots mostly unregulated," Pittsburgh Tribune-Review, January 17, 2005

19 Joe Waller, interview with author, September 30, 1999

20 Ibid

21 http://mainland.cctt.org/istf2006/accidents.asp

22 Ibid, Linn

23 Ibid

24 http://www.lrp.usace.army.mil/nav/mont.htm

25 http://www.iwr.usace.army.mil/ndc/factcard/fc02/fcdidu2.htm

26 U. S. Waterway System, The – Transportation Facts, Navigation Data Center, U. S. Army Corps of Engineers, December 2007

27 Keat, Bobby Kerlik, Reid R. Frazier, "Heroism, peril, snap decisions," *Pittsburgh Tribune-Review*, February 6, 2005

28 Gulf Coast Mariners Association (GCMA) Report #R 340-A, April 5, 2007

29 Ibid, Whitehurst

30 Ibid, Keat

31 Ibid

32 Don Hopey, "3 dead, 1 missing as towboat goes over dam, sinks in Ohio River," *Pittsburgh Post-Gazette*, January 10, 2005

33 Ibid, Keat

34 Heidi Price, "Greene man was piloting towboat," *Observer-Reporter*, February 3, 2005

35 Bill Vidonic, "Elizabeth M report released," *Ellwood City Ledger*, November 12, 2007

36 Ibid, Keat

37 Reid R. Frazier, "Pilot details rescue of 2 from towboat," *Pittsburgh Tribune-Review*, February 5, 2005

38 USCG MISLE Incident Investigation Activity Number 2271812

39 Ibid, Keat

40 Ibid, Price

41 Ibid, Frazier

42 Ibid, Hopey

43 Reid R. Frazier, "Towboat wreck still a mystery," Pittsburgh Tribune-Review, January 11, 2005

44 Ibid, Frazier, "Towboat pilots...."

45 Ibid, Frazier, "Towboat wreck...."

46 John Snyder, "Coast Guard cites mistakes of master of towboat swept over dam," "Professional Mariner," February/March 2008

47 Larry Gwin, paper prepared for Towing Safety Committee Meeting at U. S. Coast Guard Headquarters, Washington, D.C., March 17, 2004

48 Mike Wereschagin, "Towboat in fatal crash had prior power failure," *Pittsburgh Tribune-Review*, January 27, 2005

49 Gary Rotstein, "Ohio River Gets Angry in High Water" *Pittsburgh Post-Gazette*, January 16, 2005

50 Ibid, Keat

51 Ibid, GCMA

52 Ibid

53 Ibid, Frazier, "Pilot details..."

54 Ibid, Vidonic

55 Ibid, Hopey

56 Ibid, Frazier, "Towboat wreck..."

57 WTAE-TV, "Elizabeth M Towboat Survivor Recalls Tragic Day; Doesn't Blame Captain," November 14, 2007

58 Ibid, Price

59 Ibid, Frazier, "Pilot details...."

60 Ibid, Price

61 Ibid, GCMA

305

62 Ibid

63 Interview with author, July 23, 2001

64 Reid R. Frazier, "Towboat captain expected to help," Pittsburgh Tribune-Review, February 4, 2005

65 "Towboat in barge accident in Pa. defied order?," Associated Press, February 1, 2005

66 Ibid, Frazier, February 4, 2005

67 Ibid, Bill Vidonic, "Elizabeth M report...

68 Ibid

69 John Snyder, "Coast Guard cites mistakes of master of towboat swept over dam," "Professional Mariner,"
Issue #111, Feb/Mar 2008

70 Ibid, Rotstein

71 Brandon Keat and Jeremy Boren, "Locks reopen after deadly barge wreck, Pittsburgh Tribune-Review,
January 13, 2005

72 Ibid, Frazier, "Towboat pilots....

73 Ibid, GCMA

74 Bill Vidonic, "Elizabeth M report released," Ellwood City Ledger, November 12, 2007

75 Don Hopey, "New facts emerge in '05 towboat fatalities," Pittsburgh Post-Gazette, October 28, 2007

76 Ibid

77 Don Hopey, "Crucial Details Revealed In Fatal Towboat Sinking," Pittsburgh Post-Gazette, October 28, 2007, A-1

78 Ibid

79 http://www.lawboat.com/news.asp?ID=460

80 Joe Mandak, "Search for missing towboat crewman unsuccessful, called off," The Associated Press,
January 21, 2006

81 Ibid

82 www.wheelhousereport.org/to/in/elizabethm.mgi

83 Liz Zemba, "Survivor of towboat accident charged with assault," Pittsburgh Tribune-Review, March 7,
2005

84 Ibid, Hopey, January 10, 2005

85 M. Cristina Medina, "Local army captain dies in Oklahoma bridge collapse," Monterey Herald, May 28,
2002

86 National Transportation Safety Board, Highway/Marine Accident Report NTSB/HAR-04/05

87 Ibid

88 Dawn Marks, "Spiro couple lived, died together," The Oklahoman, May 31, 2002

89 Cochran Interview with author, July 22, 2001

90 Ibid, 18

91 Ibid

92 Ibid, 21

93 Ibid, 7

94 "Death toll from bridge collapse rises to 13," USA Today May 28, 2002

95 Ibid, NTSB

96 Ibid

97 Ibid, "Death toll

98

http://media.www.thebatt.com/media/storage/paper657/news/2002/06/03/NewsInBrief/Towboat.Pilot.Un

aware.Of.Heart.Condition.Before.Bridge.Collapse.On.Arkansas.Rive-517894.shtml

99 Correspondence with author, July 27, 2010

100 Rod Walton, "Tugboat captain's interview released," Tulsa World, September 4, 2003

101 Ibid, Waller

102 http://www.gameandfishmag.com/fishing/bass-fishing/gf_aa016503a/

103 ibid

104 "Bridge rescuer credits 'greater power than us'," CNN, May 28, 2002, 1:41 PM EDT

105 Kelly Kurt, "I-40 bridge collapsed a year ago," Amarillo Globe, May 27, 2003

106 Vicki Speed, "Supporting the Collapse," Point of Beginning, January 24, 2003

107 http://newsok.com/article/867320/1147960676?pg=1

108 Capt. Robert Corrales, "Day-by-day account," Engineer Update, U. S. Army Corps of Engineers, July 2002.
Volume 26, Number 7

109 Steve Lackmeyer and Sonya Colberg, "Up to 20 still trapped, I-40 closed," The Oklahoman, May 27, 2002

110 Ibid, Corrales

111 "Oh my God, the road's gone," Associated Press, May 29, 2002

112 Sarah Hart, "Two BA Residents Honored for Life-Saving Work at I-40 Bridge Collapse," Tulsa World,
October 26, 2002

113 Ken Raymond, "Final minutes draw picture of bridge collapse," The Oklahoman, June 2, 2002

114 Rod Walton, "Story of the Year: I-40 bridge plunge top newsmaker," Tulsa World, December 31, 2002

115 Correspondence with author, June 15, 2010

116 "Oklahoma barge crash - FBI investigates Army impostor," Associated Press, June 5, 2002

117 www.jerrypippin.com/140bridge.htm

118 Ibid

119 Ibid

120 Ibid, NTSB/HAR-04/05

121 http://www.tulsaworld.com/news/article.aspx?articleID=020610_Ne_a1impe

122 "Missouri man sentenced for impersonating military officer," Associated Press, August 26, 2003

123 James Justin Mercier, P.E., TxDOT- Design Division, Austin, Texas

124 United States Coast Guard (USCG), "One Person Formal Board of Investigation [of the] Allision Involving
The MV Brown Water V and the
Queen Isabella Causeway Bridge," 13

125 www.gicaonline.com/media/tools/queenisabella.pdf

126 National Transportation Safety Board, Safety Recommendation, September 9, 2004, H-04-29 and -30, 3

127 http://www.brunchma.com/archives/Forum8/HTML/000762.html

128 "Memorial held on anniversary of South Texas bridge collapse," Laredo Morning Times, September 16,
2002, 3A

129 James Pinkerton, "South Padre death count rises to five," *Houston Chronicle*, September 18, 2001, 21A

130 http://www.txdps.state.tx.us/hp/hpspecializedunits.htm

131 GCMA Report #R-276, Revision 9, June 1, 2005, 3

132 Ibid, 4

133 http://www.tattooyou.freeservers.com/custom2.html

134 http://www.usfa.dhs.gov/downloads/pdf/pcm/pcm-R508.pdf

135 Associated Press, "Divers find last auto in bridge disaster," *Amarillo Globe Times*, September 22, 2001

136 Ibid, www.usfa...

137 Lynn Brezosky, "1 year later, causeway solution still debated," *Houston Chronicle*, September 15, 2002, A4

138 http://www.tshaonline.org/handbook/online/articles/GG/rrg4.html

139 Ibid, USCG, 7

140 Ibid, USCG, 17

141 Associated Press, "Bridge collapses in Port Isabel," *The Battalion*, Texas A&M University, May 3, 2002

142 Waterways Journal, The, "Editorial: Do Bad Results Reflect Ineptness Or Intent?" June 2, 2008

143 http://greenspun.com/bboard/q-and-a-fetch-msg.tcl?msg_id=006PsW

144 Ibid, USCG, 18

145 http://www.msnbc.msn.com/id/20651147/

146 Ibid, USCG, 18

147 Ibid

148 "Bridge collapse report awaits Coast Guard's ruling," *Lubbock Avalanche Journal*, September 15, 2004

149 "Queen Isabella Causeway Hearing Cites Several Problems," Connecting Link, Fall 2001, 3

150 Ibid, Brezosky

151 http://blue.utb.edu/newsandinfo/2006%C2%AD%C2%AD_09_14CausewaymemorialService.htm

152 Rosanna Ruiz, "Humble family mourns loss of son on causeway, *Houston Chronicle*, September 17, 2001, 17A

153 http://www.texnews.com/1998/2002/texas/bridge0916.html

154 http://greenspun.com/bboard/q-and-a-fetch-msg.tcl?msg_id=006PsW

155 Ibid

156 Ibid, Brezosky

157 Ibid, USCG, 19

158 Ibid

159 https://ritdml.rit.edu/dspace/bitstream/1850/5286/1/BTownsThesis09-2007.pdf

160 Ibid

161 http://www.accessmylibrary.com/coms2/summary_0286-1403066_ITM?email=harpersferry_2000@yahhoo.com&library=

162 James Pinkerton, "Survivor recounts fall from causeway," *Houston Chronicle*, September 19, 2001, 33A

163 http://www.texnews.com/1998/2002/texas/bridge0916.html

164 http://www.gicaonline.com/media/tools/queenisabella.pdf, 13

165 Ibid, usfa..., 5

166 Ibid, USCG, 13

167 Ibid

168 Ibid, "Bridge collapse report awaits..."

169 "Tugboat relief captain testifies about signaling cars on bridge," Associated Press, October 11, 2001

170 "Tugboat captain won't testify at bridge collapse hearing," *Amarillo Globe-News*, October 10, 2001

171 Ibid, USCG, 7

172 John Gonzalez, "Stranded await ride on ferry," *Houston Chronicle*, September 18, 2001, A21

173 James Pinkerton, John W. Gonzalez, "Bridge closure could last months," *Houston Chronicle*, September 17, 2001, A13

174 James Pinkerton, "DA to review probe of causeway collapse," *Houston Chronicle*, September 20, 2001, 27A

175 Associated Press, "Tugboat relief captain testifies about signaling cars on bridge," *Amarillo Globe-News*, October 11, 2001

176 Associated Press, "Company in South Texas bridge collapse tied to 60 other mishaps," *Laredo Morning Times*, October 8, 2001, 5A

177 "Captain of Boat in 2001 Texas Crash Sues," Daily Shipping News, #179, September 16, 2004

178 Associated Press, "Company settles with families from bridge collapse," *Laredo Morning Times*, June 30, 2005, 6A

179 Ibid, "Bridge collapse report awaits..."

180 David Tyler, "Currents, tow configuration, lack of power called factors in bridge accident," Professional Mariner, August/September 2005

181 "Fiber Optic Warning System Placed on South Padre Bridge," GCMA News, #23, June 2004

182 Larry Muhammad, "Blessing Opens Boating Season, Promotes Safety," Courier-Journal, May 28, 2001

183 Chris Kenning, "Six fishing buddies stuck together in life and death," Courier-Journal, July 17, 2001

184 Terry Flynn, "Ohio River yields up sixth body from crash," *Cincinnati Enquirer*, July 19, 2001

185 Chris Kenning, "Despite fatal barge accident, increased traffic, Ohio River considered safe," Courier-Journal, July 18, 2001, 1

186 Interview with author, July 25, 2001

187 Interview with author, July 24, 2001

188 "Ingram completes Midland Enterprises purchase," Nashville Business Journal, July 2, 2002

189 http://www.lrp.usace.army.mil/nav/ohioback.htm

190 Tom Reaugh, Senior Meteorologist, National Weather Service, Louisville, August 25, 2008

191 U. S. Coast Guard, Report of Investigation into the Circumstances Surrounding the Incident Involving M/V Elaine G Collision, 4, Misle Activity Number, 1476414, MSO

       Louisville, Misle Case Number 83605

192 Ibid, 3

193 Ibid, 12

194 Ibid, 3

195 Ibid, 13

196 Bruce Schreiner, "Barge captain testifies in Coast Guard hearing on collision," Associated Press, July 26, 2001

197 Ibid, NTSB/HAR 04/05, 59

198 Ibid, Gwin

199 Chris Kenning, "6 boaters feared drowned after collision with barge," *Courier-Journal*, July 17, 2001, 1a

200 Ibid, U. S. Coast Guard, Report....15

201 John Gormley, "Six fishermen die after collision with tow on Ohio River," Professional Mariner, December/January 2002

202 Chris Kenning, "Barge inquiry finds drug use," *Courier-Journal*, July 2001

203 Ibid, U. S. Coast Guard, Report....24

204 Ibid, Schreiner, "Barge captain testifies...."

205 Ibid, 15

206 Ibid

207 Bruce Schreiner, "Investigator says fishing boat sank instantly," Associated Press

208 Ibid, U. S. Coast Guard, Report....23

209 Ibid, 23-4

210 Ibid, 24

211 Associated Press, "Skipper Of Towboat: Collision Was Not My Fault," *Cincinnati Post*, July 26, 2001, 5K

212 National Mariners Association, "Newsletter," September 2008, pg. 12

213 Jim Yardley, "Plunge Into Horror," Atlanta Constitution, September 23, 1993, A/3

214 "Evaluation of Options for improving Amtrak's Passenger Accountability System," U. S. Department of Transportation, Federal Railroad Administration, December 2005

215 "7 tries before passing," Houston Chronicle, February 4, 1994, A16

216 http://video.aol.com/video-detail/seconds-from-disaster-s01e06-wreck-of-the-sunset-limited-36/403879507

217 http://www.mtvassociation.com/files/Lowered_tugboat_bar_may_spell_spill.pdf

218 Ibid

219 Ronald Smothers, "Accident Puts Barge Owner in Spotlight," *New York Times*, September 26, 1993

220 "October 1993 Hotlines, #793," National Association of Railroad Passengers, October 1, 1993

221 National Transportation Safety Board, Railroad-Marine Accident Report RAR-94-01, Adopted September 19, 1994.

222 Stephen LaBaton, "Barge Pilot Blamed in Fatal Amtrak Wreck," *New York Times*, June 22, 1994

223 Ibid, Smothers

224 Ibid, LaBaton

225 Robert G. Knowles, "Amtrak Wreck Liability Not Close To Being Settled," National Underwriter, August 29, 1994

226 Ibid, LaBaton

227 Anthony M. Davis, International Analyst Network, October 24, 2007

228 Don Phillips, "Skipper Believes Barge Hit Bridge Before Train Fell" *Washington Post*, December 16, 1993, A.16

229 Ibid

230 Ibid

231 Martin Tolchin, "Witnesses Recall Chaos Of Crash," *New York Times*, December 16, 1993

232 "Towboat Captain May Have Hit Railroad Bridge in Fog," The Tech, Volume 113, Issue 44, September 24, 1993

233 Ibid

234 Peter Applebome, "Tracks Apparently Remained Intact When Barge Hit Bridge Before Wreck," *New York Times*, September 24, 1993

235 Ibid

236 Ibid, Tolchin

237 Ibid, Phillips

238 Martin Tolchin, "3 Heroes Recall Amtrak Disaster on a Bayou," *New York Times*, December 14, 1993

239 http://legaltechnologies.com/Axolotl%20v%20Milkweed/136fsupp2d1251.htm

240 Pam Lambert, "Hero of Car 211," People magazine, Vol. 40, No. 15, October 11, 1993

241 Ronald Smothers, "Dozens Are Killed In Wreck Of Train In Alabama Bayou," *New York Times*, September 23, 1993

242 T.J. Milling, Glen Golightly, "Everybody started screaming . . .," *Houston Chronicle*, September 26, 1993, A1

243 Ibid

244 Ibid, http://video.

245 Ibid, Smothers, "Dozens Are Killed...

246 Ibid, Evaluation of Options..."

247 Don Phillips, "Put Out the Fire. I'm Going to Die" *Washington Post*, December 14, 1993, A.03

248 Ibid, "Evaluation of options...,"

249 "Deadliest Train Crash In Amtrak History Kills 44," Emergencynet News Service, September 23, 1992 [sic]

250 Jim Yardley, "Seeking bayou's dead is heart-rending job," *Atlanta Constitution*, September 24, 1993, A/3

251 Martin Tolchin, "Report Revises Times in Train Wreck, *New York Times*, October 8, 1993

252 Ibid

253 Ibid, "Evaluation of Options....", 154

254 Ibid, Tolchin, "3 Heroes Recall..."

255 Ibid, Lambert

256 Ibid

257 Don Phillips, "Safety Board Cites Lack of Training In Amtrak Crash," *Washington Post*, Jun 22, 1994, A09

258 National Transportation Safety Board (NTSB), Highway-Marine Accident Report, June 7, 1994, 1

259 Hayes Ferguson and John Pope, "Pregnant woman killed; 2 men hurt," *New Orleans Times-Picayune*, May 29, 1993, 1

260 Associated Press, "Crews to clear tons of rubble after barge fells section of bridge," *Houston Chronicle*, May 30, 1993, A6

261 Ibid, NTSB, 4

262 Ibid, Hayes Ferguson and John Pope, 1

263 Ibid

264 Hayes Ferguson, "Victim: Lives are touched," *New Orleans Times-Picayune*, May 30, 1993, 1

265 Hayes Ferguson, "Collapse shocks drivers, residents," *New Orleans Times-Picayune*, May 29, 1993

266 Ibid

267 Susan Finch and Leslie Williams, "Coast Guard investigating tug's captain," *New Orleans Times-Picayune*, May 30, 1993

268 Bruce Alpert, "Bridge Collapse Called Avoidable," *New Orleans Times-Picayune*, June 8, 1994, A1

269 Ibid, NTSB, 21

270 News Services, "One killed when barge hits bridge," *Houston Chronicle*, May 29, 1993, A2

271 Hayes Ferguson, "Erosion suspected in Collapse," *New Orleans Times-Picayune*, June 2, 1993, 1

272 Ibid, Hayes Ferguson and John Pope

273 Louis A. Le Blanc and Kenneth A. Kozar, "An Empirical Investigation of the Relationship between DSS Usage and System Performance," MIS Quarterly, Vol. 14, No. 3,
          September 1990, 263-277

274 Gulf Coast Mariners Association, Report #R-293, Revision 2, June 2002

275 WWL-TV, July 27, 1964

276 "For a Safer Causeway," *New Orleans Times-Picayune*, August 2, 1974, 16

277 "'Passed Out,' Before Barges Hit Span, First Mate Quoted," *New Orleans Times-Picayune*, June 17, 1964, 1

278 "Tugboat's First Mate Capable Man – Captain," *New Orleans Times-Picayune*, June 18, 1964, 1

279 "Driver Thinks Bridge Was Knocked from Under Bus," *New Orleans Times-Picayune*, June 17, 1964, 2

280 Ibid

281 Ibid "'Passed Out,...'"

282 Ibid, "Driver Thinks Bridge...."

283 "Fifth Time Causeway Rammed," *New Orleans Times-Picayune*, June 17, 1964, 1

284 Ibid, GCMA #R-293

285 Emile LaFourcade, "Captain and Owner City 5th Amendment, *New Orleans Times-Picayune*, August 3, 1974, 1

286 Emile LaFourcade, "Crew Tired, Sparse," *New Orleans Times-Picayune*, August 8, 1974, 1

287 Ibid,"For a Safer Causeway..."

288 "Plans to Prevent Causeway Rammings Are Aired," *New Orleans Times-Picayune*, September 5, 1974, 4

289 Ibid, Report #R-293, Revision 2...

290 "Scarbrough is Lauded by Fellow River Pilots," *New Orleans Times-Picayune*, April 9, 1969, 7

291 U. S. Coast Guard, Marine Casualty Report, Collision Involving SS Union Faith and M/V Warren J. Doucet and Tow in Mississippi River on April 6, 1969, 6, released
          December 22, 1970

292 Ibid, 3

293 Ibid

294 Ibid, "Scarbrough is Lauded..."

295 Ibid

296 Ibid, U. S. Coast Guard…, 3

297 "At Least 20 on Freighter Picked Up by Two Tugs," *New Orleans Times-Picayune*, April 8, 1969, 6

298 Charles Boggs, "18 Ship Crash Survivors Released from Hospital," *New Orleans Times-Picayune*, April 8, 1969, 3

299 Ibid, U.S. Coast Guard…, 20

300 Don Lewis, "Family Runs Fiery Gauntlet," *New Orleans Times-Picayune*, August 7, 1969, 1

301 Ibid, U.S. Coast Guard…, 6-7

302 Tom Flesner, "Oil Recovery from the SS <u>Union Faith</u>," Underwater Magazine, July/August 2001

303 Ibid, Charles Boggs…

304 "Taiwan Line Sues In Sinking Of Ship." (1969, April 24). *New York Times* (1857-Current file),93. Retrieved September 21, 2008, from ProQuest Historical Newspapers *The New York Times* (1851 - 2005) database. (Document ID: 78343674).

305 Ibid, U.S. Coast Guard…, 6

306 Ibid, 4

307 Testimony of Captain Richard A. Block Before the House Subcommittee on Coast Guard and Maritime Transportation, Committee on Transportation and Infrastructure, Thursday July 9, 2009

308 Ibid

309 www.americanwaterways.com/about_awo/index.html

310 http://www.gulfcoastmariners.org/newsletters/HTML/may2005/may2005.htm#queen